CHARLES MAURICE

Insane Killers Inc.

THE BRABANT KILLERS MYSTERY

RAYEM

Published by Rayem Press

ISBN: 978-1-9994519-0-5
eBook ISBN: 978-1-9994519-1-2

Printed in the United States of America

www.insanekillersinc.com
www.charlesmaurice.net

FIRST EDITION

To Bruno, who left us much too soon…

Contents

We are the Dead. Short days ago
We lived, felt dawn, saw sunset glow,
Loved and were loved

—John McCrae (1872–1918)

Principal Characters

List Of Suspect Groups:

The groups are listed in alphabetic order.

These groups are not our own list of suspects; they are all groups suspected at one point in time of some involvement in the Brabant Insane Killers' crimes. Everyone listed is presumed innocent and we hope this book contributes to confirming the innocence of some suspects. Even if evidence confirms that a group listed here was involved in these heinous crimes, it doesn't mean each member listed was complicit.

Suspect Group #1: Baasrode Gang

This gang specialized in robbing post offices in Flanders, the northern Dutch-speaking part of Belgium.

Johnny De Staerke — Individually charged in the Insane Killers' crimes and then released.

Dominique S. — Cigarette and car thief.

Leopold Van Esbroek — Stolen check fraudster.

Stereo P. — Best friend of Johnny.

Suspect Group #2: The Borains

This is the only gang ever charged for some of the Insane Killers' crimes, but their case was thrown out.

Michel Cocu — Former small-town police officer; suspected leader.

Adriano Vittorio — French citizen; had a restaurant that went bankrupt.

Jean-Claude Estiévenart — Day laborer.

Michel Baudet — Unemployed.

Kaci Bouaroudj — Bar manager.

Suspect Group #3: The Bouhouche Gang[1]

A criminal gang that is well connected in the Gendarmerie.

Madani "Dani" Bouhouche — Ex-Gendarme and leader of the Bouhouche Gang.

Gangster A

Gangster B

Gangster C

Suspect Group #4: The Vincent L. Crew

This gang was linked to Gendarme Martial Lekeu.

---

[1] We have decided not to name the members of the Bouhouche Gang because not all were accused of violent crimes like key members of other gangs. They are presumed innocent. Bouhouche has relationships with a motley crew of police officers, criminals and murderers. Most of these acquaintances know nothing about the Bouhouche Gang.

Vincent L. — Junkie.

Francis V. (Crazy Pete) — Armed robber and police witness.

Vicky V. — Armed robber.

SUSPECT GROUP #5: THE HAEMERS GANG

This is a gang that specializes in holding up armed postal truck convoys and gained notoriety for having kidnapped the former prime minister of Belgium and demanding a ransom.

Patrick Haemers — Most notorious criminal in Belgium.

Thierry S. — Getaway car driver.

Philippe L. — The brains behind the Haemers Gang.

SUSPECT GROUP #6: WESTLAND NEW POST

A clandestine Neo-Nazi organization.

Paul Latinus (alias "Orf") — General and paid informant for the Sûreté.

Michel Libert (alias "Wagner") – Captain and paid informant for the Sûreté.

Marcel Barbier (alias "Von Salza") — Captain, charged in a double murder case.

Eric Lammers (alias "The Beast") – Soldier, charged in a double murder case.

Other Important Characters:

Gendarmerie

The Gendarmerie is the special police force that takes care of the most important crimes in Belgium. It's officially part of the army.

Christian Amory — Gendarme in the town of Mons.

Robert Beijer — Gendarme in the Narcotics Division then private detective.

Gérard Bihay — Detective, Wavre Gendarmerie, linked to controversial August 1985 report.

Claude Dery – Ballistics expert (officially in the intelligence branch of the army).

Guy Goffinon — Gendarme Commander; heads the Judicial Division.

Martial Lekeu – Gendarme posted in the Ardennes region.

Herman Vernaillen — Gendarme Major; in charge of discipline.

Sûreté:

Internal intelligence agency of the Belgian government, in charge of spying on extremist organizations.

Albert Raes — Director.

(Alias "The Duck") – Commissioner.

(Alias "The Rabbit") — Commissioner.

(Alias "The Dog") – Agent.

VARIOUS

Mohammed Asmaoui — Key Gendarmerie informant against the Borains Gang.

Jean Bultot — Assistant director of a jail; once a suspect.

Juan Mendez — Sales representative for gun maker FN in South America and Spain.

Willy Pourtois — International guns broker, paid informant for the Sûreté.

INTRODUCTION

THE BRABANT KILLERS RAVAGED BELGIUM BETWEEN 1982 AND 1985. They've attained international infamy for their three supermarket massacres of 1985—all for ridiculously small financial gain. In total, the Brabant Insane Killers are responsible for 28 deaths and 40 wounded. They struck in the Brabant, a rich suburb surrounding Brussels where crime is almost non-existent.

Like Jack the Ripper, who preyed on and gruesomely mutilated prostitutes, and the Zodiac Killer, who killed teenagers and young adults and sent ciphers to authorities, the Brabant Killers developed their own specific serial killer branding. They attacked Delhaize supermarkets in the evenings just before closing time, arriving in a stolen, dark Volkswagen Golf GTI. They were always a group of three with one noticeably so much larger than the others that witnesses called him a giant. The Killers wore dark trench coats, black bell hats, and carnival masks. They never hurried, never ran, and always seemed cool and collected as they emptied the front cash registers and the back-office vault. They carried pump-action rifles, which they used to shoot indiscriminately at employees and customers inside and outside the store, and they carried several other weapons strapped around their bodies. The Killers always reused the same weapons, so it was extremely easy to link all their attacks forensically. Each time they robbed a supermarket, the Killers grabbed hostages and hit bystanders. All three Killers always entered the store during a hold-up; they never left anyone behind in the getaway car. After robbing the supermarkets, the Killers would slowly walk back to their car, often parked far from the front doors, and disappear into the dark.

The public was spooked by the random attacks and the helplessness of the authorities to prevent or predict them. All the supermarkets in the country ended up preparing for attacks by the Insane Killers: the stores were all secured and the police put snipers with infrared goggles on the roofs of supermarkets. Still, the Killers found a way to strike a Delhaize supermarket—and no one could do anything about it. They didn't discriminate between men, women, or children. They killed, kicked, and brutalized, pulled hair and forced victims to walk on their knees. Horrified onlookers witnessed heads being blown off and brain matter dripping off supermarket ceilings.

Decades later, the Insane Killers mystery is still officially unsolved. It's one of the biggest unsolved mysteries in the world. In March 2018, the number of investigators dedicated to the Brabant Killers was raised to 30. There are also four state prosecutors involved. There has always been at least one investigative cell hard at work on the case since 1985, the date of the last murder. It's certainly one of the few murder mysteries where authorities have deployed such vast resources over such a long period of time and not solved the case. The case of the Brabant Insane Killers also has a major political twist, as many have long suspected the attacks were sponsored directly by Washington, NATO, or some other Western intelligence agency. Other suspects have included VIP pedophile rings and royalty.

In this book, you'll get the most complete picture and up-to-date details in the case of the Brabant Insane Killers. Unlike many other countries (including the US), Belgium does have a statute of limitations on murder. However, because of how gruesome these murders were, the government made extensions to it for this particular case. As it stands now, if the case is not prosecuted by 2025, the Brabant Killers will get off scot-free. A great deal of time is required to put together a legal case of this complexity; to prosecute this case, time is of the essence. Things need to happen now.

MOTIVE

The clock is ticking on the statute of limitations, but the motive for the Brabant Insane Killer attacks is still unknown. Several potential motives have been proposed, but there's still no agreement. Two recurrent motives put forward have been terrorism or simple robbery. Why terrorism? Because many suspect the attacks were sponsored directly by Washington, NATO, or some other Western intelligence agency. However, others profile the Killers as a gang of hoodlums trying to make money through robberies. They feel the end goal of the Killers is the cash in the cash registers and the back-office vault, nothing else. It is just coincidence the Insane Killers happened to be more violent and kill more people in the process.

The disparity between alleged motives and the lack of progress in solving the case has caused a serious disconnect; distrust grows between the population and the media on one side, and investigators on the other. While the Brabant Killers did steal money, their small gains and the extreme level of violence suggest other motives. The terrorism motive came to the forefront, particularly in the nineties when there were disclosures that for decades NATO, the CIA, MI6, and other Western intelligence services had built up, funded, and developed secret armies inside every European country.[1] These armies were not operated by each country's military. Ministers, secretaries of states, the media, and the public—no one knew that secret cells were built in each country. These secret soldiers were armed and had state-of-the-art means of communication. The purpose of these secret armies was to form a resistance against Communist Russia should the Russians invade any of these countries. But the Russians never invaded. Which begs several questions: What did these secret soldiers do during all these years? Did they just sit around, waiting? Is it possible that they decided to go rogue and commit atrocities for entertainment and/or personal gain? Were they used to commit terrorist acts on behalf of Western intelligence agencies like the CIA?

The eighties saw a series of terrorist-style attacks hit Europe, for which no one ever claimed responsibility. These included the Munich Oktoberfest bombing in Germany in 1980 that killed 26 people and wounded more than two hundred, and the Bologna train station bombing in Italy that killed 85 people and wounded more than two hundred in 1981. One year later, the Brabant Insane Killers started their attacks. Though the casualties of the Brabant killings were not as high as the Bologna bombing, the Insane Killers' reign of terror lasted three years and struck substantially greater fear in the population. Were the Brabant attacks committed by thes secret armies to foster unrest in Europe? Like the other attacks, the crimes perpetrated by the Killers have also stayed unresolved—or not resolved to the public's satisfaction—despite how terrible they were. Fall guys were prosecuted for some of the terrorist incidents but question marks about these attacks in Europe, as a whole, remain; within these series of horrific crimes, the Brabant Killers case is probably the one where the least progress was made.

There were two full public inquiries established in Belgium in 1988 and 1997 to try to understand what went wrong, but to no avail. A separate inquiry into the issue of the NATO secret armies in 1991 indirectly looked at the involvement of the Brabant Killers. The two government figures that knew the names of the secret army cell members refused to give their full names, so they could never be compared with a list of suspects for the Brabant Killers' crimes.

EVIDENCE

One perplexing aspect of this case is that no DNA evidence has been found or catalogued, despite the fact there were numerous sites where the attacks happened. How could this happen? Some key pieces of evidence that would have had fingerprints or DNA simply disappeared during investigations. Other articles tested by authorities have some DNA but are not necessarily linked to the Brabant Killers. This is discouraging for victims and observers who seek a breakthrough in the case. However, a study of many cold cases has determined that DNA has only been helpful in a minute percentage of cases where there was closure. Statistically, DNA matches and confessions are only integral to solving five percent of cold cases. Cold cases are closed in several different ways, typically by finding a new key witness, getting new evidence from an old witness that was ignored or overlooked, or building a new theory of the crime…basically classic gumshoe work.[2]

Two characteristics that substantially raise the clearance rate are absent from the Brabant Killers case: The case is missing motive and the identification of a prime suspect. Obviously, uncovering motive is not needed to prosecute someone, but helps a lot in clearance rates. The issue of motive here is symptomatic of having no agreement on several core issues around the case, which leads to vastly different analysis. Several specific actions by the Brabant Killers during each of their crimes are interpreted in very different ways and investigators didn't agree on behavior patterns.

Did their ultra-violence serve a purpose in the robberies? Did it help them accomplish what they wanted? When they assassinated certain people, was it overkill that satisfied some psychopathic need for them? Was there a pattern to how they selected victims? Were all of their behaviors "necessary to perpetrate the crime" or did they feel "compelled to act out this ritual?"[3] Were hats, coats or other objects deliberately planted at certain crime scenes?

A main issue where interpretations wildly vary in the case of the Brabant Killers is the issue of staging—fixing crime scenes to confuse investigators or for some other reason. Some of the items they stole, like cooking oil from a supermarket and alarm clocks from a jewelry store, were unusual choices for such aggressive robberies. Several times further examination of the crime scene revealed that they left smaller, and easily transported, items of far greater value. Why?

Everything regarding their serial killer branding is a source of disagreement. Why did the Insane Killers always attack supermarkets and not higher value targets, like banks or armored trucks? Why Delhaize supermarkets and no other chains? Why did they carry at least seven firearms for the nighttime break-in of a store? Was material gain their only motive? Was their first intent murder or money? One very contentious issue among those interested in the case is whether evidence found at several locations was deliberately planted by the Killers. With so many unresolved issues, the true story of the Brabant Killers has yet to be written.

While we still don't have the elusive DNA match for evidence, the goal of this book is primarily to deliver the best up-to-date evidence in the case. We have interviewed witnesses and thoroughly reviewed all the information ever made public in the case, including hundreds of police statements and the minutes of both public inquiries into the matter. By giving an accurate and complete picture of all the facts and primary suspects[1], we will attempt to sort the important details from the red herrings.

To be clear, this book is about the evidence in the crimes committed by the Brabant Insane Killers and not about the investigation. Our original intention was to correctly identify the pieces of this giant puzzle, but to leave solving the mystery up to the readers. By being as factual as possible, we intended to refrain from even giving our best opinion on the case. However, things changed as we wrote the book and we have delved much further than we initially thought possible.

Several good books have been written regarding the lapses in the investigation and there were two public inquiries. We chose not to look at what evidence we could have had access to if things had been done differently, and instead considered only the evidence that we uncovered through research.

There have been many books on cover-ups and conspiracy theories around this case. Often they describe the political situation in Belgium at the time and how the Brabant Killings could have been influenced by it; a top-down approach. This book instead looks at the case from a bottom-up approach.

---

[1]   We recommend to return to the table of contents and the list of suspects at the beginning when need be.

The only time we will look at conspiracies or cover-ups is when we strongly believe it originated from the Insane Brabant Killers themselves and is necessary to understand the case. Otherwise, we will not look at political or investigatory decisions in the case.

The Brabant Killer story is complex. To try and simplify things, we've looked at it in a mostly linear time frame. Other books will separate chapters by issues. Our approach means that we start from the beginning of the Brabant Killers criminal career, when the crimes seemed pettier. They are, however, essential to understanding all facets of the case. As you read, reflect on a few things: What do you see in these crimes? Are there patterns? Why did they use a particular modus operandi and not another? Are there already some criminal signatures?[4] The reader needs to look for something, anything, to try to understand the bigger picture. When we decide to include a detail about a small crime, it's because we feel it might ring some bells a few chapters later.

The story of the Brabant Killers is split into two distinct time periods or "waves." The First Wave took place from 1982 to 1983.[2] It's a mixed bag of crimes of varying severity, ranging from carjackings to murders. Why did they commit all these crimes? Is there any logic to their madness? The fact three of their major shootouts with police happen during this time says something about the Killers. Why do they confront police? Why do the Killers always come out on top, unscathed, while officers end up killed or wounded? Then the Killers disappear without a trace for almost two years with no explanation. They reappear with a vengeance in 1985, causing large-scale bloodbaths in supermarkets. Then, abruptly, the Brabant Insane Killers disappear again, this time for good. No one knows why.

---

[2]   There is a geographic map for each of the two waves at the end of the book.

PART I:

FIRST WAVE (1982–1983)

BEERSEL CASTLE, FLEMISH-BRABANT

CHAPTER 1

SHOPLIFTING, CARJACKING AND BREAK-IN (MARCH–MAY 1982)

J UST AS EVERY RAGING INFERNO BEGINS WITH A SPARK, THE BRABANT Insane Killers started their reign of terror with a small crime. To understand how the Killers began terrorizing Belgium, we need to start where they did and work through the crimes they committed in sequence. It took a long time before authorities realized that various crimes had similarities and even longer for ballistics to prove they were connected.

The public, the media, and the Gendarmerie didn't know who was behind the crimes and so we'll review the evidence, various leads, and suspects in keeping with the timeline. It may seem confusing and bewildering at first, but that was the intent of the Insane Killers. It takes time to sift through all the information and make sense of what has baffled investigators and the public for decades.

It all starts on the afternoon of Saturday, March 13th, 1982. Two men walk quickly along the main road in the southern town of Dinant, Belgium. The first is a tall, middle-aged man with dirty blond hair. The second is smaller, with graying hair and perhaps in his forties or fifties.[5] They are about to commit the first crime in the Brabant Insane Killers canon, a prelude to later violence.

The two men slow down as they get close to the Bayard Gun Shop, which specializes in hunting and fishing equipment. The men quickly glance to the left and to the right before opening the gun shop's unlocked door. As an automatic bell rings to let the shopkeeper know someone has come in, the two men quickly hide in a corner of the hunting showroom.[6]

The owner is in his workshop. He isn't visible at first, and then he hurries into the showroom from another area of the shop. He glances around but doesn't notice the two intruders hiding in the corner, so turns around and returns to his task.

It is at this moment the two men come out of their hiding place. They grab a long, double-barreled duck hunting rifle from the front display window and bolt out of the store. As the bell on the door rings again, the owner returns to the empty showroom. Puzzled, he steps out the front door looking left, then right, until someone on the street points towards two men running with a brand new duck hunting rifle in their hands. Unfortunately, the men are too far off and there's nothing left to do. The owner balls his fists as the men run off into the distance.

Clearly, the Bayard Gun Shop was targeted for its ease of access. The Brabant Insane Killers banked on the fact it took the owner a minute to go from one side of the store to the other, giving them ample time to shoplift the rifle.

THE DUCK HUNTING RIFLE

This crime is way out of the zone where the Brabant Insane Killers usually operate. It is miles south of Brussels and the Brabant. Shoplifting that duck hunting rifle is the first known crime of the Brabant Insane Killers, and it's also their only known crime in this area. There is speculation they sawed the long barrel off this rifle and used it in some of their other attacks.

We don't know if the Insane Killers were armed when they stole from the Bayard Gun Shop. This is also one of the only times their getaway car is not seen in the vicinity and there are only two perpetrators. In most of their subsequent crimes, there is a trio of Insane Killers.

The stolen rifle is a 10-gauge Faul Duck-Hunting Rifle. It's one of only 17 Faul rifles produced by the Belgium firm, Centaure, to hunt small game. The 16 other rifles are later accounted for. Not only does this Faul rifle have very little firepower, it is also extremely bulky with a heavy recoil.[7] Consequently, this particular rifle would garner little interest on the black market.

There are various theories to explain why they took the Faul. The most common is that the two men just grabbed anything they could get their hands on. They were not picky and were unsophisticated when it came to gun knowledge. This theory is supported by the fact that one hunting rifle next to the Faul was worth well over five times as much.[8]

Another theory is that the men stole the Faul because it looks very impressive and intimidating, reminiscent of the weapon carried by Mad Max in the legendary action movies—even more so after the barrel and stock were sawed off. It is double-barreled and each barrel boasts an almost one-inch diameter, so it is readily maneuverable and can easily be hidden under a coat or jacket. Additionally, the heavy butt of the Faul can be used to beat victims, which could have been a consideration at the time. That's despite the way the Insane Killers ended up targeting their victims in a terrorizing spree of violent attacks.

Was the Dial-Budget Robbery a Warm-Up for the Insane Killers?[9]

A few weeks later, on Thursday, May 6th, two armed men come through the front doors of a small grocery store called Dial-Budget in the Brussels suburb of Anderlecht at 6:50 p.m. The intruders demand money from the cashier and force three clients to lie down on the ground. The men then go to the grocery's back office, where they force two store employees to open the safe. No shots are fired, and no one is hurt. The robbers leave with a loot of 100,000 BEF[3] (around $2,816) and flee on foot. There is no getaway car.

---

3   Belgian Francs, which were subsequently replaced by the Euro.

It is important to note that Dial-Budget is a niche grocery store that is part of the supermarket giant Delhaize's chain of stores. What's significant is that this is the first time a grocery store in the chain is ever held up in Belgium—despite being a small grocery store it shares some similarities with the layout of the larger Delhaize supermarket outlets.

The robbery is not widely regarded to be part of the Insane Killer canon of crimes; however, the modus operandi is strikingly similar to the pattern they'll use in their later attacks. The robbery happens early in the evening. The intruders go to the cash registers first, where they force everyone to get down on the floor. Then they head to the back office to force employees to empty the safe contents into a bag.

But there are also differences to the later crime spree of the Insane Killers, notably that no shots are fired at the Dial-Budget and no one is hurt. Like the earlier Dinant rifle theft, there are only two perpetrators, there's no getaway car, and they flee by foot. This Dial-Budget robbery happens in the western suburb of Anderlecht, which is outside the zone of their later attacks.

Without definitive proof, this robbery cannot be placed in the Insane Killer canon. Unfortunately, because no shots were fired there is no ballistic evidence that the same weapon was used to commit this robbery as was used in known crimes of the Brabant Insane Killers. However, the similarities could show that two members of the Insane Killers were involved with grocery store hold-ups much earlier than originally believed. It would also show that some of their earlier crimes were motivated by profit, not violence.

IXELLES

On Monday, May 10th, at 10:20 p.m. in the Brussels suburb of Ixelles, two Insane Killers walk up to a man who is in the process of parking his car in his building's parking lot. They are armed. One of them has black hair, a mustache, and a knitted sailor's cap. The second one sports a mustache and graying, frizzy hair.[10] Both seem to be in their forties, and while neither wears a mask; it is likely they have used makeup and wigs to disguise their identities. Both perpetrators carry what appear to be long-barreled revolvers. One could be the rifle stolen in Dinant, with the barrel sawed off. Or it could be an entirely different weapon with a silencer attached. Note that Ixelles is located in southern Brussels, which is the home base of the Insane Killers.

One of the robbers points a long-barreled revolver, ordering the man to hand over the keys to his metallic gray Austin Allegro. The man is also forced to hand over his wallet and get down on the ground on his stomach.[11] Having the victims lie flat on their stomach is a technique the Insane Killers use in all their robberies.

While the stolen Austin Allegro is in a very bad state and with practically no gas left in the tank, the two carjackers take off.[12]

LEMBEEK

The two middle-aged robbers drive the stolen Austin Allegro about 15 miles, parking it near a Volkswagen dealership in Lembeek. Once they reach the dealership, they force the lock at the bottom of a glass door to gain access to the showroom floor. They quickly steal a 1982 dark blue Volkswagen Santana; the dealership has conveniently left the keys on the vehicle's dashboard.[13] They leave the stolen Austin Allegro behind.

THE MOTIVATION FOR STEALING CARS

When the Insane Killers steal a car, it is used to commit a crime. They never steal a car to resell it. According to reporter Gilbert Dupont, the Killers break into another car on the same Ixelles Street before they target the man parking the Austin Allegro, but leave without stealing it. According to Dupont, they tried stealing it and gave up when they couldn't hotwire it.[14] This is the only known incident of the Killers trying to steal a car without the keys. In the eighties, any common thief could hotwire a car, so car-jackings were extremely rare. Every single car used during their subsequent crime spree is stolen with the keys.

Some theorize that once the two men left Ixelles with the Allegro, they realized it was too beat up and contained little gas in the tank, so they decided on a whim to steal another vehicle. Perhaps they went to the dealership in Lembeek to steal a new car that wouldn't give them any problems.

Another theory is that the two robbers planned to use the Austin Allegro only as a means of conveyance to the dealership. If they had already scouted the dealership, the Austin Allegro was simply a target of convenience because any beat-up car that could get them to the dealership would have done.

VOLKSWAGEN SANTANA

The Volkswagen Santana they steal at the dealership is quite a rare model. There are only 358 Santanas in Belgium at the time, all of which were dark blue or metallic colored.[15] The Santana has a big trunk with a greater storage capacity than other regular cars, making it a very convenient and practical choice for men looking to transport stolen goods after a crime.

The Santana is spotted several times in Ixelles in the following months, always with false plates that copy the plate of another Santana in the city. This proves to be part of the modus operandi of the Killers, who fix false plates on all the cars they use. The fake license plate number is always from a car of the same color and make as the stolen car.

CHAPTER 2

GROCERY STORE IN MAUBEUGE
(AUGUST 14, 1982)

I N THE EARLY HOURS OF FRIDAY, SEPTEMBER 13TH, THE INSANE KILL-ers drive the stolen dark Volkswagen Santana with Belgian plates into the French town of Maubeuge. It is 3:30 a.m. and only about five miles from the Belgium border.[16] They drive with the car's lights turned off to a little square surrounded by some shops and a residential building, where they park the Santana near a sports apparel shop.[17]

Two armed men step out of the Santana and walk towards the small Piot Grocery Store, which is not far from the sports apparel shop. This time, a third man, also armed with a weapon, waits near the getaway car. The two men try to open the side door of the grocery store, but when that fails, they break into the shop by smashing through the window of the front door.[18] After quickly ripping out the building's telephone wires, they stuff the trunk of the Santana to full capacity with hundreds of bottles of wine and champagne.[19] They also take some tea and foie gras.

Twenty minutes later, the local French police station receives an anonymous phone call.[20] The caller tells the officer working the phones that there's something happening at the Piot Grocery Store. Three police officers are dispatched to take a look, but because the grocery store is only about a hundred yards from the police station, the officers go on foot.[21] Officer Christian Delacourt leaves first and two other officers follow a few moments later. They each take a different street to get to the grocery store.[22]

When Officer Delacourt gets near the grocery store, he spots the blue Santana parked in front and notices the man wearing a ski mask keeping a lookout. Sensing he might need backup, Officer Delacourt turns back to get the two other officers. Bullets start ringing out in his direction. Officer Delacourt throws himself behind a fountain, but he's hit in the stomach. He lies, critically injured, on the pavement.[23]

At this point, the second police officer arrives in the square, a few steps ahead of the third officer. He's shot at three consecutive times and barely has time to hit the ground to avoid the barrage. Alerted by the sounds of gunshots, the third officer returns fire. Now, a second Insane Killer starts shooting at the officers.

Still shooting, the Insane Killers jump back into their Volkswagen Santana getaway car. One of the Killers continues to fire from the back seat of the car as it rolls away from the scene. The Santana heads towards an intersection that leads back to Belgium. Despite calls to police forces around the border region, the Insane Killers slip back into Belgium without being apprehended.[24]

STEALING ALCOHOL

The Maubeuge shootout outside the Piot Grocery Store is the first crime committed by the Insane Killers where there are injured victims. It's also their first firefight with police officers, and while there will be a few more, this is the only shootout when the Killers don't massively over-power the security forces who try to stop them. The reason could be that at this time they still have a limited arms arsenal to use for their crimes. Like the French police officers who are firing the standard 7.65 mm handgun issued to police forces at the time, the Killers are using small caliber guns. The sawed-off shotgun used by one of the Killers was not effective at long-range.

One of the three Brabant Killers is bigger than the other two. Even though it's a nighttime break-in, all three men wear ski masks or face covers. They're quite conscious of the risk of being identified. In some daytime robberies, they use makeup, wigs, and other props instead of masks to prevent being identified. Sometimes the wigs and the makeup are obviously fake. Because of their penchant for disguise, it makes the dozens of police witness sketches created after their attacks of limited value.

While the Maubeuge firefight is probably just a break-in gone bad, there are several theories that the trio really showed up to get into a shootout with police. There was a public phone in the small square not far from the grocery store, so one of the Brabant Killers could have made the anonymous phone call to lure the police with the break-in just a pretext. The anonymous caller has never been identified.

Although the Piot is called a grocery store, it actually specializes in the sale of alcohol and the shelves inside the shop were filled primarily with rows of wine, champagne and hard liquor bottles. The Insane Killers left with hundreds of bottles, which were worth a good deal of money and comparable to the monetary gain they'd netted from robbing cash registers.

The way the Insane Killers immediately ripped out the Piot Grocery Store's telephone lines upon breaking into the building becomes a habitual precaution they take in all of their subsequent break-ins and robberies.

While the break-in at the Piot Grocery Store happens in France, the region could be considered an extension of the Borinage border region in western Belgium. There's no open border between France and Belgium in 1982; all the main thoroughfares had border guard posts. The fact the perpetrators crossed back into Belgium by using side-roads only known by locals, points to one of the killers having some close connection to the Borinage region.

BRAINE-LE-COMTE

At 3:00 a.m. on September 18, 1982, intruders park near the outdoor car lot of the Volkswagen dealership in Braine-Le-Comte on Soignies Lane. When they break into the yard, they wake up the elderly dealership owner who lives right across the street. The dealership owner looks through his bedroom blinds and sees two armed intruders, one of whom carries a rifle. The owner grabs his own hunting rifle, opens his bedroom window, and shoots into the air to scare away the intruders. One of the intruders shoots back at the owner's window without any kind of warning, hitting the older man in the head and stomach. The owner collapses on his bedroom floor and is later found in critical condition; he barely survives and is left with a serious incapacity. The bandits jump in a getaway car and leave.[25]

SHOOTING AT WINDOWS

The unsolved Braine-le-Comte attack was never officially linked to the Insane Killers' canon of crimes. However, this is another unsolved crime with strong similarities in the modus operandi—an attack that seems like a blueprint plan for a portion of their Temse fabric attack one year later in September 1983 when they shoot at residential windows in the Temse neighborhood, not to scare but to kill. Who does that?

The Braine-le-Comte dealership had seen a recent uptick of break-ins prior to this attack. Tires and other items had disappeared and a car had been recently stolen. There were no witnesses able to identify the car the intruders parked near the car dealership, so it's impossible to know if it was the Santana. However, when paper clippings from the Insane Killers are found in October, the Killers seem to refer to this attack. The words, "Braine-le-Comte" and "Soignies" are written down along with part of a license plate number. The plate could be a reference to a car they targeted in the dealership lot or one of the false plates they would put on a stolen car.

CHAPTER 3

WAVRE GUN SHOP
(SEPTEMBER 30, 1982)

ON SEPTEMBER 30TH, 1982, SHORTLY BEFORE 10:30 A.M., THE OWNER of the Dekaise Gun Shop is chatting with two customers in his store. This gun shop is located on a busy, narrow, one-way commercial street in the city of Wavre, the capital of the Belgian province, Walloon Brabant.

The Insane Killers park the stolen blue Volkswagen Santana, which now sports false French license plates, a few yards away from the Dekaise Gun Shop and three armed men step out.[26] Two of them walk straight to the store, one at a short distance from the other. The first man has a hand hidden in his coat. As he opens the shop's front door, he whips out a pistol and points the barrel in the owner's face.[27] He shouts: "Don't move!"

The second man crosses the street. He pulls a sawed-off, double-barreled shotgun out of his trench coat as he enters the shop and smashes the owner's face with the butt end. The owner falls to the ground, bleeding profusely. The assailant then violently beats the faces of two clients that happened to be in the shop with the butt of his weapon. He screams, "On the ground, or I kill you!"[28]

The Killers take a quick glance around the shop and then ask the owner for the counter keys. The owner tries to get up in order to retrieve them but is beaten to a pulp by the second intruder, who likes to use the butt end of the sawed-off shotgun. The attacker then points the barrel of the gun at the back of the owner's neck and says menacingly, "Now you're going to die."[29] At this point, the third Brabant Killer arrives and acts as a lookout near the window while one of the Brabant Killers finds the counter keys himself.

The perpetrators pull out the telephone wires and the man with the sawed-off shotgun smashes all the glass counters. The Killers steal handguns and submachine guns, completely ignoring the assault rifles and shotguns. They dump a total of 18 firearms in two bags before forcing the three severely injured victims on the floor to hand over their wallets.[30] The owner gets more butt ends to the face, which breaks his orbital bone and knocks him into a coma.

A pedestrian notices something is happening in the gun shop and runs to a nearby garage, asking the mechanic to contact the authorities. The mechanic notices a police van driving past the gun shop, and alerts Officer Claude Haulotte in the van. The officer double parks his van and rushes to the gun shop with his gun out. In his haste, Officer Haulotte leaves the van's door open with the keys in the ignition.[31]

The third perpetrator, still acting as a lookout, notices the police officer running towards the store and slips out the door, on the attack. Only a Toyota truck separates the lookout and the officer, so the lookout shoots a 7.65 mm bullet through the truck's window. It misses Officer Haulotte, who uses the truck as a shield and returns fire, but misses.[32]

A second gangster exits the store and joins the lookout on the store side of the Toyota truck. One of the gangsters directs the other to go around the back of the truck, while he goes around the front. Officer Haulotte, caught between the two, is hit with a bullet to the upper body and crashes down to the pavement. The gangster walks right over the writhing police officer on the ground and finishes him off with a 7.65-caliber bullet.[33]

THE GETAWAY

The Insane Killers hastily return to the dark blue Volkswagen Santana, dumping their two bags of stolen weapons in the trunk. Two perpetrators get into the Santana while the third takes the wheel of the double-parked police van to move it out of the way.[34] He then jumps into the Santana and they flee north towards Brussels.[35]

By then, all police cruisers in the vicinity have already been alerted. They're advised to keep an eye open for a dark Audi 80—the Volkswagen Santana is rare and easily mistaken for the Audi 80. Two Gendarmerie officers in an unmarked Renault R4 head to a busy intersection that connects with the thoroughfare to Brussels.[36]

They notice the dark blue Santana with French plates zooming by and give chase, but are quickly left behind by the much more powerful Santana. Once out of sight, the Santana hides in a parking lot. The Brabant Killers remove the French plates and replace them with Belgian plates that match another blue Santana from Ixelles. They then exit the parking lot to resume their escape to Brussels.[37]

By dumb luck, the unmarked Renault police car stumbles on the Santana again, right as it turns back onto the road. The high-speed chase starts again near the town of Overijse, which is located roughly midway between the Wavre Gun Shop and Brussels. The unmarked police car manages to keep up with the Santana for a good ten minutes.[38] Both cars swerve around other cars and zigzag around obstacles in the narrow streets of Overijse, with the Santana barely missing a bus. The police officer driving the unmarked Renault 4 needs to hop over the sidewalk to avoid the bus. The officers try to call for radio backup, but the airwaves are now too clogged. The passenger in the backseat of the Santana often glances back at the police car.[39]

HOEILLART INTERSECTION

By 10:50 a.m., both cars approach a traffic jam at the corner of a busy intersection in the town of Hoeillart; the buildings are so close to the four corners of the intersection that it's impossible to get by.[40] The Renault 4 cuts right in front of the braking Santana, which causes it to fishtail, bump the back of the Renault and grind to a halt.[41] The officers pull out their Gendarmerie regulation 7.65 mm sidearms with an eight-bullet charger.

Only a few feet away, the Insane Killers also exit the Santana with their weapons at the ready. They take cover behind the Santana and the open car door. Dozens of witnesses who are stopped at the intersection watch the scene as it unfolds. Officer Campinne and the front passenger of the Santana exchange fire. Campinne empties his whole eight-round clip, but his 7.65 mm bullets aren't powerful enough to pierce through the Santana's passenger door and stay stuck in the metal frame.

The Santana's passenger's 9mm bullets do much more damage. Of the nine bullets fired, four hit Campinne. He's hit twice in his left thigh, once in his forearm and once his stomach just between the liver and a lung. A fifth bullet ricochets off his belt. The bandits get closer and shoot another bullet under the officer's knee, which ricochets and lodges in his groin.

His partner, Officer Sartillot, also empties his whole eight-bullet clip of small caliber 7.65 mm, but not one hits a Brabant Killer. With no ammo left and his partner down, Officer Sartillot tries to run away. One of the killers aims and tries to fire a kill shot toward the retreating officer, but had already fired his last bullet. With his clip empty and no more ammo, the Brabant Killer takes out the sawed-off shotgun and fires. Officer Sartillot is hit in the lower back with 72 buck shots, leaving both police officers seriously hurt. Fortunately, the three Brabant Killers are out of ammo and step back into the Santana, quickly swerving out and around the unmarked Renault R4. As the Santana disappears towards Brussels, smoke from the radiator pours out from under the hood.

While they weren't wearing masks, the Brabant Killers probably had makeup and props to alter their appearance. A witness believes one of the Killers was wearing a wig.[42] Because the Santana's radiator was hit and was smoking after the shootout at the intersection, some observers believe the criminals probably hid nearby and never made it to Brussels. According to Officer Thompsin, if a bullet pierced the radiator, the Santana could have only driven a maximum of five miles from Hoeillart.[43]

Building an Arsenal

The Brabant Killers used two 9mm caliber handguns to overpower the Gendarmes. They also used the 7.65 caliber FN pistol that they had fired at the grocery in Maubeuge, France on August 14th and a sawed-off shotgun. It's suspected to be the 10-gauge Faul that was shoplifted at the Dinant Gun Shop on March 13th. This could explain why Officer Sartillot survived as the Faul is intended to be used to hunt small game like fowl. The Killer who shot the sawed-off shotgun is the one who carried the two bags of stolen guns out of the gun shop. The lookout carried the 7.65 mm pistol and the third gangster used a 9mm.

The Brabant Killers didn't bother trying to get the contents of the cash register and so the most likely motive for this crime was to steal guns to use in crimes. Earlier that year, thieves attempted a nighttime break-in attempt into the same gun shop but weren't able to get in the store. There is speculation that the Brabant Killers, escalating their criminal activity by this point, felt they had no choice but to hold up the gun shop. The only other gun that can be traced to them was shoplifted directly from the Dinant Gun Shop. The Brabant Killers never buy guns off the black market, preferring to steal them. Either they have no black-market contacts or they're very conscious of the risk of having the guns traced back to them.

Among the 18 weapons stolen are nine revolvers, five pistols, and four submachine guns. The guns are for their own personal use not for resale. Some are assumed to have been used later as the calibers match up perfectly, such as a Smith and Wesson revolver capable of shooting both .38 Special ammo and 357 Magnum bullets. A few of the pistols likely used by the Brabant Killers during their later crimes include a 45-caliber Colt Government, a Smith and Wesson 9mm Para Model 559, an FN 22-caliber LR, 150 Concours, and a 7.65 mm Bernadelli Model 60.[44] They also probably used some of the submachine guns and an Ingram silencer prototype they stole.

THE WAVRE GENDARMERIE INVESTIGATION

A team of three detectives from the Wavre Gendarmerie station leads the investigation and produces their first report by July of 1983. The detectives determine the motive was not to steal guns, but most likely to steal the Ingram silencer prototype. One of the witnesses from the gun shop robbery said that when the Killers stole the weapons, they also picked up the silencer and the witness heard one bandit tell the others, "Okay, let's go! We have what we want."[45] This leads the detectives to believe the Killers came for something specific like the prototype. They also believe that the owner could have been targeted because he was known to be a big player in the international weapons market. However, the owner tells investigators he did not recognize the perpetrators.

When looking over the gun shop's accounting, investigators determine that in-shop sales were only a fraction of the owner's revenue because he produced all kinds of high-tech gadgets and specialty products for the international market. The prototype silencer the Killers stole was one the owner had recently designed. It was a custom-made silencer prototype for Ingram submachine guns and the detectives believe a dispute related to the silencer transaction may have prompted the attack on the Dekaise Gun Shop.

The detectives discover that the owner of the Dekaise Gun Shop contacted arms broker Willy Pourtois to find buyers for his silencer prototype. Pourtois allegedly brought representatives from the Lebanese Christian Phalange—one of the major factions embroiled in the Lebanese Civil War—to take a look. Additionally, Pourtois worked for a Belgian firm with links to the New York firm International Security Associates (ISA), which represented a Columbian client interested in 250 Dekaise silencers. The parties came to an agreement that Dekaise got US $1000 up front, then 400,000 BEF (around $11,268) in September 1982 to cover the initial production costs. The total value of the deal amounted to 1,250,000 BEF (around $35,211). To facilitate production, Pourtois loaned five Ingram submachine guns to Dekaise to work with. By the end of September

1982, Dekaise still hasn't received the 400,000 BEF for the initial production costs. Apparently, ISA's European rep disappeared with the money from the head office. Dekaise halts production of the silencer.

The Wavre investigators speculate that Dekaise refused to return the US $1,000 advance and the five Ingram submachine guns on loan from broker Pourtois. The detectives speculate that one of the parties involved may have retaliated and punished Dekaise. Under their scenario, the Insane Killers may have stolen the silencer prototype so another gunsmith could reproduce it. The rest of the weapons are stolen as a diversion.

Because ISA was involved, some sources speculate that the beating of the gun shop owner was done with the knowledge of American intelligence authorities. Furthermore, Willy Pourtois is known to be a paid informant for the Sûreté, the Belgian intelligence gathering agency. The Sûreté was likely informed of every interaction Pourtois had with the Wavre Gun Shop, which would lend credence that it was because of some Western intelligence operation.

There are holes in the theory, however. First, Pourtois asked Dekaise for the five Ingram submachine guns after the attack, they were returned to him. Second, these types of deals fall apart all the time and violence rarely follows. Furthermore, Dekaise only received US $1,000 as an advance—and he's not the one who broke the contract. It isn't very likely that someone would put together a hit squad over US $1,000 and five weapons. Another thing that doesn't make sense is the time delay. If Dekaise stops production in September, why is the beating only 30 days later? Finally, there's never been any evidence that silencers based on Dekaise's prototype have been mass-produced by anyone.

VINCENT L. CREW

The search for suspects in the Dekaise robbery begins to bring in leads. In 1983, Francis V. tells police his friend, deceased junky Vincent L., committed the robbery. While investigating the allegations, a picture of Vincent L., Francis V., and convicted criminal Vicky V. is found. In the background, there's an Enfield machine gun decorating the fireplace of Vicky V.'s home. Police determine that the Enfield in Vicky V.'s home is a similar model to the one stolen from the Dekaise Gun Shop.

There's a search and seizure at Vicky V.'s home and investigators find the Enfield above the fireplace, just as in the picture. It's demilitarized and has no serial number, so no ballistic link can be established. Investigators are suspicious that Vicky V. won't say who he bought the Enfield from. They can't pursue the matter any further as this particular demilitarized Enfield is very common and can be easily purchased.

A while later, authorities suspect that Vincent L. and Francis V. delivered three weapons from the Dekaise Gun Shop attack to Gendarme Martial Lekeu, who becomes a major suspect in 1989. Lekeu worked as a narcotics detective in the Gendarmerie until 1978. After his stint there as a detective, Lekeu was transferred for disciplinary reasons back to regular patrol duty.

After this allegation, Lekeu moved to the countryside. 1He wanted to leave the atmosphere of Brussels

Bruno Van Deuren

Small-time criminal Bruno Van Deuren boasts that he was involved in the Dekaise attack. His confession is plausible, but he gives different versions of the story and then recants. He claims either he participated in the Dekaise Gun Shop attack or just helped transfer the stolen weapons after the attack. His claims resonate because they match the Wavre investigators' theory that the gun shop was attacked because the owner was punished for breaching a contract after taking a cash advance.

Authorities initially don't follow up because Van Deuren has a solid alibi. The alibi later turns out to be inaccurate.

When authorities decide to investigate Van Deuren further in the late 1980s, they find out he has just been murdered. He received one bullet to the back of the neck and his murder goes unsolved. This suspect lead is still popular because Van Deuren links up with other leads in the case.[46] The weapons transited through Ixelles, which is the suspected home base of the Insane Killers. Van Deuren also hung out at Pub De Pomp where other suspects were seen. However, aside from some circumstantial elements, there's not enough to definitively link Van Deuren to the others and consider him a serious suspect.[47]

DANI BOUHOUCHE

One of the Gendarmes in the unmarked Renault who chased the Insane Killers in the stolen Santana between the gun shop and the Hoeillart intersection believes he identified one of the perpetrators. Officer Campinne has always claimed the suspect in the back seat was a Gendarme colleague of his, Dani Bouhouche. According to Campinne, his colleague had dark makeup on his face.

Bouhouche is a street cop who worked out of the Uccle Gendarmerie station at the time of the Dekaise robbery. It's within walking distance to Flagey Square in Ixelles, the epicenter of the home base for the Insane Killers. He was originally a narcotics detective, but because of disciplinary problems, he was transferred to street patrol in 1981. In a bizarre incident, Bouhouche had hidden an electronic listening device to listen in on a discussion other detectives had with an informant. He was otherwise considered a good detective whose reports are well done, who doesn't drink or do drugs, and never goes out clubbing.

Prior to this undercover gaffe, Bouhouche did have one other disciplinary issue that was quickly covered up. In 1980, while Bouhouche was riding in an R4 van with two other Gendarmes in downtown Brussels, a taxi cab speeds past the van and cuts it off. A switch suddenly flips in Bouhouche's brain; he pulls out his own personal GP 9 mm and empties two full clips of illegal explosive Dum Dum hollow point bullets into the taxi, right in the middle of a busy street. The taxi driver, a man named Costas Giannakis, miraculously survives unscathed despite his headrest being pierced by a bullet.

The hollow point bullets bore large two-inch holes into the body of the taxicab. The Gendarmerie begins an internal review of the incident. Bouhouche claims that for a split second he believed the taxi driver was actually a gangster, as if that justified his behavior.

The ballistic expertise is supplied by Commander Claude Dery, who is a close acquaintance of Bouhouche. They both love firearms and frequently run ballistic tests together. Dery covers up the troubling detail that Bouhouche used his own personal 9mm handgun instead of the less powerful regulation 7.65 mm. He also omits the fact that Bouhouche used the illegal hollow point bullets and instead writes in the report that the ammo used is standard Winchester High-Velocity bullets. The Gendarmerie closes the internal review of the incident.

SOIGNES FOREST

Later on September 30th, 1982, the evening of the Wavre Gun Shop incident, the Insane Killers drive the stolen busted-up Volkswagen Santana to Soignes Forest in the southern suburb of Brussels. The gang douses the vehicle with gasoline and lights it on fire. It is found still smoldering at 10:30 p.m., the burned metal carcass riddled with bullet holes on the side and the dashboard. Inside the car, the backseat has been removed and eight shell casings are still on the floor. The shell casings come from both 9mm handguns fired earlier that day by the Brabant Killers during their shootout with police. Also found inside are the metallic marbles used to close the barrels of the stolen weapons while exposed in the gun shop. There's also a small scale.[48]

Dumping Ground

According to Gendarme Charles Thompsin, the intention could have been to drive the Santana into the water but it was stuck in the mud.[49] The Brabant Killers were forced to set it on fire to cover their tracks. Regarding the small scale, there are two theories: One theory is that the small scale could have been used to measure drugs. Another is that it could be used to reload munitions because the Insane Killers sometimes shoot with recharged ammunitions.

The spot in Soignes Forest where the car is abandoned is the same place where the contents of a stolen Toyota van were dumped right after it was stolen from the Ixelles perfume shop Paris-XL. Years later, it is found that the theft of the van is linked to the Gendarme Dani Bouhouche. A couple of months after the 1980 shooting incident with the taxi driver, Bouhouche had allegedly gone rogue and moonlighted as a gangster, assembling a small crew and acquiring a basic criminal infrastructure. The Bouhouche Gang rents garage boxes to store their getaway cars and weapons and also rents safe houses. The rentals are centered in two areas of Brussels, the southern Ixelles area and a western suburb Woluwe[4]. The Bouhouche Gang uses stolen IDs.

The Bouhouche Gang stole the Paris-XL store's Toyota van on October 7th, 1981. They had also stolen a Mazda the previous week on the same street using the same modus operandi. When the van's driver had come to stock the store in Ixelles, he left the keys in the ignition with the motor running. The Bouhouche Gang just had to step in and ride away. The white Toyota HiAce van was stocked full of Paris-XL merchandise—the contents dumped in Soignes Forest. They store the van in a rental unit they just rented in Ixelles. The Gang modifies the van to use as a mobile base of operations by drilling a hole in the roof, putting stickers on the van body, and affixing two fake license plates to it.

An ordinance map of Soignes forest is found years later in Bouhouche's house. The specific place on the map where the Volkswagen Santana is abandoned and torched after the Dekaise robbery is marked with a cross. Bouhouche never had an alibi for the Dekaise attack. He used a sick day.[50]

---

[4]   It it actually a very small enclave that overlaps a couple of municipalities like Woluwe Saint Lambert. In this enclave is the Catholic University of Louvain (UCL) Medical school campus.

SOIGNES FOREST REDUX

On October 16th, two weeks after the Dekaise Gun Shop attack, a series of items related to the robbery are found in a different spot of Soignes Forest, far from the area where the smoldering Santana was found the day of the attack. Among the items found are a bank card from the gun shop owner and another card from one of his clients. There are also documents and checks in the owner's name.[51]

The Santana's fake Belgian license plate is found, its number copied from the plate of another Santana in Ixelles of the same color. The plate is cut into several pieces in a peculiar crisscross pattern. Other items discovered include two back headrest frames and blocks of foam from the Santana's back seat, as well as eyeglass frames without lenses. This suggests that the Insane Killers were altering their appearance.[52] There's a card taken out of a 1970s Esso calendar, as well as a plastic bag from the gadget shop, Casine, in Waterloo.[53] A cut-up shoe is found, a copy of a Spanish newspaper, and a dirty polo shirt superficially buried at the foot of a tree.[54] The shirt, when analyzed, has drops of animal blood on it, which could suggest the person is a hunter. There are size 11 (size 44 in Europe) designer Ambiorix shoes.[55] There are also hints that a suspect likes shooting at shooting ranges, due to the discovery of pieces of a shooting range club membership and a sticker from a garage that directly faces another shooting range.[56]

HANDWRITING

A significant finding is bits of handwritten notes written in a very elegant cursive style. The notes seem like directions for a rendezvous. They include the words: "Wauthier-Braines," "Soignes," "lez" and "Pilori." These words are probably all place names. "Beside the word "Pilori" is the French phrase, "*gendarmerie à côté*", which means "beside the Gendarmerie station". There also might be the faded word "*quel était la consigne*" (what was the instruction) or "*qui était le soussigné*" (who was the undersigned)."

It seems likely that it concerns the Braine-le-Comte attack of September 18th. The Gang would have met beforehand at a place called the Pilori, which is located beside the Gendarmerie station.

CHAPTER 4

HET KASTEL INN RESTAURANT
(DECEMBER 23, 1982)

SHORTLY BEFORE MIDNIGHT ON DECEMBER 22ND THE INSANE KILL-
ers break into the restaurant at the Het Kasteel Inn by prying open
the kitchen door with a crowbar.[57] It's located in Beersel, on the southern
outskirts of Brussels, in an isolated area with nearby neighbors. It's right
in front of a castle from the Middle Ages and a park.

A 71-year-old, live-in caretaker named Jose Van Den Eynde is sleeping on the second floor and wakes up when he hears noise coming from
downstairs. The robbers realize someone else is in the building. They
stumble on Van Den Eynde, who is wearing just a T-shirt and under-
wear. The assailants beat him with many violent blows to the head.
Van Den Eynde tries to fight back but is overwhelmed. The Killers use
the telephone wires they ripped out of the walls to hog-tie Van Den Eynde.[58] The knots used to secure Van Den Eynde are the same knots used by
certain special police units. The Killers also use a scarf found in the room
to tie the victim to the bed.[59]

The intruders aren't done with Van Den Eynde yet. They use cigarette butts to burn the older man on his thighs and upper body and
beat him. At some point, the thieves stick a plastic glove in his mouth to
stop Van Den Eynde from screaming and cover his head with a brown
sheath. One of the intruders then shoots eight 22 long rifle bullets into

Van Den Eynde's left ear area at point-blank range.[60] The sheath splatters with blood.

The assassins go back downstairs, where they drink some champagne, chomp on a deer leg, and eat a fruit pie. They leave the Inn, taking several bottles of alcohol with them. They also take a dozen Royal Schwab plates, some bags of coffee, a trench coat, washcloths, and some utensils.

GRAND CRU WINE

Investigators suspect at least two perpetrators were involved in the attack on Van Den Eynde at the Inn because of the way the fight unfolded on the second floor. The caretaker Van Den Eynde slept with an alarm-pistol under his pillow, but he was never able to get to it. According to an early report, investigators suspected the meal was a put on by the intruders to make it look like small-time criminals.[61]

The motive could have been a simple robbery. The loot of expensive alcohol and goods is similar to what was stolen during the Maubeuge, France break-in of August 1982. It includes Champagne Roederer and Grand Cru wines. The estimated value of the robbery is 150,000 BEF (about US $4,225).

There were no break-ins for 30 years at the Inn. Now, this devastating event is the third break-in in the last year[62] always using a crowbar to force the back door. Each time it's expensive bottles of wine and the best champagnes that are stolen. December of the year before, 40 bottles of Grand Cru wine and the cash register were robbed. The register was dumped in a small lake in Sint-Genesius-Rose. Because of that first robbery, the Inn hired the cook's father, José Van Den Eynde, in July to provide some nighttime security. He's given space on the second floor with a bedroom and a private bathroom.[63]

On November 30th, robbers struck again and completely emptied the wine cellar, stealing 12 bottles of Cristal Rose Champagne and a few dozen other champagnes.[64] The total damage amounts to about $3,400. Van Den Eynde slept through the whole robbery. As it's a popular restaurant, the Inn has no choice but to refill the cellar.

During the third robbery, the Brabant Killers beat Van Den Eynde, perhaps to force him to disclose if he had money or valuables hidden on the property. The burnt cigarette marks on the dead body suggest the Killers could have been trying to force him to talk. The use of improvised devices like the telephone wires and a scarf to bind Van Den Eynde suggests that this was not the Killers' initial plan. They then shot him with eight bullets. The .22-caliber LR pistol they used for the murder could have been the FN Concours 150 stolen at Dekaise on September 30th.

Inspectors also looked into different possible motives. They looked in Van Den Eynde's personal life and determined he gambled regularly. If the Killers knew him beforehand, perhaps they believed he could have a large quantity of cash on him. A neighbor saw a white vehicle leaving the parking lot heading towards the highway around the time of the murder. The Brabant Killers don't have a known car in their possession. Their stolen Santana was abandoned and burned in September 1982. A while after the break-in, false police officers showed up to look for things inside the Inn. No trace of the imposters is ever found and they are never identified.

The following investigation is sloppy. Several pieces of evidence disappear. Of note, Gendarmerie Officer Bouhouche participates in the investigation.

Vincent L. Crew

In late 1983, Francis V.—who had accused his dead friend Vincent L. of being involved in the Wavre Gun Shop attack—also accused Vincent L. of taking part in the Het Kasteel Inn murder. According to Francis V., 71-year-old Van Den Eynde was in Vincent L.'s crew. Van den Eynde had to be murdered because he knew too much about the crew's activities.

In an April 1984 report, the investigation uncovers the tenuous link that the Het Kasteel Inn owner (not Van Den Eynde, who was hired as the security guard) was a former star soccer player for the Anderlecht soccer club. This is something of interest to investigators because the father of another alleged Vincent L. crew member had once been the Vice President of the soccer club.

CHAPTER 5

TAXI RIDE FROM IXELLES TO MONS
(JANUARY 9, 1983)

THE NIGHT OF FRIDAY, JANUARY 9TH, TAXI DRIVER COSTA ANGELOU advises dispatch that he has a street pickup at Flagey Square in Ixelles at 1:15 a.m. A Brabant Killer sits on the taxi's back seat, right behind the driver.[65] Within the first 6 miles of the ride, the taxi suddenly stops on an empty stretch of road on the Southern outskirts of Brussels. The passenger shoots four .22 LR bullets directly into the back of the taxi driver's head, three right above the back of his neck and one slightly under the left ear. The bullets don't completely travel through the taxi driver's skull. There is no evidence of a struggle in the taxi.

Angelou's body is hauled along the chalky ground on the side of the taxi. His bloodied body is then folded over and dumped inside the taxi's trunk. The Brabant Killer then heads toward the western Borinage region, which is near the Maubeuge France grocery shootout of August 1982. The attacker steals the cab driver's wallet, which has about 10,000 BEF (about US $282) inside.[66]

A few days later, on January 12th, Angelou's abandoned taxi is found in the center of the town of Mons, the capital of the Borinage region, about a sixty miles from Brussel.[67] It's left illegally parked in the street in a reserved diplomatic parking spot right next to the Consulate of France offices. It still carries the standard Brussels Taxi plate.[68] Angelou's dead body is found in the trunk.

IMPULSIVE RAGE OR PREMEDITATION?

There was no CB radio in the taxi because Angelou considered it too expensive. Instead, he would call from pay phones to advise dispatch of his pickups.[69] The taxi meter is torn out by the assassin, but the 57 miles recorded on the meter matches the approximate distance of the drive.[70] Angelou usually limited his taxi runs to the Greater Brussels area only. The Taxi Bruxelles sign is left in the feet area of the backseat, as are Angelou's shoe and vest, both of which are covered in blood. Authorities notice drops of blood inside the car and on the car's body. The Brabant Killer must have chosen to hide Angelou's body in the trunk rather than drive around with it on the seat. It can be assumed that this murder and theft were committed by only one Brabant Killer because he pulled Angelou along the ground instead of carrying him.

The Killer drove the whole distance in a cab drenched with blood and brain tissue, and probably had some spattered on his face. The fact he drove to Mons in the Borinage is significant; the killer probably lived in the Borinage or there was an accomplice there available to help him clean the mess up, give him access to a shower, and provide him with new clothes. In that scenario, he probably called his accomplice from a pay phone to ask for help. There were sightings of the black Mercedes in a couple of places in Mons the night of the murder.[71] Importantly, because the taxi cab ended up in Mons, the Mons Gendarmerie will conduct the investigation even if the murder was committed in the Brussels area.

The .22-caliber LR pistol is believed to be the FN Concours 150 stolen at Dekaise in September 1982—the same weapon used to kill the Beersel Inn caretaker in December 1982. This likely signals the murder was not premeditated. The Killer became angry and unhinged; the need to kill was stronger than the risks of being caught over the matching ballistics. This Brabant Killer may have pulled out a gun and told the taxi driver to stop on the side of the road. As soon as Angelou stopped, the trigger-happy Killer finished him off. It seems unlikely that the Killer's motivation was to get whatever cash Angelou made that day.

The Brabant Killers now have a second, separate series of attacks that are linked ballistically. For simplicity's sake, we'll call them the "Public Attacks" ballistics versus the "Serial Killer" ballistics. The Public Attacks ballistics link the Maubeuge grocery shootout of August 1982 with the Wavre Gun Shop attack of September 1982. The Serial Killer ballistics now links the Het Kasteel Inn Restaurant Murder from December 1982 to the taxi driver murder. The purpose of separating both series of ballistics is that the Brabant Killers build on each series for months; and, to begin with, certain attacks seem unrelated to the others.

The fact the Killer had to reuse the .22 LR in a fit of unstoppable rage makes some sense. But why would he have carried a weapon that was already used in another murder in the first place? He could have carried many of the still unused handguns stolen from the Wavre Gun Shop. The answer is probably that the only small caliber handgun among their stolen arsenal that had a silencer was the .22 LR. The risk of leaving extra witnesses now was perhaps a greater consideration than the risk of them being caught with the ballistics link later on. Or maybe they deliberately start linking their murders to one another.

In the search for another motive, the victim's past is carefully reviewed. Maybe the murder was in fact premeditated? There were rumors that Angelou worked for drug traffickers.[72] A convict claimed that Angelou would ride around Brussels in his taxi to sell heroin.[73] Another link was made between the victim, Angelou and the Het Kasteel Inn's caretaker;[74] both had worked as taxi drivers and there were reports they might have known each other. But nothing more was ever found.

Saint-Lambert Woluwe Delhaize

On Friday, January 21st, 1983, bandits step into the Delhaize grocery store in Saint-Lambert-Woluwe and yell out "Cash!" They walk to the back office and are given the contents of the safe, leaving with an amount of 1.3 million BEF (or about US $36, 620). No shots are fired.[75]

The Woluwe Delhaize armed robbery is the first robbery in a large Delhaize supermarket in Belgium.[76] Because no shots are fired, there are no ballistics to compare to the other attacks by the Brabant Insane Killers. However, there are similarities to their subsequent armed robberies of supermarkets. They steal the money from the cash registers in front and then go back to the safe in the manager's office. They don't steal cartons of cigarettes or alcohol. This Woluwe holdup is also perpetrated right before they start their first string of supermarket robberies. However, this incident doesn't fit the geographical pattern of the other attacks.

WATERMAEL

On January 28th, at 8:30 p.m., Raymond De Wee parks his Peugeot 504 in front of his home in Watermael. As he steps out, he's confronted by an Insane Killer with dark curly hair and dark-framed glasses. The Brabant Killer points a rifle with a wooden handle towards him. De Wee is ordered to hand over his car keys and to lie down on the ground. Because he's in an awkward position between the Peugeot and the wall, De Wee only gets down after the Brabant Killer repeats himself.[77]

The Insane Killer steps in the driver's seat of the Peugeot and immediately opens up the passenger door. Another man that was hidden in the dark gets in the passenger seat. The passenger has a flashlight in his hand. Before leaving, the driver exits the car, points the rifle again at De Wee, and orders him to hand over his wallet. Once they have the wallet, the Insane Killers take off with the Peugeot.[78]

NORTH AFRICANS?

As every other time they steal a car, they steal the Peugeot with the keys rather than hotwiring an unattended vehicle. They also always insist the victim lie down on the ground on his stomach. At this point in time, the Insane Killers are not known to own a car. The last time we know for sure they had a car was back in September 1982 when they torched the stolen Volkswagen Santana. The only other vehicle linked to them is from a witness report that a white van was seen in the Het Kasteel Inn parking lot in December 1982. They clearly need another car to commit their various crimes.

The Watermael carjacking is used in support of a theory that one or more Insane Killers are North African. The one with the rifle has thick curly hair, wears dark-framed glasses, and is sharply dressed. He addresses the victim with an Arabic accent. The other has an afro and wears horn-rimmed glasses. The wife of De Wee, when interviewed years after the crime, refutes this assertion. "Wrong. They had black hair, but didn't look Arab."[79]

Once again, the value of police sketches in the Brabant Killer case is debatable. The problem is that the Killers are very careful not to be identified. They often wear makeup. They are known to try to pull off a foreign accent, such as Arabic, Romani (Gypsy), Moroccan, etc.—usually unsuccessfully. Some witnesses and victims specifically mention the Killers using a contrived or fake accent.

With this Delhaize car theft, we again see the characteristic lack of impulse control of one of the Killers, only this time he is the driver. While the Killers often seem super organized, one of them seems to act very impulsively. Here they came for the car, but stop and demand the wallet as an afterthought to get a few extra bucks. As more crimes are committed by the Brabant Killers, it becomes more obvious that there's at least one psychopath. He's called "Le Tueur" by French investigators and "Killer" by Dutch investigators. Let's call him "Psycho" for a couple of reasons. First, it's confusing to call him Killer when also referring to others in the group as a Brabant Killer or an Insane Killer. Second, they're all killers; one is just arguably more mentally disturbed.[80] Several murders are presumed to have been committed by the "Psycho" had no witnesses. It's just informed speculation. For the record, the investigators have named the two others the "Old Man" and "The Giant."

CHAPTER 6

DELHAIZE SUPERMARKET IN GENVAL
(FEBRUARY 11, 1983)

A T 7:10 P.M., ON FEBRUARY 11TH, THE INSANE KILLER'S STOLEN PEUgeot 504 enters the parking lot of the Delhaize supermarket in Genval. The car stops a short distance from the front door and the three men inside head into the store.[81] Two Brabant Killers wear carnival masks and the third wears a dark gray ski mask. The carnival masks are smiling men with glasses, a big nose, and round cheeks.[82] Two carry handguns and the third carries a rifle.

The two men wearing carnival masks have curly hair and tanned skin. One of the two looks to be about 40 years old; the other man looks younger and smaller. When the trio enters, they threaten a woman just ahead of them with their weapons and hold her as a hostage. The two men with handguns force her to lead them to the manager's second-floor office.[83] Meanwhile, the man with the rifle, who is wearing a trench coat, walks to the area where the cash registers are located. The store manager, the cashiers, and the customers are ordered to freeze.[84]

Upstairs, the two other Brabant Killers find two employees in the office counting cash. The employees are ordered to unlock the office safe and then to lie down on the ground. One of the Insane Killers stuffs the cash from the safe into a plastic bag.[85] The gunmen sever the telephone wires and shoot at a mainframe computer. When they get back down the stairs, they come face-to-face with the store manager. Apparently, the gunman at the cash registers let him walk back towards the office. The two push him back from where he came from. When the manager reaches the front, he's ordered to lie down again.[86] They shoot once at the ceiling and leave the store with 692,384 BEF or about US $19,478.

An unsuspecting shopper named Jacques Culot is in his parked Audi 100 when he notices the three masked armed robbers in his rear-view mirror. He starts his car, and one of the Killers screams at him to stop. The attacker starts shooting his caliber .38 Special at the Audi. Several bullets hit the Audi's body, side panel, and tires. Culot slips under the dashboard just in time. Both front windows shatter and bullets perforate the front seats. "Forget it, let's go!"[87] calls out one of the shooter's accomplices. The shooter screams out to Culot, "If you try to follow us, we'll shoot you down."[88] The Peugeot 504 exits the parking and drives towards the South of Brussels.

OBSERVATIONS

This is the first supermarket hold-up that is officially linked to the Insane Killers. It happens in the Brabant region, which is their calling card. As mentioned before, Brabant is comprised of the rich suburbs that make a ring around Brussels. However, to be more technical, most of their crimes are committed in the southern French-speaking part of Brabant called the Walloon Brabant. The Brabant Killers are French speakers, even though the Giant is also known to express himself in Dutch. However, most of their 28 murders occur in Dutch-speaking areas in the close vicinity or a bit north of, Walloon Brabant, also in comfortable, peaceful neighborhoods.

The Genval Delhaize robbery bears many familiar characteristics to their other robberies. It happens in the early evening, just before closing time. They use a stolen car with false plates. They cover their faces. They're a group of three perpetrators and all three participate in the hold-up. No one stays back in the car. This is their typical way of operating. They don't typically use a driver that stays back in the getaway car.

They are very familiar with the supermarket's floor plan and likely scouted the location beforehand. Every perpetrator has a role. One of the Insane Killers goes to the cash registers while the two others go to the manager's office. One of the employees is ordered to unlock the store's safe. All the other employees are ordered to lie down on the ground. They systematically sever telephone wires and find a hostage they parade around the store during the duration of the holdup. Anyone who gets in their way, or does not immediately comply, is met with violence. A lady is shoved, and in a ridiculous overreaction, a shopper's Audi is riddled with bullet holes. They shoot wildly everywhere; at the ceiling, and a mainframe computer.

However, there are marked differences here than with later hold-ups. No one notices a "Giant." The Insane Killer in charge of staying back near the cash registers lets the store manager get up and go back to the office. This would be unimaginable and would never have been tolerated in later attacks. He would have been immediately beaten or shot if he tried to stand up and leave.

As for weapons, they use two new calibers—a .38 Special and a .357. According to Prosecutor Jean-Claude Lacroix, the .38 Special gave them some headaches. "We were dealing with recharged ammo and we did not know the charge of powder."[89] The Insane Killers carry a longarm and also reuse a 9mm handgun fired during the Wavre attack. Until the Wavre Gun shop attack in September 1982, the Brabant Killers probably had no choice but to reuse a weapon or two due to their limited selection of available weapons. However, after the Wavre Gun Shop attack, they've built up an arsenal of weapons and there is no burning necessity to reuse a weapon. However, it seems they consciously linked the 9mm to the other attacks by choice.

This 9mm should connect Genval to the "Public Attacks" ballistic links. If you're keeping score, the grocery in Maubeuge (France) in August 1982, the Wavre Gun Shop in September 1982, and the Genval Delhaize all link together. But they don't yet in the eyes of the investigation, as Prosecutor Guy Wezel, who is assigned the case of the Genval Delhaize in February 1983, mentioned later on: "At the time, there was not yet any link with the Dekaise case in Wavre (September 1982)."[90] There are, of course, no other obvious links to connect these attacks to the murder of the Het Kasteel Innkeeper in December and the Mons Taxi driver in January, as the weapons used in these crimes are entirely different.

LASNES

On February 14th, at 7:00 p.m., Geneviève Van Lindt drives home from her workplace in Ixelles. She's driving a brand new, dark-colored Volkswagen Golf, fresh off the dealership floor. Twenty minutes later, she turns into the driveway in front of her home. That's when she notices a dark Peugeot stopping close behind her car.[91]

When she steps out of her car, one of the Insane Killers jumps out of the dark Peugeot 504 and pulls a gun out of his trench coat. He points the gun to her stomach and says, "Lady, don't move…leave your keys on the car."[92] The carjacker appears to be in his thirties and of average build. His accomplice stays behind the wheel of the Peugeot.

Van Lindt leaves the keys on the car as instructed. The carjacker takes the keys and steps in the brand-new Golf. He puts it in reverse and drives away. His accomplice, still in the Peugeot 504, makes a speedy U-turn and quickly catches up with the Golf.

Printing Company

The armed carjacker has a dark complexion with thick, black, curly hair and white skin. He looks fit. The Brabant Killers now have two cars, this new Volkswagen Golf, and the Peugeot stolen on January 28th. The dark gray Golf is a four-door hatchback with a sunroof and tinted windows.

As a rule, the Insane Killers always steal new cars. The exception was the old Austin Allegro that they used to get to a dealership to steal a new car. When they steal from the buyer, it means they need to do some basic scouting on their target. As always, they steal the car with the keys.

A Gendarme friend of Dani Bouhouche is a client of victim Genevieve Van Lindt's printing company in Ixelles.[93] The friend later opens a business in Ixelles not far from Van Lindt's printing company.

WATERLOO

On February 15th, the smoldering remains of the Brabant Killers' stolen Peugeot 504 are found abandoned in the Waterloo countryside, an area of large green fields interspersed with nice homes. It's abandoned less than half a mile from the chic restaurant Les Trois Canard. They leave the Peugeot 504 in a narrow countryside lane, hidden by thick trees on both sides. It's impossible for anyone on the main road nearby to see through the trees to the lane. The car speakers, radio and the lighter are removed, but cigarette butts are left inside.

SHOOTING THE RESERVOIR

Before abandoning the stolen Peugeot 504, the Insane Killers try several times to ignite a fire by shooting the gas reservoir. It doesn't work. There are several items the Killers typically remove from their getaway cars when abandoning them. The radio is always removed. The investigation determines that the Peugeot has been driven less than 100 miles since it was stolen, which suggests the Killers used it only for their hold-ups and otherwise hid it. The Volkswagen Golf GTI they have just stolen is a better car. Perhaps the Killers can only hide one stolen car and had to make a choice.

AUDI 100[94]

On February 22nd, thieves break into the back of a Volkswagen dealership in Waterloo. Once inside, they move an Audi Quattro to clear a passageway to get a damaged white Audi 100 out of the garage door. The thieves enter the unlocked Audi and start the motor with keys, which have been left in the ignition, and drive out of the garage. The alarm goes off at 4:00 a.m.

The stolen Audi 100 is the car that was riddled by bullets by the hot-tempered Insane Killer in the Genval Delhaize parking lot. It was pierced with several bullets and authorities were poised to extract them for analysis.[95]

UPDATE

For a very long time, this robbery has been considered linked to the Brabant Killers—mostly for circumstantial reasons. The investigation's website still includes this robbery in the Insane Killers' list of crimes. If it is them, it suggests the Killers had inside information as the Audi had only been there for a week and the bullets were about to be extracted for analysis. It's a brazen crime, one they may have committed not to procure a car, but rather to hide forensic evidence or thumb their noses at authorities.

Decades later, a thief claims he stole the damaged Audi with three friends.[96] If the story is true, the Audi theft should be removed from the Brabant Killers' canon of crimes. It's important to note that the thief's story doesn't exactly match the police file—and it's not the first time people have falsely claimed responsibility for crimes attributed to the Brabant Killers, usually seeking street cred or attention. The most glaring example is Jean-Marie Tinck, who recently falsely implicated himself as being a Brabant Killer. But we'll still put an asterisk on this robbery.

CHAPTER 7

DELHAIZE SUPERMARKET IN UCCLE
(FEBRUARY 25, 1983)

ON FEBRUARY 25TH, AT 7:30 P.M., THE INSANE KILLERS ARRIVE IN THE parking area of the Delhaize supermarket in the upscale neighborhood of Uccle, driving the stolen dark Volkswagen Golf. Two men wearing ski masks exit the car, one noticed by a witness is the tall man authorities dub the Giant. A third man stays behind in the getaway car. The Giant carries two firearms, while his accomplice has a two-foot-long nightstick.

When the Giant enters the store, he shoots wildly, injuring an elderly person pushing a grocery cart. Shoppers and employees in the store start panicking when they see him in the khakis, ski mask, and vest. The Giant, who is broad-shouldered and looks like a bodybuilder, screams out, "Everybody freeze!" He forces everyone to get down on the ground and then demands the money from the cashiers in front. When one of them starts sobbing, he pushes his weapon to her temple and says, "You shut the fuck up."

The man carrying the nightstick goes to the manager's office. He wears a Bomber jacket and a turtleneck shirt pulled up to cover half his face and khaki rain boots. Once in the office, he grabs an employee by the shoulder and pushes her towards the store's vault.[97]

Using a poor imitation of an Arabic accent, he orders her to open the vault. She can't find the keys. The Insane Killer smashes the phone in anger with his nightstick.[98] Another employee quickly digs up the keys to calm him down. As the employee opens the vault, the attacker shouts, "Quick you bastard!" The cash is emptied into a plastic bag. The assailant then heads back to the front of the store.

The Giant keeps everyone in the front of the store in check until his accomplice comes back. Before he leaves, the Giant fires another wild shot into the shelves. The Brabant Killers steal 600,000 BEF or approximately US $16,858.

They walk out of the store, sweeping their firearms from side to side. An elderly man notices them and runs to the gas station next door. One of the attackers takes a few steps towards him and shoots twice. A bullet hits the elderly man's knee, crippling him permanently. Another bullet barely misses a garage attendant.[99]

The two attackers jump into their getaway car, where the third accomplice waits for them. The VW Golf heads out of the parking lot.

THE INCREDIBLE HULK

It's the first time witnesses ever refer to "the Giant." He's not just very tall; but he is also physically massive, a monster of a man who looks like actor Lou Ferrigno when he played the Incredible Hulk. The size between the tallest and the other Brabant Killers has never been this marked, though a tall man had also been seen when they shoplifted a rifle in Dinant in March 1982.

The Brabant Killers exhibit some of their typical hold-up behavior: People are forced to get down on the ground, there's pointless shooting, both at inanimate objects and people, and there is no hesitation to shoot and cripple an elderly man to prevent him from alerting authorities. They also try and fail to mimic a foreign accent.

It's the only supermarket hold-up in the Brabant Killers' canon where only two attackers enter a supermarket. The third man in this scenario plays the role of getaway car driver and waits while the other two go inside. The most common explanation for this is that the store is situated at less than five kilometers from Flagey Square in Ixelles, which is the epicenter of the Brabant Insane Killers' activities. One or more of the attackers likely live or work there and the risk of being recognized is that much higher.

The Insane Killers use the caliber .38 Special fired in their first supermarket attack ever at the Genval Delhaize on February 11th, which links this crime to the series of Public Attacks ballistics. It includes the shootouts in Maubeuge, France in August of 1982 and the Wavre Gun Shop in September of the same year. It can be assumed they are aware of this link but do it anyways. So now, Maubeuge, Wavre, Genval, and Uccle are all linked together—in theory, as the only two crimes that authorities will connect together in the short run are the Maubeuge and Wavre attack. As for the Serial Killer ballistics of Het Kasteel Inn in December 1982 and Mons taxi in January 1983, they are still completely separate. In terms of other weapons, a witness reported seeing the Killers carrying what looked like a sawed-off shotgun.

The investigation is botched. The Gendarmerie tell supermarket employees to wipe the crime scene even before the Judicial Police get there. The caliber .38 Special ammo was recharged, which was a hindrance. Since the Gendarmerie take the bullets and they were subsequently destroyed, the police are unable to make a ballistics comparison.[100] The attack happens about a hundred yards away from the Uccle Gendarmerie, which is where Bouhouche worked.[101] Also, a short walk away is the spot in Watermael where the Renault was carjacked.

FLAGEY SQUARE

On March 3rd, at 11:00 a.m., the Audi the Killers shot at in the parking lot after robbing the Genval Delhaize supermarket is found parked in Ixelles off Flagey Square.[102] The car body is fixed; all of the bullet fragments are removed, and the bullet holes are filled. Remember that the driver of this Audi just barely had time to slip under the dashboard to avoid being hit. It was seized by police and was awaiting forensic analysis in a dealership garage when it was brazenly stolen.

As mentioned previously, including this theft from the repair shop in the canon of Brabant Killers crimes is still debated. If it is unrelated, it's quite coincidental that it was found in Ixelles, the Gang's epicenter. Furthermore, the thieves were a special kind of stupid to break into a dealership, move cars inside and steal a car with several bullet holes if they weren't trying to impede an investigation. If this was not linked to the Brabant Killers, it seems odd other criminals would keep the Audi even when they realize it's been part of a violent crime, fix the bullets holes, and then use it in downtown Brussels.

CHAPTER 8

COLRUYT SUPERMARKET IN HALLE (MARCH 3, 1983)

ON MARCH 3RD, AT 7:30 P.M., THE BRABANT KILLERS DRIVE THE stolen Golf GTI into the parking lot of the Colruyt supermarkets in Halle. Inside are three men. The attackers exit the car and make their way to the front doors of the supermarket, all wearing black ski masks with yellow sides and holes for the nose and the mouth. They have dark commando makeup around their eyes.[103]

Once they enter, one of the gunmen fires two warning shots at the ceiling. They did the same in their two previous supermarket robberies. One of the attackers stays by the cash registers in front, threatening the staff and customers with a short-barreled gun and forcing everyone in the vicinity to get down on the floor. This Killer, who is tall and stocky, wears a used grayish-blue trench coat with dark gray pants and black shoes. He shoots at a hanging "Butcher" sign to get people to obey his order to lie down before demanding that the cashiers open the cash registers for him.

The two others walk across the store to get to the second-floor office. The wiry-looking one carries a nightstick and the other slightly shorter man in a dark trench coat and dark turtleneck holds a revolver. The box-shaped office overlooks the first floor. When the pair enters, they find the store manager, an employee, and a supervisor from the Colruyt chain's head office.

One of the assailants shouts, "The money, the money, on the ground, on the ground!"A The manager realizes what's happening and says, "This can't be serious?"B The Killer with the gun says, "You, come with me!"C As the supervisor moves to obey the gunman, he leans on the desk right near the office phone. He's immediately smashed on the hand and over the head with the nightstick. The supervisor sustains a traumatic brain injury and several bones in his hand are broken.[104]

Meanwhile, the manager is led to another room where he's forced to open the store's vault. The vault room is about 60 feet away from the first room. The Killer quickly stuffs the cash into a large travel bag. Once he's done, he shoots the manager in the throat before leaving the vault room. The manager does not survive his injury.

The Brabant Killers leave with a total of 1,182,115 BEF (approximately US $33, 252). The first assailant to reach the Golf turns the engine on and waits for his two accomplices. As they leave, they fire more wild gunshots toward witnesses looking at the scene. They speed toward the highway.

KILLING THE MANAGER

Because the vault room is so far and isolated from the main office where the supervisor and the employee are still lying on the ground, no one knows if there were words exchanged or if there was an altercation between the victim and his murderer. Only the gunshot was heard. Did the murderer consider the manager a hindrance? Did the manager provoke the Killer in some way? It's by far the most senseless murder in the First Wave attacks of the Insane Killers.

A particularity of this attack is that it happens in a Colruyt supermarket. It's the only time the Insane Killers ever hold-up a different supermarket then a Delhaize. The Colruyt's layout is different from that of the Delhaize chain. The rows and the offices are not positioned the same way. Another anomaly is that none of the witnesses report seeing a Giant. In terms of similarities to their previous attacks, warning shots are fired on entry and people are forced to get down on their stomachs.

The Brabant Killers shoot the same 9mm that they used during the Wavre Gun Shop shootout in September 1982 and at the Genval Delhaize robbery on February 11th. They also shoot the caliber .38 Special that has now been used in all three of their supermarket robberies. This links the Colruyt robbery to their Public Attacks ballistics. In theory, this now links up Maubeuge-Wavre-Genval-Uccle-Halle. While the authorities still don't know it, the Insane Killers are self-aware enough to realize these crimes can be linked, yet don't seem to care. The Beersel-Mons Serial Killer ballistics are still separate.

The attack disturbs Colruyt management. They're shocked by the death of their branch manager. The day following the attack the Colruyt chain of supermarkets put out an offer to pay out 5 Million BEF (approximately US $140,000) to whomever can give information that will lead to the arrest of the perpetrators.[105]

HAEMERS AS A POSSIBLE SUSPECT

While watching TV in 1989, supervisor Jules Knockaert, the employee who had his head and hand smashed with the nightstick, sees a report on notorious criminal Patrick Haemers. He believes Haemers could have been one of the attackers.[106] By 1989, Haemers has become the most famous criminal in the country. He had just kidnapped an ex-prime minister for ransom.

Patrick Haemers is very tall and handsome, a fixture of the nightlife scene in Brussels who boasts striking blond hair and blue eyes. He comes from a very wealthy[107] family from a rich western suburb of Brussels. Haemers always carries wads of cash to spend on drugs and women and is often high on coke, which he washes down with alcohol.

In his youth, Haemers is left to his own devices. His parents are workaholics, always busy running their many businesses. Haemers stays home and receives little supervision while his parents overcompensate for their absence by showering him with gifts and cash. This is a young man who has always had what he wanted when he wanted. Haemers dropped out of school to become a full-time party animal, alcoholic, and junky. His life is basically spending lots of his parents' money.

In the seventies, Haemers is charged in the gang rape of a prostitute. He'll maintain his whole life that she pressed charges against him only when she found out his father was rich. He receives a three-year sentence, but ends up serving only 14 months. After he gets out, his father Achille tries to get him involved in his businesses. He's given a clothing apparel store to manage. Achille owns twenty of these stores in Brussels.

Haemers ends up spending very little time in the store. Instead, he takes stacks of bills out of the cash register and goes clubbing, indulging in bottles of Champagne at 10,000 BEF or US $282 a pop and allegedly up to 5 grams of cocaine a day. Eating at four-star restaurants, he leaves ridiculous tips for waitresses. At one point, Achille gets upset: "Without even looking at refunds for your personal expenses, your car, your rent and whatever else, you still need more cash for your own enjoyment: April: 76,110 BEF ($5,206 in 2018 dollars)—huge. March: 116,380 BEF ($7,964 in 2018 dollars)—no receipt!"[108]

Aside from clothing businesses, Achilles also owns nightclubs and gives his son another chance by handing him the management of his club "Happy Few." He seems intent on making his son a success at something… Anything… Really anything… When running the Happy Few nightclub is a dismal failure, his father Achille helps Haemers transition into armed robberies.

In October 1981, Achille pitches an armed robbery idea to his son Patrick. It's a hare-brained scheme to rob the BBL Bank in Deerlijk, which is Achille's hometown. According to Haemers, "he had told me it would be a piece of cake. He explained to me how we opened the safes."[109] Haemers didn't even own a gun at the time. He borrowed his brother Eric's registered handgun. In a rare moment of self-reflection, Haemers will say: "It's bizarre for a father to treat his own son that way."[110]

Haemers steals a BMW immediately before the robbery. The improvised crew has now two cars: The stolen BMW and… Achille's own car.

The plan is to get to the bank in two cars. When he's finished robbing the bank, Haemers will dump the loot in his father's car and use the stolen BMW as his own getaway car. Really…

On October 22nd, 1981, at 2:00 p.m., Haemers enters the bank with an accomplice. He holds up the tellers and jumps over the counter. Talking about his father's plan, Haemers says, "Once inside, his explanations were obviously wrong. We left with 350,000 BEF (about US $9,860). We were furious. That mess for so little cash."[111] Haemers stuffs the cash in a plastic bag and runs back outside, throwing the bag through the open window of his father's car. The two cars bolt as fast as possible.

Haemers and his father Achille are quickly arrested, and Haemers later says, "My stupid dad had no better idea than to park his own car to see how his son was doing. Obviously, someone wrote down his license plate number and the next morning, they got me."[112]

Haemers is significant because he will decide to form his own Gang that will become active in 1984. They will become suspects of the Insane Killers attacks, mostly those of the Second Wave of 1985. Haemers is sentenced to two years of jail, but is released after serving only one year.

This is important to know, as jail is a great alibi for Haemers for all the 1982 Insane Killers crimes. The court is more lenient to his father Achille, who just gets time served. It seems that Achille's curious parenting leads to a breakthrough because, for once in his life, Haemers discovers something he really likes to do: Armed robberies. However, Haemers decides against further criminal joint ventures with father Achille given that, "…he only had bad ideas."[113]

THE BORAINS

In late April, in a pub near the French border, in a small Borinage town, a seemingly innocuous sale of a second-hand gun unleashes a whole series of events. The salesman Michel Cocu sells his Ruger Police caliber .38 Special to welfare recipient Jean-Claude Estiévenart for 10,000 BEF (or approximately $ 280). The deal will change their lives and the trajectory of the Brabant Killers' story. Like Estiévenart, Cocu was often on welfare but just recently got a job driving a funeral car. Both Estiévenart and Cocu spend lots of their time with other locals. Cocu is down on his luck and is looking for cash. Earlier that April, he passes the word to patrons that he'll sell his gun. He initially purchased the Ruger in 1979 from a local gun shop. After purchasing the gun, Estiévenart shows it if off to the patrons at the pub.

The Borinage Region is situated in southwest Belgium. The French town of Maubeuge, where the Killers had their first shootout with police in August 1982, is just across the border. The Borinage's capital is Mons, which is where the dead taxi driver Costa Angelou was found crumpled in the trunk of his taxi in January 1983. It's also the poorest and most disaffected part of Belgium; having suffered an industrial decline a couple of decades ago, that has left troubled lives with few opportunities in its wake.

Estiévenart, the purchaser, alternates between welfare and short periods of day labor. He left school at fourteen and has been evaluated as having below-average intelligence. He's separated from his wife, Josiane De Bruyne, but they're still forced to see each other because they have several children together and other family connections—Estiévenart's sister married De Bruyne's brother. Estiévenart is a heavy drinker and when he sees his estranged wife, they butt heads. The Mons Gendarmerie station has been called in a couple of times to break up their violent disputes.

Agent Coulon is the officer in charge of the couple's file. He gets help from his teammate, Christian Amory, who used to work with Dani Bouhouche in the Brussels Narcotics Unit. Amory left Brussels because he wanted to get back to the Borinage, the area where he grew up. To work on the Estiévenart file, Amory has an informant, Mohammed Asmaoui. He's been infiltrating Estiévenart and his friends for the past year.

Word gets around to Josiane De Bruyne that her husband purchased the Ruger. On May 25th, she finds the Ruger in one of Estiévenart's pants pockets. She hands it to her social worker, who drops it off at the local Gendarmerie station of Colfontaine. The reason given to the police officer when the gun is dropped off is that De Bruyne's scared of her husband having a gun because he's sometimes violent. The Mons Gendarmerie station immediately finds out about the drop off of the Ruger at the Colfontaine Gendarmerie Station.

Agent Beduwe, who is Agent Coulon and Amory's boss, goes to pick up the Ruger in Colfontaine and bring it back to the Mons station. Standard procedure mandating that the gun must then be deposited in the Criminal registry is completely ignored. Beduwe jots down informally on a notepad, "Estiévenart—Ruger 9 (…) cal. 38 special—12 Inox cartridges." Beduwe then dumps the Ruger in a drawer. The Ruger will remain in the Mons station for months.[114]

The Ruger will become critical to the Insane Killers file in a few short months. The loose network of people affiliated with the seller Michel Cocu and the purchaser Jean-Claude Estiévenart will gain nationwide infamy under the moniker, the Borains. They are, like the Haemers Gang, major players in the Insane Killers case.

BOUHOUCHE

Amory still meets his ex-colleague Bouhouche regularly. Bouhouche left the Gendarmerie on April 1st to change careers. A couple of weeks after leaving, Bouhouche co-founded a private detective agency in Ixelles with ex-Gendarme Bob Beijer. It's christened the Agency of Research and Information, or ARI, for short. ARI takes over the client base of another detective agency that closed down. This gives the duo a foot in the door with law firms that handle contested divorce cases, which was big business back then for detective agencies. Altogether, they invest 250,000 BEF (or approximately US $7,042) in the startup. Many of the funds are spent on spy gadgetry and they have staff on payroll.

In terms of detective gadgets, ARI has access to everything imaginable—bugs, wiretap equipment, disguises, and computers—all rare at the time. They also have an impressive array of technical resources. They are experts taping phones. For apartments, they tap the building's telephone box. For homes, they open up the neighborhood telephone box. Once they find the right line in the box, they attach a transmitter that's picked up by a van parked close-by that records the calls. They use authentic phone company uniforms and their van is stocked full of listening devices and electronic gadgets.

ARI outsources part of their illegal tapping operations to a phone company employee on the payroll. He has easy access to the wiring information of residential neighborhoods. That way, ARI saves time and energy and can focus on other aspects of their business. Altogether, they have the capacity to have several transmitters in telephone boxes taping conversations in several different towns simultaneously. They can also listen in on private conversations by planting bugs in rooms connected to recording devices.

The detective agency has the external appearance of being quite active. However, the firm's books tell another story. ARI makes only 52,000 BEF of profit in 1983 (approximately US $1,465), 76,000 BEF in 1984 (US $2,141) and 50,000 BEF in 1985 (US $1,409). In 1986, the balance sheet of the agency shows a loss of 188,000 BEF (US $5,296). This suggests that ARI has been a disastrous venture. Bouhouche has just quit the Gendarmerie; he doesn't collect his Gendarme salary, and has just invested lots of money. However, the reality is different. Bouhouche and his partner have a progressively more lavish lifestyle. They have visible signs of wealth like luxury apartments, cars, and in Bouhouche's case, an expensive art collection." Of note, they pay their large contractor bills with cash.

BOUHOUCHE GANG

Now retired from the Gendarmerie, he devotes a larger chunk of time on running his Gang. He's already set up the storage locker network used to facilitate his Gang's criminal activities. The total cost of the network is estimated at one million BEF (about US $28,000). The locker network was started in 1981 when Bouhouche was still a detective in the Narcotics Division. The paper trail details how Bouhouche made most rentals himself under an alias. However, from the beginning, there were traces of others.

The networks' first rental ever is an apartment in the Woluwe neighborhood. It was leased from July 1981 to January 1982 by an Asian presenting a false ID. The Asian comes from London, just like the good friend of a Gendarme in Bouhouche's entourage. A handwriting analysis is done on four separate payment slips for the lease. The analysis determines that two notes on two separate slips were written by the Asian from London. After first denying it's his writing, he'll claim that while it is, it could only have been at the request of the Gendarme.

Their second apartment rental in the Woluwe neighborhood is in September 1981. The handwritten words on the phone company's contract are, according to handwriting experts, "very certainly" from that same Gendarme. The other marks are from Bouhouche.

RAIDING THE GENDARMERIE

When Bouhouche leaves the Gendarmerie, he takes with him a whole toolbox of misappropriated items. These include a duplicate of his Gendarmerie permit with the seal of the Brussels brigade, blank documents with Gendarmerie letterhead, and stamps. He also brings arrest orders and a document from his Gendarmerie brigade that is proof a license plate was lost. In addition to a blank order from a prosecutor, which is what's required to retrieve someone from jail or to transfer a prisoner from one jail to another, he also takes Gendarmerie drug identification kits.[115]

The Bouhouche Gang has scanners to listen to police radio frequencies. One of their scanners includes the frequency list of all the codes for the Gendarmerie, the Judicial Police and for local security firms.[116] They have specialty trade documentation on Gendarmerie style antennas, as well as a tubular antenna and three police-grade antennas in their possession. The Gang installs a radio-communication antenna on an apartment's terrace in 1983, which allows them to keep radio contact during some of their early attacks. The lease for the apartment is terminated in July 1983.

They have materials to set up highway roadblocks, such as their own road signs and cones.[117] Not only do they have a system to dress up a white car to look like a Gendarmerie car, complete with orange stripes and a blue light on the roof, they also have real Gendarmerie uniforms, including official Gendarmerie raincoats. In preparation for criminal activities, the Gang also has ski masks and silencers, including a .22 LR silencer. They get license plates pressed to use for stolen cars from a store called L'Autac and develop a technique to quickly replace one fake plate with another. Clearly mindful of forensics, they have kits to produce false leads, like bags of fired cartridge cases, and a vast array of makeup, wigs, and fake mustaches. Their careful planning includes having geological survey maps, access to details about individuals based on license plate numbers, and dry powder extinguishers to wipe off all fingerprints.

As mentioned, the Bouhouche Gang has developed this elaborate box and apartment network since 1981. The most major shift in the network's operations occurs in the summer of 1983 when they shut down their Woluwe base and shift all their holdings to Brussels, in the south-central area of Ixelles. They have already had Box 179 in the Ixelles Complex since 1981 and so the Gang builds around this centrally located box. On July 10th, they rent Box 144 and Box 150 storage units, tripling their holdings in the Ixelles Complex. Ten days later they shut down all their rentals in the Woluwe area, presumably to transfer the contents to their boxes in Ixelles. They also relinquish their apartment with the transmission antenna.

Members of the Gang have large cans of unused gunpowder, plus several boxes of gun primers of various sizes and brands. They have ammo recharge equipment like a Hydro Punch. Bouhouche, personally, boasts almost everything needed to reload every type of ammo and keeps these things at his home.[118]

ARMS TRAFFIC

Bouhouche is a licensed gun dealer, which allows him to traffic in firearms. With all the money that he seems to pull out of thin air, he has built his own arsenal. Bouhouche also has a friend named Juan Mendez, who he first met in 1975 at the Uccle shooting club. They hit it off because of their shared passion for guns and their wives also develop a close friendship. Mendez works as the FN gun manufacturer's sales rep for South America and Spain. Bouhouche uses Mendez to misappropriate weapons from the gun manufacturer.

Bouhouche devises a system to launder stolen firearms from the FN with the help of Mendez, who is sometimes entrusted to give guns off the books to foreign decision makers. It is very easy for Mendez, who is well informed of the details, to pocket many of the gifts and obviously there's no paper trail of these transactions anywhere. The misappropriations mostly happen during deliveries to South American countries. After the weapons are smuggled out of the FN, they end up listed on Bouhouche's official weapons registry, but under a false origin. The process goes as follows: Bouhouche writes down that ten weapons (three pistols, three guns, two machine guns, and two submachine guns) have been acquired from a gun dealer. Sometimes he hasn't even met the dealer, but having a name gives the firearms an appearance of legality. They are then flipped back to Mendez, who can add them to his personal weapons collection.

GANG HISTORY

The Bouhouche Gang's operations began while Bouhouche was still a Gendarme. Now, more than two years later, and unbeknownst to the public and authorities, they've already accumulated an impressive resume of crimes. At the time of the publication of this book, the following are crimes to which they have confessed or were found guilty of.

On May 22nd, 1981, a fake police officer presents himself to the criminal Court Registry in Brussels. He flashes a stolen Gendarmerie ID and hands the clerk a series of fake documents. In turn, the clerk gives the fake officer over three million BEF in cash (or about $85,000), which is one of the court exhibits in an upcoming transnational drug dealing trial. The impostor signs the necessary paperwork and the authorities only find out about the swindle much later.

On July 11th, 1981, they break into the Town Hall of Chaumont-Gistoux to steal ID cards and other documents. Among the stolen ID cards are cards that had been discarded for minor technicalities. They also steal a stamp and a dry stamp. This is a critically important robbery for the Bouhouche Gang as it provides them with a veritable treasure trove of all the essentials required to create all sorts of false personas. They'll make all sorts of false IDs including fake driving licenses and foreigner ID cards, which they can use to rent apartments and storage units for their network, buy guns, and facilitate arms transactions.

On October 1st, 1981, Bouhouche receives a disciplinary sentence for the listening infraction mentioned earlier, when he bugged the interrogation room where other narcotics detectives were talking with an informant. Bouhouche is demoted to a street cop and is suspended for six days without pay. While he liked to stalk around with holsters in civilian clothes, he's now forced to wear a cop uniform and drive the streets in a police cruiser. He's steaming mad and all of his anger is directed toward Major Herman Vernaillen, the Commander of the Brussels District of the Gendarmerie.

Before he was sentenced, Bouhouche had received a lateral transfer from Narcotics Detective to Judicial Division Detective. There he spent a few months under the direction of his new boss Staff Sergeant Guy Goffinon. But this transfer was done behind the back of Vernaillen, who had final authority on discipline. Vernaillen insisted Bouhouche receive a full hearing and a sentence proportionate to the severity of his infraction.

Another Gendarmerie leader who also raised Bouhouche's ire was his interim superior, Goffinon. During the few months Bouhouche spent working in the Judicial Division, he developed a strong enmity towards Goffinon.

Shortly after Bouhouche is informed about the October 1st decision that puts him back on the street as a regular police officer, both Vernaillen and Goffinon start receiving anonymous death threats by telephone. A prosecutor known to work on cases with Goffinon is also warned by an anonymous caller that, "Goffinon will die!"

TIME OF RECKONING

The members of the Bouhouche Gang make plans to assassinate both men and their first target is Goffinon. They build a remote-controlled bomb and fill it with nails to ensure maximum damage, using a nylon cord as a receptor. On October 10th, 1981, an anonymous caller places a call from a downtown Brussels tavern to the Gendarmerie station where Goffinon works, saying he has a tip to give on a murder that happened a few days prior. "My information could interest officer Goffinon,"A says the caller. The officer working the phones calls around to find Goffinon, but he can't get a hold of him. A Peugeot 405 police cruiser with three officers is dispatched instead.

The Bouhouche Gang waits in ambush with the remote control. Two hundred yards away from the station, a small explosion blows up in the trunk and some shrapnel hits the three Gendarmes inside. While the nails completely mangle the trunk, all three officers survive with just a few scratches and minor injuries. The investigation determines the bomb maker's lack of in-depth knowledge likely saved the lives of the three Gendarmes because a couple of amateur mistakes caused the bomb to malfunction.

The anonymous death threats against Goffinon resume immediately after the failed attack. According to Prosecutor Duinslaeger, "a couple of days after the fact, on October 13, 1981, telephone threats were professed against [Goffinon]."[119] And, according to Prosecutor Huinens, "we had the conviction that Adjutant Goffinon was targeted by this attack. He should have been inside the BSR car that exploded."[120]

The Investigation

Bouhouche is part of the Gendarmerie team investigating his own Gang's bombing. The investigators trace some of the parts used for the bomb to the manager of a local army supply shop, who is charged with attempted murder on October 24th, 1981. During their investigation, the Gendarmerie put a caller trace on the suspect's phone to nab accomplices and notice several phone calls between him and officer Bouhouche. They confront Bouhouche, who acknowledges that he is a high school buddy of the suspect. Because Bouhouche has no alibi for when the bomb went off, the Gendarmerie make a search and seizure at his home on November 27th, 1981, but fail to find any further evidence that links Bouhouche to the crime.

The investigation of the army supply shop manager suspect quickly loses steam and they feel they can't prosecute with what they have gathered at this point. The suspect is released on February 5th, 1982. It will take a couple more years before there are any new developments in the case. Because Goffinon is involved in the high-profile prosecution of undercover cops involved in a drug trafficking case, it's just assumed the motive must have been related to that.

Vernaillen

After going after Goffinon, the Bouhouche Gang goes after their second target, Major Herman Vernaillen, the Brussels District Commander of the Gendarmerie who Bouhouche blames for his demotion to street cop. They won't play with explosives this time, however. Their plan is to simply ambush Vernaillen's car and kill him as he drives home after work.

On October 25th, 1981, Bouhouche Gang hit men park their stolen Mazda 626 on the side of the road along the road Vernaillen must take to get home. It's late at night and they keep their lights off. Vernaillen notices the car with the two men inside because it's the first time he's ever seen a car there. Fortunately for Vernaillen, he's being driven home that night and doesn't use his own car. The hit men were looking for a different model.

Vernaillen is dropped off at home and goes straight to bed. After a while, the hit men realize he must have gotten home some alternate way and decide they'll get him in his house. They boldly ring the doorbell past midnight. Vernaillen gets out of bed and walks up to the front door, peeking through the window curtains beside the door to see who is ringing the doorbell. "Who's there?"A Vernaillen asks. An assailant tries to break through the front door by smashing it with the butt-end of his rifle. Hearing the noise, Vernaillen's wife makes her way through the house to see what's happening.

When breaking in the door doesn't work, the hit men fire bullets through the window and the door. As several bullet rounds burst in succession from a Remington-style rifle, Vernaillen dives for cover in the living room. Unfortunately, a bullet strikes him in the back and he's down on the floor, bloodied. The attackers fire several more bullets through a living room window, exploding shards of glass everywhere. Bullets lodge into the walls and the ceiling of the front hall and the living room. The attackers go to another window on the side of the living room and fire even more rounds into the home. Vernaillen's wife is struck by several bullets in the living room hall.

Vernaillen's daughter rushes to pull her mother out of the way. After the hit men have emptied all their cartridges, they run back to their car and drive away from the scene. Despite shrapnel in his back and arm, Vernaillen sustains only nerve damage and manages to avoid a major injury. His wife Magda, however, is critically wounded when bullets pierce her lungs and intestines. She pulls through in the end but is permanently disabled after the attack.

The intruders shot eight .22-caliber Remington Magnum cartridges and two 9mm bullets. Investigators find the ten rounds were fired from two to four assault-style rifles and a 9mm pistol. Almost all the ammunition has been recharged.

Investigation

The attack at the Vernaillen home occurs only 15 days after the attempted bombing of Goffinon. According to Prosecutor Huinens, "Afterwards a link was immediately established between both cases."[121]

The Brussels Gendarmerie dispatches an investigative team and the prosecutor is sent to review the crime scene. When the prosecutor arrives, Bouhouche is there waiting for him.[122] Just as Bouhouche was one of the officers dispatched to investigate the Goffinon bombing, he is again on duty at another crime his own Gang has just committed.

Claude Dery is tasked to lead the ballistic tests, with Bouhouche to assist him in the research and verification. Dery and Bouhouche have several encounters during the investigation and it's Bouhouche who brings the reference shot results back to Dery from the lab. The results are compiled in an October 29th police report.

Just like officer Goffinon, Vernaillen and his wife continue to receive anonymous phone calls after the attack. The frequency of calls increases just before Vernaillen testifies in two parliamentary commissions and a case that implicates the Bouhouche Gang.

For the first few years, the case investigating the attack at Vernaillen's home goes nowhere. Similar to the Goffinon case, the working theory in this case, is that Vernaillen was a target due to his involvement in the same international drug case and the prosecution of undercover cops. The disciplinary sentence of Bouhouche is not on the radar.

Looking back at the two Bouhouche Gang attacks, Goffinon believes the Gang replaced the Mazda's radio with a sophisticated Jet Radio to eavesdrop on frequencies used by the Gendarmeries. A Jet radio stolen in May 1981 from the Gendarmerie could have been the one installed in the car used for the attack.

Dyane Break-In

Sometime between December 31st, 1981 and January 3rd, 1982, members of the Bouhouche Gang slip into the Dyane building, which houses an elite special forces unit of the Gendarmerie that oversees the most dangerous public security operations throughout Belgium. The elite officers who work here are called for hostage cases and the most dangerous arrests. This building houses all the best equipment in the police force.

Bouhouche Gang operators get to the second-floor garage where six specially equipped swat vehicles are parked. Inside each of the cars are special weapons for on-the-road Swat interventions. The intruders use a metallic rod to pry open the driver's door of each swat vehicle just enough to slip a wire into the cabin to unlock the vehicle. Careful not to leave fingerprints, the culprits empty all the Swat firearms, ammunition, and equipment from the special cars and load it all into a green-colored Gendarmerie Mazda car that is parked in the garage.

The Bouhouche Gang exits the building's gates with the stolen Mazda and the guards never notice them leaving. The thieves drive the vehicle only 6 miles to their Ixelles box where they empty the stolen weapons before abandoning the Mazda on a nearby street. Authorities find the Mazda on January 4th, 1982 with one clip from the Dyane robbery inside. The thieves pepper sprayed the car, probably to hinder police dogs from catching their scent.

The Bouhouche Gang collects an important stash of high-tech arms from this latest robbery, which includes five HK machineguns, 10 HK submachine guns, five automatic Faul guns, and four state-of-the-art FN automatic Riot Guns. They also take 28 HK clips, each containing twenty-five 9mm para cartridges. The thieves also score a car siren light and two signal pistols to add to their extensive collection of police equipment. The total value of the loot is somewhere around 500,000 BEF (approximately US $14,084).

Among the most valuable items are the ten Heckler Koch submachine guns, the only ten in the country and used solely by the special forces to shoot during special operations because they don't make any noise. According to Arsene Pint, the founder of the Dyane unit, "They were made specifically for German units. No one else in Belgium had those weapons and you couldn't buy them. They were the cream of the crop."[123] The drawback to acquiring these submachine guns for the Bouhouche Gang's state-of-the-art arsenal is that they are too conspicuous for everyday crimes and it's dangerous to resell them.

Pint adds: "I was extremely embarrassed when they were stolen. We had given our word when we bought those weapons. They were not allowed to end up in the hands of anyone else, especially of gangsters or terrorists. At GSG 9 [the German swat unit] and at Heckler, they must have been steaming mad!"[124]

INVESTIGATING HIS OWN GANG AGAIN

Investigators suspect the thieves had made copies of the keys of the Green Mazda when they used it once beforehand. The original keys and documents were still in the Dyane stockroom. Investigators quickly speculate that the thieves are members or ex-members from Dyane or the Gendarmerie because they had to be well acquainted with the Dyane premises. Most Brussels Gendarmes were, as they regularly visited the site and many officers used the building's parking lot.

Bouhouche had shown lots of interest in the Dyane weapons. He would show up regularly to chat with Warrant Officer Evance Collard, the Dyane gunsmith and logistics manager who was responsible for taking care of the Dyane's arms and the vehicles. Bouhouche would drop by specifically to see if a new item had come in and would always ask lots of questions about the various specifications of anything new. He and Collard were known to get along very well. Bouhouche also participated in shooting practices with the Dyane unit, where he gave the unit pointers.

Once again, Bouhouche is part of the team investigating his own Gang's break-in. He participates in at least one search and seizure.[125] In 2000, after the statute of limitation has run out, Bouhouche confesses he stole the Dyane weapons. In terms of timeline, all the major crimes listed, like the Goffinon bombing, the Vernaillen home attack, and the Dyane robbery happened before the Brabant Killers started their crime spree.

MECHELEN

The first suspected crime from the Bouhouche Gang that overlaps the attacks by the Insane Killers is the Mechelen robbery of a security company agent. However, unlike the other Bouhouche Gang crimes, they were not found guilty and never confessed to it even after the statute of limitations had passed. Unlike the other Bouhouche Gang crimes, this one has an asterisk.

By the summer of 1982, the Insane Killers have already started their activities. On July 6th, Antoine Brouwer, a security guard for the Kirschen company, is driving a company Volkswagen Golf on the highway just northwest of Brussels to transport valuables to the Brussels airport. A white BMW with an orange stripe along the side quickly passes in front of his Golf. Inside the white BMW are three fake police officers.

An imposter officer signals to Brouwer to stop along the highway. When both cars stop, the three fake officers get out and one of them walks up to Brouwers's door and sticks the barrel of a revolver to Brouwer's head. Brouwer is forced to step out of the car, where his attackers quickly shackle him and stuff him into the fake police car. Both cars leave, with one of the fake officers driving Brouwer's Golf. Both cars take the next exit and drive towards the town of Perk, which is not far from the Brussels airport.

In an abandoned street, the fake officers pull Brouwer, whose feet and arms are bound, out of the white BMW. They put a bag over his head and stuff him back into his Golf. The fake officers then transfer the valuables from Brouwer's car into the trunk of their white BMW.

They push Brouwer's Golf into a ditch on the side of the road. Brouwer believes he hears a second car when the fake police officers drive away. The loot includes diamonds, 30 Kilos of gold bars, BEF and several other currencies. There's also 736,000 BEF (approximately $ 20,732) in coupons and a check for four million BEF (approximately $ 112,000).

Investigation

The Kirschen robbery bears a striking resemblance to the Zaventem Airport Heist, a later robbery committed by the Bouhouche Gang. In terms of the timeline of attacks committed by the Insane Killers, the confrontation with French police in Maubeuge in August 1982, and the Wavre Gun Shop robbery and subsequent shootout in September 1982 fall between the Mechelen and Zaventem heists.

Zaventem Heist

Their Zaventem heist occurs on October 25th, 1982 at 8:35 p.m. at Brussels International Airport in Zaventem. A Sabena security employee named Francis Zwarts is given the task to transport valuables from a Zurich flight. It's a daily flight from Zurich that's known to always carry valuable cargo. He's a last-minute replacement who must take the place of the regular team member, who may have been called to resolve an incident on board a plane from Munich. He uses a plain van to transfer the valuable cargo, as the usual armored truck is being repaired.

The road from the unloading area to the guarded warehouse is several hundred yards and it passes through a tunnel under an airplane landing track. At 9:20 p.m., Zwarts starts unloading the special vault inside the airplane's hold. At 9:26 p.m., he informs dispatch that he's done loading the valuable cargo and drives toward the secured warehouse.

A white Ford Taunus is stopped in the tunnel that Zwarts must travel through to get to the warehouse. The Taunus has a painted yellow-orange stripe that looks like a Gendarmerie car without a siren light. Three Bouhouche Gang cronies are standing beside it, dressed in Gendarmes uniforms and carrying sub-machine guns.

The three fake Gendarmes wave along another Sabena vehicle coming from the other direction. Then Zwarts enters the tunnel and disappears. Dispatch radios Zwarts a couple of minutes later to inform him that there's freight to unload from an incoming plane from Germany.

They get no answer and try to make radio contact with Zwarts three more times. On dispatch's fourth attempt, the answer is, "Ja! Ja!"A It's the last contact ever with Zwarts. Dispatch alerts the airport Gendarmerie when they realize Zwarts has gone incommunicado.

The van leaves the airport premises in tandem with the Bouhouche Gang's white Ford Taunus with the yellow-orange stripe. The next day, the Sabena Volkswagen van is discovered in a public dump in Diegem. The precious cargo of gold, diamonds, valuables in various forms, and twelve Cartier watches is gone. The total value of the loot is somewhere between 80 and 90 million BEF (or approximately between US $180,000 and $225,000). Zwarts' body is never found.

INVESTIGATION

According to Gendarmerie logbooks, it was impossible that it was a real Gendarmerie vehicle in that tunnel. The fake Ford Taunus used by the Bouhouche Gang is found on June 6th, 1984 by their Woluwe boxes in Woluwe-St-Lambert (near the UCL campus and St-Luc Hospital). The Taunus has a two-centimeter-diameter hole pierced in its roof exactly where radio antennas are usually placed on Gendarmerie vehicles.

The Gang splits the money among participants, suddenly improving their lifestyles. Bouhouche uses some of the cash to renovate his family home. According to a forensic accountant, the couple rakes in revenues of 413,000 BEF in 1982 (or approximately $30,433 in 2018 dollars) that cannot be accounted for. In 1983, the couple purchases a new house, spending a total of 1,600,000 BEF that year (or approximately 114,231 in 2018 dollars). Bouhouche also keeps a few stolen watches for himself and other accomplices split the rest.

The Zaventem robbery bears a striking resemblance to the Mechelen robbery the previous July 1982. While the Zaventem Heist is attributed to the Bouhouche Gang, no definitive link has ever been made to the Mechelen robbery. However, in each case, it's three fake officers who commit the robbery. They use a white car with an orange stripe and tie up the victim before stuffing the bound victim in the white car. One of the officers then steps in the security guard's car. The two cars leave together. Both the Mechelen and the Zaventem loot includes gold and diamonds and the valuables were all transported on Swissair.

The Ford Taunus used for the Zaventem Heist was stolen in late February 1982. It's suspected that on February 26th, the same vehicle is used to go on a reconnaissance mission at the airport. When they also trail a security agent who is transporting money and valuables offloaded from an airplane from Zurich, the alarmed guard alerts authorities by radio. The car leaves, but he notices there were three men in the Taunus.

On November 10th, 1982, the office of the prosecutor taking care of the Mechelen case is broken into. The thieves steal the entire Kirschen file. Today the case is way beyond the statute of limitations, but it is still interesting. Was the Bouhouche Gang involved? Did the fake police officers in July also use submachine guns? If not, where did the Bouhouche Gang find the submachine guns used in Zaventem? Remember that similar weapons were stolen a few weeks before at the Wavre Gun Shop by the Brabant Killers.

Like the Haemers Gang and the Borains, the Bouhouche Gang will become suspects in the Insane Killers case a few years later.

END OF CYCLE OF SUPERMARKET ROBBERIES

Fast Forwarding to 1983, after the three supermarket robberies of February and March 1983, the Insane Killers change their pattern of crimes. During the rest of the First Wave (1982-1983), they'll only hold-up one more supermarket, in November 1983. Before they were committing supermarket hold-ups they started off with night-time break-ins for alcohol, like at the Maubeuge (France) grocery store and at the Het Kasteel Inn in 1982. There are no more night-time break-ins for alcohol after this. The remainder of their crimes target objects, rather than money. Besides continuing to steal cars to commit their crimes, they'll steal bulletproof vests, a blowtorch, large cans of oil, and bags of coffee. They'll also steal alarm clocks and worthless jewelry. Everything is done with extreme violence.

BRAINE BLOWTORCH

At 2:00 a.m. on May 28th, 1983, the Brabant Killers drive up to the hardware store Centre du Bois Paul André in the town of Braine-L'Alleud. They exit their car and walk behind the store where they remove the window frame on the back door, which releases the glass pane. Once the glass is off, they slip into the store and reach the front showroom. They pick up an Oxypack blowtorch with two cylinders. They leave everything else behind.[126] The alarm rings at 2:20 a.m. They take off in their car.

TECHNICAL QUESTIONS

It's strongly suspected that the Brabant Killers are responsible for this break-in and the stolen blowtorch is later found in their possession. It's the only thing they steal that night. Why go through the risk of a break-in for only a blowtorch and two cylinders? It's a significant crime because they didn't come to steal money or as many other items as they could from the store. They came specifically for what they needed and nothing more. Money was not the motive; getting the blowtorch and cylinders was. If they had been surprised by police would they have shot their way out to escape? Despite the insignificant loot?

The owner remembers a customer had visited the store a couple of days prior to the theft and asked lots of technical questions about the blowtorch. There might be a link, as the store rarely rented blowtorches. The customer who made inquiries about the blowtorch was well dressed and in his thirties. He didn't wear glasses or a mask. He spoke well in French, not in a regional slang. If it is indeed one of the Killers, he likely wore a wig, false eyebrows or other elements of disguise. The Insane Killers still have the Golf, which they stole in Lasne on February 14th.

CHAPTER 9

BRAINE CAR DEALERSHIP
(JUNE 8, 1983)

A T 1:00 A.M. ON JUNE 8TH, THE BRABANT KILLERS DRIVE TO A CAR
dealership in Braine. One of the Killers goes to the back of the
building to access the roof. There he stumbles on Ben, the German Shepherd guard dog. He shoots the dog 11 times with .22-caliber LR bullets.
Yes: An excessive 11 bullets are fired to kill a guard dog.

He then climbs onto the roof. He opens up a trap window that gives
access to the workshop. He drops down on a work table. Once in the
workshop, he opens a sliding door for his accomplices. The office is in a
corner of the workshop. They attempt to pry open the office door but fail,
so opt to break an office window pane instead. One of the Killers slips a
hand through the broken window and grabs all of the keys hanging near
the door. One of the keys is for a Saab 900 Turbo.[127]

They go through the double doors that give access to the showroom.
Once in the front showroom, they move several cars, creating a passageway for the Saab 900 they want to steal. One of the Brabant Killers exits
the showroom and takes off with the Saab.

OBSERVATIONS

The FN .22 LR pistol used to shoot the guard dog was also used in the
murder of the Beersel Inn caretaker and the taxi driver in Mons. The Se-

rial Killer ballistics now include Beersel Inn, Mons Taxi, and the Braine dealership. It's still completely separate from the Public Attacks ballistics; there is no crossover of firearms used between the series of crimes. In theory, police should now be aware they have a violent, murderous gang on the one hand and a serial killer on a spree on the other hand. In reality, the only two crimes linked by authorities are Maubeuge in August 1982 and the Wavre Gun Shop in September 1982. Everything else is still a string of unrelated crimes.

No one heard the guard dog being shot 11 times, even though potential witnesses were sleeping close by. This indicates that the .22-caliber LR they use for close range encounters has a silencer. It's likely their only small caliber handgun with a silencer. The Gang has no choice but to use it under these circumstances, presumably deciding it's better to leave a ballistic link to another crime scene than to get caught because of a loud bang. Notably, authorities do not prioritize these crimes for forensic testing.

The Braine dealership break-in happens just ten days after the theft of the Braine blowtorch. Both robberies happen on Ophain Street in Braine, which does not have much traffic. To get to Braine, the thieves likely use the Golf stolen in Lasne on February 14th. Unlike their other stolen cars, the Killers will use the stolen Saab 900 a lot, criss-crossing Belgium to do night-time break-ins for sundry items. No more hold-ups. No more stealing alcohol.

THE COUPLE

Later that October 1983, a cop working the case visits the dealership owners and brings pictures of potential suspects to see if anyone rings a bell. The husband believes he recognizes criminal Istvan Farkas and his wife Berthe De Staerke, who is the sister of the currently incarcerated and notorious criminal Johnny De Staerke. According to the male dealership owner, Farkas' face seemed familiar but he couldn't say when or where he had seen him. His wife, who also works in the dealership, doesn't recognize anyone.

It's not much in terms of a lead, but this alleged identification will be, ex-post facto, the first sign that criminal Johnny De Staerke could be linked to the Insane Killers. He'll later become a major suspect in the case although in 1982, when the Insane Killers start their crimes, Johnny has jail as his best alibi. Johnny was released on May 10th, 1982, the day the Gang steals their first car in Ixelles. However, he doesn't stay out long and he's back in jail for Maubeuge in August 1982. And in December of that year, Johnny receives a three-year sentence for a violent robbery. At the time of the Braine dealership incident, he still has a couple more years to serve.

Johnny is the youngest child of a large Gypsy family of Romani descent. His oldest brother, Leon, is already a well-known gangster. Most of the family has followed in the older brother's footsteps; even his sister Berthe married into a life a crime when she married Farkas. The family lives the traditional nomadic lifestyle of the Romani, though Johnny ultimately completely abandons the old Romani life and makes Brussels his criminal home base.

By 1980, Johnny already has an extensive rap sheet and is continually in and out of jail. In 1972, he's embarked on his life of crime and is arrested for break-ins. By 1975, he's arrested for an armed robbery and in 1976 he's sentenced to two years of jail for armed robberies. Shortly after getting out, he goes right back in for aggravated assault. He's later in trouble for illegal arms possession and fencing illegal weapons.

Johnny corners drug trafficking in a busy neighborhood in Brussels. With some of his criminal earnings, he invests in a nightclub. But most of his money is spent quickly. He's a regular at horse races and builds up a fearsome reputation, though he's never charged and found guilty in a murder case. It's just a lot of hearsay. In October 1980, a jeweler was shot in the back and robbed in his home. Three gangsters suspected of being involved in the robbery are murdered shortly after. It's suspected there was a disagreement among the thieves and the three gangsters were involved in joint criminal ventures at the time with Johnny's older brother, Leon De Staerke. Some people suspect Johnny is associated with the hit, but there's never been any tangible evidence he was. No one is ever charged with the triple murder.

HOURPES FOREST

On June 9th, 1983, the Killers torch and abandon the dark gray Golf they stole in Lasnes back on February 14th. It's dumped in Hourpes Forest, which is located south-east of the Borinage Region, about 20 miles from Mons. Everything that can be removed from the Golf is removed. Like the other hatchback cars they use and discard, the back seat is removed. The Blaupunkt car radio, the speakers and the amps are gone. They also removed the headlights, the battery, and the steering wheel.

OBSERVATIONS

The day before the gray Golf is abandoned, the Saab was stolen in Braine. The Golf is now disposable because they have another car to use when they commit their crimes. The torched Golf was a four-door hatchback in mint condition with a sunroof and tinted windows. Because the steering wheel, the battery, and the lights are removed, it can be assumed they removed those items at the dump site and put them in another car.

VIOLENT ARGUMENT

On August 16th, 1983, Brussels resident Marcel Barbier gets into an argument with his brother Robert. They've been drinking for a few hours in Marcel's apartment. Things start getting nasty and the brothers continue their argument outside in front of the apartment building. Marcel hits his brother and pulls out a gun. Courageous bystanders try to intervene to separate them, but Marcel becomes unhinged and threatens to shoot one of the bystanders. In a fit of rage, he fires a bullet that narrowly misses a foreign worker. Marcel then tries to carjack a passing car, but fails.

Police quickly show up and take Marcel Barbier into custody. They search his apartment and they're very concerned with what they find. First, there are weapons. But they are more alarmed when they also stumble on some curious membership paraphernalia for a Far-Right organization called Westland New Post. Because of a spike in Far-Right incidents in the past couple of years, Belgian authorities had dusted off an old law that made private militias illegal. Everything they see in Barbier's apartment points to some type of private militia.

Very worrisome to investigators is the discovery of several dozen classified NATO intelligence documents, including NATO Intelligence Summaries. The discovery of the underground militia makes the front page of all the newspapers. The full extent of their criminal activities is not known. Disclosures about the movement have continued for decades and they are long suspected of being involved in the Brabant Killings.

WESTLAND NEW POST

The public will soon learn several details about this alleged private militia, which is known to its members by the innocuous name Westland New Post. The Westland group is led by founder Paul Latinus, who is already known to authorities as a top member of the Youth Front movement, which was the most important Far-Right movement in Belgium before it was abolished under the private militia legislation. The Youth Front was an anti-communist and anti-immigrant movement that spread leaflets and organized rallies. Latinus was partly responsible for the downfall of the movement as he introduced more extreme, hard-core political ideas when he joined in 1979.

Latinus molded the most violent and impressionable members of the Youth Front to commit political attacks. No more passing leaflets. No more arguing in smoke-filled halls. Suddenly, Far Right attacks start making headlines regularly. A teenager participating in a communist rally is kidnapped and beaten to a pulp. The offices of a Far-Left organization are firebombed. The embassy of the pro-Soviet country of Angola is attacked. Latinus had just obtained the embassy's floor plan a couple of weeks before and prompted other Youth Front members to sketch and list all the important landmarks around the building. No arrests are ever made.

With authorities cracking down on them, Youth Front leadership saw the writing on the wall and made an effort to go mainstream. Leader Francis Dossogne tries to go legit by starting a political party called New Force but Latinus and the violent wing of the movement are not interested. The death knell of the Youth Front sounds on December 5th, 1980, when two Latinus protégés go out together to the Bar La Rotonde in the Laeken suburb of Brussels.

An argument breaks out with four Algerian foreign workers. One of the Front members shoots at them, killing Hamou Baroudi on the spot and critically wounding his friend. A third is hit by shards of exploding glass. The newspaper *Le Soir* blares out the headline "Racist Crime in Laeken" and the crime garners national attention in Belgium. Across the country, roughly 50,000 demonstrators participate in a march against racism. Latinus' name is exposed in the media as a person of interest in the Laeken murder. He disappears from the public eye that December 1980.

With the Youth Front disbanded, a splinter cell of the most violent members follow Latinus when he creates the Westland New Post in 1981. Unlike the Youth Front, the Westland movement is underground. To be initiated into the group, new members are required to commit a crime. This leaves the new member open to blackmail by Westland. Some members of the movement are recruited from the Belgian military, most in the communications department. At least seven of these Westland military members are involved in stealing a hundred NATO documents. Among these, 70 documents are classified confidential and 17 documents are classified secret. There is no rhyme or reason about what has been taken; it appears that opportunity determines which documents are stolen. The Westland New Post will later become major suspects in the Brabant Killings.

CHAPTER *10*

TEMSE FABRIC
(SEPTEMBER 10, 1983)

O N SATURDAY, SEPTEMBER 10TH, 1983 AT 2:30 A.M., THE BRABANT
Killers drive the stolen Saab 900 turbo up to the Wittock textile
factory in Temse.[128] The factory is located in an industrial pocket surrounded by rows of houses. It's impossible to see the buildings from the
street. There's a long narrow alleyway connecting a residential street and
the factory, but the Saab doesn't enter the alleyway. Instead, the Killers
park it on the street on the side of a bike path right before the alleyway.

The Brabant Killers walk the whole length of the alleyway, which is
about a three-minute walk. After they break into the factory building, they
head to the warehouse and open up boxes. When they don't find what
they're looking for, the men go to the lab in another area of the building.
Jozef Broeder and Linda Van Huffelen, the factory's resident janitorial couple, live in an adjoining apartment.[129] Broeder hears noise and jumps out of
bed to check what's happening. As he opens the door to his apartment, he
sees the heavily armed men. Broeder tries to fight back, yanking blond hair
from the head of one the Brabant Killers, but he's overwhelmed. Breaking
free from his assailants, Broeder runs back into his apartment and shuts
the door behind him. The Brabant Killers chase him and fire through the
apartment door with a pump-action shotgun, hitting Broeder in the stomach. He drags himself to the bedroom to warn his wife.

The killers burst into the apartment at this point and finish Broeder off with four bullets to the head. Broeder's wife, Linda Van Huffelen, sees the killers coldly execute her husband and somehow has the reflex to pull her hand near her face to protect herself. A bullet ricochets off her thumb and is lodged in her lung. Van Huffelen crashes down to the ground. The couple's three-year-old daughter Sharon walks out of the room. One of the gangsters picks her up and drops her back into her bed. Both Sharon and her two-month-old sister Patricia are left crying alone. Their father is dead and their mother ends up in a coma for two months and spends a year in a hospital.

The Killers then reach the lab where they continue their search. They eventually leave with seven bulletproof vests, a smoke-colored vest and camouflage overalls. They shoot all four tires of the live-in janitors' Toyota, as well as all the streetlights along their exit route.

As the Brabant Killers make their way back through the alleyway, a noise wakes up an elderly man who lives in a house near their parked stolen Saab. The man, who believes it's the sound of a car with motor trouble, slips out of bed and peeks through his bedroom window. He sees the Saab parked close to the factory's alleyway access and calls out to see if anyone needs help.

One of the Killers shoots his shotgun at the man's bedroom window, shattering the glass. The projectiles miss the old man, who barely has time to dive and take cover.[130] A streetlight that turns on automatically for passing cyclists is also shot out by the Killers. The commotion wakes up another neighbor. When they notice the drapes moving in the neighbor's bedroom, the Killer fires his shotgun towards the house. The shotgun buckshot slams on the front of the house, but doesn't claim another victim.[131]

The Killers drive away towards downtown Temse, making a few weird detours before disappearing.

Bulletproof Vests

The Killers use the Saab stolen at the Braine dealership on June 8th for this robbery. The Temse factory location is unusual, hidden behind houses. If you don't know where you're going, you won't find it. The Killers had clearly cased the place before. Sources indicate some Killers were wearing ski masks, but there's no consensus.

The Killers use a pump-action shotgun to fire through the door and hit the caretaker. Investigators label this shotgun SG-1 (RG-1 in French and Dutch). The SG-1 is also determined to be the weapon used to shoot warning shots at the neighbors looking through their windows. The janitor is hit with fatal shots to the head with the same caliber .22 that was used in Beersel on December 23rd, 1982; in Mons on January 9th, 1983; and in Braine on July 8th, 1983.

This Temse factory attack only links to the Serial Killers ballistics, not the Public Attacks ballistics, now becoming Beersel Inn, Mons taxi, Braine dealership, and Temse factory. However, these crimes won't be connected immediately by authorities and no one attributes these attacks to the Brabant Insane Killers at this time. There are only several unrelated crimes. Only Maubeuge and Wavre from the previous year are linked by ballistics.

Once in the factory, they know exactly what they are looking for; they head straight for the vests and ignore the safe stacked with money. They search a couple of places and find the protective vests in a metal cabinet in the office. After they left the couple for dead and the two kids alive, they didn't panic. They returned to finish off the robbery, located the vests, and left. We don't know how long they stayed.

Why were the vests so important to them? In some early reports, the insignificant value of the stolen goods is brought up to emphasize how senseless the crime was. The *De Voorpost* newspaper reports on September 9th, 1983: "There was an unbelievable massacre that happened. For a few pieces of clothing. Because the company safe didn't interest them." Why would people kill for this?

Quickly, the story changes. The type of stolen bulletproof vest was a recently finalized prototype, so novel and rare that it actually had an intangible value. These vests had cutting-edge technology, made with an ultra-light fabric traditionally used to make sails. Their existence was a closely guarded secret inside the company, so there is speculation that the fact the Killers knew to steal the prototypes points to inside information.

However, the prototype vests are the latest upgrade, but not drastically different from previous models. In the local yellow pages, the ad for Wittock boasted: "Bullet-proof vests—Camouflage filets." Employees at Wittock's Temse factory likely knew about the vests, but not the exact metal cabinet where they were hidden. Given that Wittock was promoting their latest upgrade to a large swath of the market, many of the firms' clients had been informed about them and many reps came to see them. These included the army, reps from Securitas and other security firms, a few police departments, and arms dealers.

Articles were also published in the press that the Gendarmerie was also interested in the vest. The Wittock technical rep responsible for the flak jackets confirmed people presenting themselves as Gendarmes visited him, but the Gendarmerie vehemently denies visiting the factory to see the new product. Some have suggested that officers might have come outside of their work capacities or the people who visited the rep could have been fake Gendarmes.

WILLY POURTOIS

Arms broker, Willy Pourtois had recently visited the Wittock textile factory to look at the flak jacket prototypes with a Lebanese purchaser. Remember that Pourtois had been embroiled in the Wavre Gun Shop attack investigation when the Wavre Gendarmerie found out he had acted as a middleman for the Wavre Gun Shop silencer sales. It was still their working theory that the motivation for the Wavre attack was to steal the silencer prototype. However, at the time of the

Temse fabric attack, Pourtois is in jail. He had been arrested for illegal traffic of weapons. Pourtois was also a paid informant for the Belgian intelligence agency, the Sûreté. There's speculation that the Sûreté could have been aware of his dealings with Wittock, which opens up a completely new can of worms.

Vincent L. Crew

In late 1983, when criminal Francis V. is arrested for a series of crimes, he tells police he suspects his recently deceased friend Vincent L. of having been involved in the Temse Fabric break-in and the Brabant Killings. Francis V. gave the name of an accomplice who told Vincent L. the spot in the Wittock factory where the vests were warehoused. In a 1984 report, police document that the accomplice's stepsister worked in the factory's management. However, when they find out, the accomplice's family claims that the police report is wrong and the stepsister didn't work there.

Francis V. claims that after the Temse fabric factory attack he drove with Vincent L. to the deep south of Belgium, to the Ardennes Region. There Vincent L. hands a Gendarme three bulletproof jackets stolen from Temse and a bag with three arms from the Dekaise attack. According to Francis V., the Gendarme had worked previously as a detective in the Brussels Drug Department. Investigators put two and two together and come up with the name of Gendarme Martial Lekeu.

Later, Francis V. also claims that Vincent L.'s drug pusher, Hage Maroun, gave two flak jackets to Staff Sergeant Guy Goffinon, the officer who was targeted in a Bouhouche Gang bombing in 1982. Both Goffinon and Maroun denied the transaction ever happened.

Additionally, Francis V. claims that a small-time criminal of Romani heritage named Robert "Balou" Becker is part of Vincent L.'s crew. When police walk around the Temse neighborhood to interview suspects, they bring a series of pictures of likely suspects. Two witnesses believe they recognize "Balou" Becker. One or both believed to have seen Becker near the Wittock premises earlier on the day of the Temse attack.

CHAPTER 11

COLRUYT SUPERMARKET IN NIVELLES
(SEPTEMBER 17, 1983)

ON SEPTEMBER 17TH, 1983, SOMETIME BETWEEN MIDNIGHT AND 1:00 a.m., the Brabant Killers discreetly drive the stolen Saab Turbo to the back of a Nivelles Colruyt supermarket building. The Colruyt supermarket is a long rectangular building, only 300 feet away from the highway access ramp.[132] The Saab parks right next to a metallic door at the back and three Killers step out of the car. One of them starts to use a blowtorch to make a hole through the door.[133]

Earlier in the evening, a middle-aged couple, Jacques Fourez and Elise Dewit, leave Paris in their Mercedes to go back home to Belgium. Fourez, a businessman, and Dewit, a secretary, were in Paris to review a paint job completed in a rental apartment. During the drive back, Dewit takes off her shoes to be more comfortable. Once the couple gets to Nivelles, they exit the access ramp to fill up at the Colruyt's self-serve gas station. It's right on the side of the building the Killers are breaking into.

The Mercedes reaches the gas pumps at 1:10 a.m. Fourez steps out to fill the tank while his wife waits in the car. One of the Insane Killers notices the Mercedes at the pumps. He takes a few steps towards the Mercedes and tries to fire his 7.65 mm pistol at Fourez, but the pistol is stuck. He ejects two casings from the pistol, takes a few more steps and shoots Fourez right in the face. Fourez crashes down to the pavement and the shooter finishes him off with two .22 LR bullets to the head.

Dewit watches the horrific execution-style murder and steps out of the car. She doesn't even take the time to put her shoes back on, she opens the door and tries to get away. The Killer immediately shoots at Dewit once with his 7.65mm but misses. The casing falls to the pavement to the right of the Mercedes.

The murderer tries to grab her instead of shooting again right away. Dewit puts up a fight and loses her glasses in the struggle. The Killer pulls her to the back of the Colruyt building where he shoots two .22 LR bullets at her head and she collapses. The Brabant Killers ignore the expensive jewelry she wears and drag her body farther towards the back of the Colruyt building.

One of the Brabant Killers steps into the couple's Mercedes and drives it over by the back metal door being blowtorched. The Killers drag Fourez's body behind the building, where they shoot three more .22 LR shots into his head and attempt to flip his body over the fence. When that doesn't work, the Killers leave his body right along the back wall of the building. A few yards away, one of the Killers also shoots three more .22 LR bullets into Dewit's head. They then bring her body close to Fourez's body and hide the bloodied corpses as well as they can with a few shopping carts.

The Killers then get back to using the blowtorch to gain access through the back door. A couple of minutes later they finally succeed in making a square-shaped hole in the door. They slip through the hole and enter the back of the store. A silent alarm connected to security headquarters is triggered at 1:23 a.m. Security calls the local Gendarmerie station at 1:26 a.m. to advise that a robbery is in progress.[134]

A Gendarmerie patrol is dispatched to the supermarket. The alarm continues to pick up people moving inside the store until 1:35 a.m. The intruders steal only 4,100 lbs. of coffee in large pouches, five 50-liter cans of peanut oil, five 50-liter cans of corn oil, five boxes of pralines, and two bottles of gin. The Killers load the loot into both the stolen Saab Turbo and the dead couple's Mercedes.

While the robbers finish loading the two cars, a police van enters the gas pump area at 1:30 a.m. The police officers flash the van's high beams and make their way to the back of the building. They spot the two cars a few yards away from each other and stop 300 yards away from the dark blue Saab 900 Turbo. At this point, the criminals are nearly finished loading their loot.

As soon as they notice the police exiting their van, the Killers immediately fire a heavy barrage from several weapons. Gendarme Lacroix takes cover behind the open driver's side door of his van. A volley of 12-gauge shots hits the top left of the van door. Lacroix returns fire with his 7.65 pistol and shoots at least twice.[135] He then moves to the back of his van to shoot some more.

The thieves keep blasting the cops with shotgun blasts and .22 LR bullets. Gendarme Morue, who is beside his van's right door firing his UZI submachine gun, screams to Lacroix: "Call for backup!" A few seconds later, Morue is hit on the right ankle by two caliber .45 ACP bullets. He falls to the ground and his UZI clinks on the pavement. He's then killed when he's hit in the throat by the shotgun.

The killers then concentrate all their fire on Officer Lacroix. They shoot a 9mm, .357 Magnum, seven caliber .45 ACP bullets, and eight shots from a pump-action shotgun. A Killer with a beard and a long, light-colored trench coat starts creeping up towards the car. Lacroix shoots twice more towards the bearded criminal before he's hit by several bullets to the left hand.[136] He crumbles between the dashboard and the passenger seat of his van. Lacroix has the presence of mind to leave his legs dangling out of the van to play dead. When the Killers realize the police have stopped returning fire, they hold their fire and walk up to the police van.

Though injured, Lacroix is still conscious. He hears a Brabant Killer say of Morue: "Oh, the bastard, he had an UZI."[137] The Killer shoots again at point blank range at Morue's head for good measure. A total of 34 pieces of lead are now in Morue's body. One of them grabs officer Lacroix by the belt and flips him over. He unbuckles Lacroix's belt and removes the holster. However, before they leave, one of the Killers goes up to Lacroix and pulls the 7.65mm out of Lacroix's right hand before shooting him in the neck to finish him off. Miraculously, the bullet ricochets off Lacroix's shoulder strap and, unbeknownst to the Killers, he survives. The Killers leave, taking the keys out of the police van's ignition, as well as the weapons and walkie-talkies from both police officers.

LEAVING

The assailants leave the Colruyt in two cars, their stolen Saab Turbo and the murdered couple's Mercedes. Officer Lacroix, who survives with only an injury to his left thumb, radios at 1:34 a.m. that Morue has been killed and reinforcements are needed. The police station sends a general alert to all the police brigades in the Walloon Brabant. They also contact first responders, who arrive at the Colruyt to find the three dead bodies and dozens of spent casings littering the pavement.

THE CHASE

Police set up roadblocks all over the region and issue an order for all officers to be on the lookout for the white Mercedes.[138] Unfortunately, Officer Lacroix could not identify the second getaway vehicle. Six minutes later, a VW Golf driven by Officer Marc Lemal accompanied by officers Ben Ruys and André Bernier is in the vicinity and they stumble on two cars driving at full speed along a secondary highway. The officers are not sure if these cars are the right target, but they give chase anyway.[139]

Their reaction time makes them lose precious seconds. The two cars are already far ahead and only the backlights can be seen. But the fugitives only drive another 100 yards on the country highway, which is lined by trees and fields on both sides. They slow down near an oddly located nightclub called *Le Diable Amoureux* (The Devil in Love). The Mercedes stops on the left side of the road and the Saab stops a few yards further on the right side.[140] The Killers wait in ambush for the police's Golf.

Twenty yards before reaching the Mercedes, Officer Ruys sees the driver exit the car. He has combed back dark hair with a slightly receding hairline. The police officers, confused by this maneuver by the Insane Killers, slow down a bit and hesitate about what to do next. The Insane Killers unleash their weapons on the approaching police car. The Mercedes driver shatters the police car's windshield with his pump-action shotgun. The driver, Officer Lemal, is hit on the shoulder and grazed on the head. Hiding behind the Saab on the other side of the road, another Insane Killer also blasts his pump-action shotgun but misses the police car.

Despite his injuries, Officer Lemal keeps control of the car as he passes the Killer's improvised roadblock and then bolts ahead, out of range of the Brabant Killers. Instead of escaping with both stolen cars, the Killer driving the Mercedes leaves it and the loot inside and joins the two other Killers in the Saab Turbo. The Saab does a U-Turn and drives in the opposite direction.[141] Once out of sight, the Killers veer right into a little known narrow side street and head to the other side of town.[142]

Alone

The Killers drive the stolen Saab a few more kilometers when a valve in the motor splits. The fugitives can't shift into third gear and the Saab now maxes out at 45 miles per hour. They make it to a gas station. The Brabant Killers take some toilet paper from the restrooms and probably use it to wipe the blood from hauling the dead bodies.

They leave the gas station, driving the Saab to a long dirt driveway entrance in Braine and stop. The Saab has a flat tire, so they take the carjack from the toolbox and try unsuccessfully to replace the flat tire. They chuck the spare tire over a fence and abandon the Saab, leaving the carjack strewn on the side. They shoot twice into the tank with a pump-action shotgun to set the car on fire. It doesn't work, so they just leave the Saab there as is.

LEAVING

Investigators believe the Killers spend a couple of hours in the vicinity of the abandoned Saab, perhaps taking some time to strip the Saab of clues. They wait for the cops to relax their surveillance of the area and possibly arrange for an accomplice to pick them up in another vehicle. A neighbor reports hearing a noise coming from the dirt driveway at 7:00 a.m. and there is speculation that it was from the Insane Killers shooting the car tank. The neighbor sees the Saab, but doesn't notice anyone around it and goes back to bed. Authorities are only alerted later.

Police find the Saab at 9:30 a.m. Dozens of fingerprints are left inside and outside the car. There are bloodstains from the victims and a strand of hair. Authorities also recover the carjack, toolbox, and the car's fifth wheel. They left a few items inside the car, including a khaki green 10-liter gas tank with metal spout, two gas tanks from their blowtorch, and a green safari hat. The vehicle has a pair of CIBIE anti-fog chrome headlights, which the Killers removed. Other items left behind include the UZI stolen from the dead officer at the Colruyt, 100 lbs. of coffee, and the 50 liters of oil stolen from the Colruyt. Fifteen other oil containers are found in the Mercedes.

The Killers have taken the two 7.65mm caliber pistols that were stolen from the two Gendarmes. They also leave with their arsenal of weapons and the police walkie-talkies.

The headrests and the seat belts were removed from the Saab to facilitate shooting and the 'stop' bulbs had been taped over. This kept the element of surprise when the Killers stopped to ambush the police, who had a severely limited reaction time. The radio antenna is removed, and the antenna hole is carefully filled up. The Saab's two-tone car horn and matching 6-volt battery are removed. So is the original stereo system with one amplifier, two loudspeakers, one Jenssen (vs.) equalizer, and one Blaupunkt car radio.

The Saab's turbo was boosted. It had false plates with the number copied from another Saab 900 in the vicinity of Ixelles and Soignes Forest and had been driven roughly 500 miles since it was stolen and 24 miles that day. The spoilers are gone.

ENTER THE INSANE KILLERS

The Nivelles attack is huge national news. No one can grasp why they killed so many people for so little. The Gang is officially christened following this attack; the French-language media call them, "The Walloon Brabant Insane Killers" and the Dutch-language media call them the "Nivelles Gang." The Brabant Insane Killers are born as a media concept and this is the first day the public finds out who they are.

The attack is disturbing on many levels. They killed the couple in the Mercedes a full ten minutes before they actually entered the store. We know this because the driver, Fourez's watch stopped working 10 minutes before the silent alarm rang at headquarters.[143] According to Prosecutor Jean-Marie Schlicker: "Everything indicated the couple that was killed came to get gas and fell by accident on the robbers."[144]

Just like in Temse, the Killers violently murdered victims and then just resumed breaking into the supermarket as if nothing had ever happened. Criminal defense lawyer Jean-Paul Moerman wondered during the first Commission: "Why did the robbery in Nivelles resume after the killings? We would think that panicked, robbers would normally leave."[145] After a double murder, the Brabant Killers just went on stealing tanks of cooking oil and large bags of coffee—just like they continued looking for the flak jackets with a modest market value.

Any criminal knows the most lucrative items to steal during a night-time supermarket break-in are alcohol and cigarettes. And the Brabant Killers know this, as they did just that in 1982; we know they stole alcohol in Maubeuge that September and at the Beersel Inn in December. But that's clearly not what they're looking for—and it wasn't cash they were after either. Despite all the time they spent in the store and having a blowtorch, there's no sign they attempted to crack the store's safe.

They had filled up grocery carts with bottles of whiskey and packs of cigarettes but it looks like it was an afterthought. They never had time to transfer in the couple's Mercedes when they were surprised by the Gendarmerie van. We can tell what they valued the most that night by what they stored in the stolen Saab Turbo: Cooking oil and bags of coffee! They had no plans to leave with a second car before getting there that night and stealing the Mercedes, so they had no intention to steal alcohol and cigarettes. The Mercedes just gave them extra space to steal more stuff. And they put in more cooking oil! Then, when they had enough cooking oil and still had room remaining, they stole whiskey and cigarettes just as an afterthought. They did the polar opposite of what any normal thieves would have done.

As the blowtorch was stolen almost four months before during their May 28th Braine break-in, it seems very unlikely that the initial motive for stealing it was piercing a hole in the metal door of this Colruyt. The Saab stolen in Braine on June 8th had little storage space and was less maneuverable than the Golf. However, it packed more speed and horsepower, which made it more useful during a long distance chase. In 1982, their priorities were different; they stole a Santana with a large trunk to load as many valuables as possible.

The odometer showed the Saab Turbo had driven for 500 miles. It's speculated the Killers had driven to the Temse factory and back. However, there was not a single supermarket attack or nighttime break-in for alcohol linked to the Brabant Killers during that time period. Their break-ins now are for very specific items, such as the single blowtorch and tanks, seven bulletproof vests, and now tanks of oil and bags of coffee. The market value of the items stolen is minimal. However, the Killers must consider them valuable for some reason.

SEVEN FIREARMS

When news of the Brabant Insane Killers hits the newsstands, the public is struck by the assailants bringing so much firepower to their crime scenes. Defense lawyer Moerman, who will be involved in the case later on, observed, "Why the use of seven different weapons for a nighttime store break-in?"[146] Prosecutor Schlicker also couldn't make sense of it, saying, "We didn't understand the number of calibers used, to steal food…"[147]

The couple in the Mercedes was each shot first with a 7.65 mm pistol and finished off with several bullets to the head with a .22-caliber LR pistol. The FN 7.65 pistol was used in Maubeuge and Wavre. So when you add up all the Public Attacks ballistics, that also includes all the supermarket holdups.

Very significant is the .22 LR FN pistol that they use. It's the same gun that is used for the assassinations of the Het Kasteel Inn caretaker in December 1982, the taxi driver found in Mons in January 1983, the German Shepherd guard dog at the Braine car dealership in June 1983, and the Wittock factory janitor in September 1983. This makes these crimes all part of the Serial Killer ballistics series. For the first time ever, all the known Brabant Killer attacks are linked by ballistics. The 7.65 was used in the Public Attacks ballistics. The .22 LR was used during the Serial Killer attacks. This latest crime, the Nivelles attack, now merges both tracks of ballistics. Everything is now connected to the same weapons being used in violent crimes.

The Insane Killers use a new Colt .45 Semi-automatic 1911. The Colt .45 was shot seven times at Officer Morue and hit him twice in the ankle. They use a .357 that was shot before at the Delhaize Genval on February 11th. It's probably a Smith and Wesson .357 Magnum Revolver. They also use a 9 mm pistol that links Nivelles to their other Public Attack ballistics of the Halle, Genval, Uccle supermarkets, and the Wavre Gun Shop. A 7.65 was also used.

The Brabant Killers used two tactical pump-action shotguns, which are commonly called Riot Guns in Belgium. They're identified with the Riot Gun initials by investigators: RG-1 and RG-2. For simplicity's sake, we'll call them SG-1 and SG-2. The SG-2 is shot several times on the Gendarmes behind the Colruyt supermarket. It's a 12-gauge with a charger that can hold at least six 3-inch., 12-gauge cartridges. It had never been used before.

During the Diable Amoureux ambush, the Killers fired three SG-1 and seven SG-2 cartridges. It's the first time SG-1 shot that night, but it had already been used at the Temse factory attack. It's a .12-gauge shotgun with similar characteristics to SG-2.

THE AMBUSH

Their ambush technique has spilled lots of ink, with assessments running the gamut from pronouncing the Insane Killers mere amateurs, to asserting they were professional criminals. What people usually agree on is that the Killers use an unusual tactic.

If it was used deliberately, experts debate whether it was a bad technique to use. The ambush technique can just be improvised, but it also had doctrinal foundations. For example, it's called the 'V' formation in American military lingo used by the U.S. Marine Corps.[148] Like other ambush formations such as the Line Formation and the Box Formation, the goal is to "isolate, trap and destroy the enemy."[149] According to the Marines manual: "Its main advantage is that it is difficult for the enemy to detect the ambush until it is well into the killing zone." But there are precautions to take, as it is not without danger: "Care is taken to ensure that neither group (within the "V") fires into the other."

There's a debate about whether the Brabant Killers even deliberately used that ambush technique or if they just stumbled into it as a crime of opportunity. Perhaps, as they fled the scene, the Killers noticed the distant, flickering lights of police cruisers setting up a roadblock. They just happen to stop on either side of the road and, when the police car shows up on the road near them, they impulsively open fire. When they've finished their ambush, they leave in the direction they came from.

ACCOMPLICE

The most likely explanation for how the Killers evaded authorities searching the area for them is that they called an accomplice to come pick them up, probably using a pay phone. A black taxi was seen in the area after 4:00 a.m. and so was a BMW. In both cases, if they did leave early, there's still the 7:00 a.m. gunshot heard by the neighbor.

Another explanation for how they would have escaped the tightening noose is that they had a safe house in the area. One interesting tidbit is that police from Braine and Waterloo received an anonymous phone call concerning a fight at a party in Ophain that was false but successfully diverted forces away from the chase of the Killers.

Bouhouche Gang

Officer Lemal, who drove the van during the ambush, is sure that he was shot at by a Gendarme that he knew. He also believes he recognized a second shooter but unlike the other Gendarme, he isn't certain. Both suspects are in Bouhouche's close entourage. He noticed the Gendarme was losing his hair and had a beard, just like one suspect close to Bouhouche who had just received a special permission to wear a beard while on duty as a Gendarme. He had skin problems on his face and wore a beard for about three months during that time period and had been losing his hair for a few years already. The Saab Turbo carried false plates with the same technical glitch used in the mold of the other Bouhouche Gang fake license plates. The license plates were also all aged artificially using the same process.

The ambush technique used seems very much like the technique a Bouhouche-led commando had devised in case they were caught red-handed. It was related to the robbery of a dinghy that happened not too long before the Nivelles attack. A friend of Bouhouche, well aware of the dinghy robbery, when asked by a journalist if the police interception plan used during the dinghy robbery was the same as the one in Nivelles, answered, "It was something like that."[150]

Vincent L. Crew

According to Francis V.'s narrative, the Vincent L. Crew are responsible for the Colruyt attack. They wanted to steal the cooking oil and other foodstuffs to supply one of the Vincent L. Crew's alleged members. Things derailed when they were interrupted first by the couple getting gas for their Mercedes and then by the police officers.

DE STAERKE ESCAPE

Five hours before the Nivelles attack, several criminals escaped from the Doornink high-security prison. The prison guards were on strike that day and ten Gendarmerie officers were forced to take over. The inmates took advantage of the situation and pierced a hole in the jail wall. They then used ladders and ropes to scale a four-meter-high wall. By 7:45 p.m., 38 prisoners were on the run. The alarm only went off at 9:00 p.m. Johnny De Staerke, who one day becomes an important suspect for the Brabant killings, is one of the fugitives. Most inmates are quickly picked up, but Johnny is successful in his escape.

Johnny is kind of a bogeyman. In his later years, he's notorious, considered one of the most hardcore criminals in the country.[151] Part of it is Johnny's self-promotion as a bad hombre. Just the fact he's out of jail makes him a suspect for various crimes, including the Nivelles attack. As there are no eyewitnesses or serious leads that put him in Nivelles, there's not much to go on, other than gauging the odds of him being there. How likely is it for someone to break out of a high-security jail under fortuitous circumstances, hook up with accomplices, gather stolen weapons, a stolen car and a blowtorch, and make his way to the Colruyt in just five hours? According to Leo Van Esbroek, a recently released jail acquaintance of Johnny's, the truth of that night was not too exciting. Van Esbroek says Johnny showed up at his apartment a couple of hours after the jailbreak with nothing but the clothes on his back.

SELF-DESTRUCTION OF THE WESTLAND NEW POST

On September 23rd, the Westland New Post movement is in the news again. The Far Right militia is being investigated for the stolen NATO documents and other suspected infractions. The Westland New Post leader Paul Latinus makes headlines with statements concerning an unsolved double murder that happened in February 1982. A couple, murdered in a particularly gruesome way in their second-floor apartment on Pastorale

Street in Brussels, were shot and then their throats were slit. They were found on their knees in the middle of the living room facing each other. Witnesses had seen two unidentified men enter the apartment. Authorities quickly determine nothing was stolen from the property and are baffled by the viciousness of the murder. They make background checks on the murdered couple, follow a bunch of leads, and never get anywhere.

Latinus says the two murderers are part of his Westland New Post and he even gives their names. One is Marcel Barbier, the man involved in the drunken incident that opened up the whole Westland affair. The other is Eric Lammers, nicknamed the Beast. Latinus will even convince Barbier to confess to police. Both suspects are arrested. Authorities and the public start wondering what other violent crimes could this underground private militia could have committed. Could they be involved in the Brabant Insane Killers attacks?

CHAPTER *12*

AUX TROIS CANARDS RESTAURANT (OCTOBER 2, 1983)

O N THE NIGHT OF OCTOBER 1ST, 1983, JUST AFTER MIDNIGHT AT 12:30 a.m., the owner of Aux Trois Canards Restaurant, Jacques Van Camp, exits the restaurant to give lifts home to students who don't have cars. The employees have just finished closing up for the night and the four-star restaurant is out of the way in the countryside. He's barely crossed the door's threshold when two armed intruders with carnival masks surprise him.

Van Camp is ordered at gunpoint to follow one of the intruders outside to the front parking area. The second intruder, wearing a mask with a black eye and crooked teeth, directs the rest of the staff to go in the kitchen right next to the front door. He holds a long-barreled pistol and wears pink rubber gloves on his hands. He's of normal build and wears blue bell-bottom pants.[152]

He barks in French with a fake Romani or an Arabic accent,[153] "Everyone lie on the kitchen floor."[154] He tells them to hand over their cash and car keys.[155] The cook, who thinks this is all a big joke, hesitates to lie down, so the gunman shoots at the fridge to make the cook understand this is dead serious.[156] The only one who has car keys is the cook and none of the employees have cash in their pockets.[157]

Meanwhile, the other intruder is in the front parking area with Van Camp, who offers some resistance.[158] The Killer shoots a 7.65mm bullet to the back of Van Camp's head. Van Camp has the keys to his daughter's new red Golf GTI, which the Killer steals. His accomplice leaves the kitchen, where the employees are still lying down on the floor, without asking for the money from the cash register.[159] After shooting the tires of all the cars in the parking lot, the Killers leave with the Golf GTI.[160]

THE KEYS

The Aux Trois Canards Restaurant is in the countryside south of Brussels, far removed from the urban area and about 500 yards from where the Insane Killers abandoned one of their stolen cars a few months earlier. The Inn is managed by a well-to-do, middle-aged couple, architect Jacques Van Camp and his wife Germaine Doom. Their 27-year-old daughter Catherine, who just returned from a trip to Australia, also helps run the Inn. Almost all the Inn's employees are students.[161]

According to Prosecutor Schlicker, Van Camp offered resistance and perhaps was killed because he didn't obey right away. Van Camp's daughter Catherine believes it's a possibility, "Maybe he really tried to defend himself and ripped off the perpetrator's mask? Then he would have gotten a look at him and become an annoying witness."[162] Another theory is that Van Camp wouldn't hand over the keys to the car. Would he have been killed if he obeyed?

An important question is which car the Killers came to steal. They left with the Golf, but there's some evidence they wanted the Porsche. According to the victim's daughter, who owned the Golf. "I believe that the perpetrators really wanted the Porsche. Maybe they got furious when they noticed that my father didn't have the keys?"[163] Van Camp was leaving to drive young employees back home in his daughter's red Golf.

The stolen red Golf GTI has black stripes on the side and the sticker "I Love Australia" on the window. The Brabant Killers were not known to have a car after they abandoned the stolen Saab during the Nivelles attack on September 17th. The dark Porsche would have made more sense if they were looking for an expensive car like the Saab Turbo, and the Golf was a flashy bright red, not ideal for nighttime break-ins. However, they'll repaint the car black and Golf cars come to be associated as the preferred choice of the Brabant Killers.

Van Camp is shot with one of the two pistols stolen from the Gendarmes they killed or left for dead in the back parking lot of the Nivelles Colryut supermarket. It's a Gendarme regulation FN 7.65 mm pistol. A light beige Burberry raincoat is later found on site. It may or may not have been left behind by the Killers. Initially, investigators believed the 7.65mm was the same 7.65 that killed the Gendarme in Nivelles and the media reported it as a sure thing because the Nivelles attack was still on everyone's mind and the authorities had noticed that the Killers reused some of their guns. Ballistics testing confirmed it wasn't.

Investigators looked into the Inn's accounting. Some of their luxury foodstuffs were bought at a very low price and had originally come from a robbery of the Sabena airline. However, no link could be found between the Sabena robbery and the Killers.

VINCENT L. CREW

According to convict Francis V., the police's key witness against the Vincent L. Crew as Insane Killers suspects, Vincent L. had told him that the Aux Trois Canard owner Jacques Van Camp was part of his crew. It might seem surprising at first that a 19-year-old drug addict would be in the same criminal gang as a successful architect and businessman, but investigators follow up the leads they get. There is speculation the Vincent L. Crew killed the Het Kasteel Inn's caretaker in December 1982 for knowing too much about Van Camp's criminal activities. Van Camp is the one who told Vincent L. where the bulletproof vest prototypes were kept during the Temse attack of September 1983. The cooking oil and other foodstuffs stolen during the Nivelles Colryut attack were to allegedly stock Van Camp's Aux Trois Canards Restaurant. The Crew was afraid Van Camp would snitch, so he had to be killed and the car's robbery was just a diversion. Vincent L. killed Van Camp with another thief, Balou Becker. Some witnesses from the Temse factory robbery picked Becker out of a photo lineup as someone they saw that day.

Vincent L. could have sold the murder weapon, a GP 9mm, to Lebanese drug trafficker Hage Maroun. Investigators look into the alleged sale of the GP 9mm and confirm that Vincent L. did indeed sell a GP 9mm to Maroun, who paid with jewels and a watch. Maroun then resold the gun to a buyer from Lebanon. Belgian Justice takes steps to reach out to Lebanese authorities for their help. Lebanese police trace back the buyer and find he still has the GP 9mm in his possession. Belgian authorities do not pursue the matter any further and don't do any ballistic tests.[164]

Francis V. started talking about the Vincent L. Crew when he was caught in a police sting, perhaps hoping for a favors from police. It doesn't work, as he gets a seven-year sentence. Francis V.'s narrative on Vincent L. has some shaky aspects, his participation being one. He also refuses to sign his police statement, which is a common practice in Belgium to confirm validity. Eventually, Francis V. even retracts the statements he never signed and validated. No material evidence is ever found to verify any of Francis V.'s allegations. When Vincent L.'s sister was arrested along with Francis V., she claimed Francis V. made it all up.

But instead of wasting police time, the Francis V. statements have huge consequences, uncovering two other major leads that take on a life of their own. Which begs the question, if Francis V.'s statements are all made up, what are the odds that it leads them to the right suspect? Because Gendarme Martial Lekeu's link to the Temse factory attack and Vicky V.'s link to the Wavre Gun shop attack are entirely built on Francis V.'s uncorroborated statements. Lekeu did, in fact, know of both Francis V. and Vincent L. from his time working in Brussels, but their interactions, which happened in the course of a narcotics case, were limited.

Westland New Post and Sûreté

On October 7th a new earth-shattering story breaks in the media, that the Far-Right clandestine militia, Westland New Post, was thoroughly infiltrated by the Sûreté, the Belgian government's internal spying agency. Just recently, Westland confessed to the gruesome Pastorale Street double murder from February 1982. Three Westland members had been paid informants for the Sûreté, including the leader Latinus and his top lieutenant, Michel Libert.

At least three Sûreté agents have had regular contacts with the Westland New Post since 1981. Their code-names are the Duck, the Dog, and the Rabbit. But even more incredible, is the disclosure that the Duck, a management-level agent, had been a card-carrying member of the Westland group under his own name. He had given private casing lessons to the Westland members including at least one practical exercise out in the field on how to case a target.

The news sends shockwaves through the country and will shake the Sûreté to the core. Investigators investigating the stolen classified NATO documents and the Pastorale Street double murder now need to probe if the Sûreté was involved or even directed both crimes. The public and the media now scream for answers from the Sûreté and the government. Did they create Westland so they could have their own team of assassins that they could keep at arm's length? Rumors also start growing about Westland's involvement in the Brabant Killings and the responsibility of the Sûreté and even the Belgian state itself.

When the Westland leader, Latinus, is interviewed, he gives cryptic, often contradictory, answers.[165] On the one hand, he blames the Westland for being controlled by the Sûreté through the Duck, and claims they sponsored the Pastorale Double Murder. On the other hand, he also claims that the whole purpose for the Westland New Post was to smoke out communist spies in the Sûreté, namely Director Albert Raes and the Duck. Latinus suggests he received this mission from American Intelligence.

Westland members Marcel Barbier and Eric Lammers are in jail for the Pastoral Street double murder. Lammers will stay behind bars until June 1984, when he'll be freed awaiting trial. The second-in-command in Westland, Michel Libert is also detained during this period, as he worked in the military department where the Classified NATO documents were stolen. This means that for the tail end of the First Wave of Insane Killers attacks, Barbier, Lammers, and Libert are in jail, which is a reasonable alibi.

CHAPTER *13*

DELHAIZE SUPERMARKET IN BEERSEL (OCTOBER 7, 1983)

ON FRIDAY, OCTOBER 7TH, 1983, AT 7:50 P.M., THE INSANE KILLERS drive the red Golf GTI, which they've repainted black, to the Beersel Delhaize supermarket. The Golf stops in the far corner of the parking lot. Three armed men wearing hats[166] and masks of French political personalities exit the car. Two are tall, but one is much larger than the others. One man is much shorter. The Giant wears a dark colored raincoat[167] and carries an axe with a long handle. Another assailant wears blue bell-bottom pants and has a tattoo on his forearm.[168] They all wear gloves.[169]

They walk the whole length of the parking lot. One of them lingers, hanging back, while the two others walk towards the front door. When the two men get close to the store, the man who stayed behind moves forward. On their way to the front door, the Killers cross a young employee putting away shopping carts in the parking lot.[170] One of them puts the barrel of his pump-action shotgun to the back of the neck of the employee, forcing the young employee to walk in front of him towards the store. The other two wait by the front door for their accomplice and his new hostage.[171]

They enter the supermarket as a unit with their hostage, shooting indiscriminately anywhere and everywhere. Store manager, Freddy Vermaelen hears the noise from his office and goes to take a look. As he approaches the first cash register, he notices the young hostage kneeling with the barrel of the gun held to the back of his neck. He opens his arms to calm down the Killers down[172] and he tries to push one aside.A The Killer with the axe gets ready to hit the manager, but another Killer shoots Vermaelen with a pump-action shotgun,[173] ripping off half of the manager's face. Vermaelen's body crumples down in a heap. Pieces of his flesh are stuck on the ceiling. Flying buckshot and shrapnel hit and injure a cashier[174] and a middle-aged customer.

The Killer with the hostage walks to the cash registers while the two accomplices head for the store's vault. The hostage is forced to his knees again, the barrel pressed to the back of his neck. He's yanked from cash register to cash register still walking on his knees. The Killer walks very slowly and deliberately. He orders two employees to get the money from the 11 cash registers. The cashiers receive the message loud and clear; they quickly and quietly empty the cash registers and drop the money in his bag. More shots are fired.

When the two Killers reach the offices, one stays back at the edge of the corridor while the other enters the vault room.[175] He severs the phone lines with his axe and then grabs cash lying on the table. He then orders an employee to open the safe. The loot is dumped in a red plastic bag. He also has a small green bag to hold checks and more money.[176]

The two robbers return to the cash registers, where their accomplice is still holding the hostage. They exit the supermarket and calmly proceed toward their Golf in the outer reaches of the parking lot. They bring their hostage all the way up to their getaway car. It's only then that they release him.[177] They leave in their repainted Golf GTI without any sense of urgency. The Killers have stolen a total of 1,200,000 BEF (approximately US $33,758).[178]

THE TATTOO

The supermarket is within walking distance from the Het Kasteel Inn Restaurant, where the security guard was beaten and killed in December

1982. Curiously, although one Brabant Killer has a tattoo on his forearm, he keeps his forearm exposed. That's despite the precaution to wear gloves to avoid being identified by fingerprints. One of them also has a noticeable birthmark. It seems from one attack to the next the birthmark travels to different parts of the body and jumps from one Killer to the next.

The Killers operate very carefully, moving more deliberately now than in the three supermarkets hold-ups in early 1983 (Genval Delhaize, Uccle Delhaize, and Halle Colruyt). It is the first attack in the First Wave that seems more like a structured commando assault than an armed robbery. It's been called their practice run for the Supermarket Massacres of 1985. They used one of the same shotguns as at the Nivelles Colruyt. The ammo is 12-gauge Winchester Western.

They always rip the telephone wires from the office. But in this attack, it's the first and only time they ever bring an axe. It's as if they want to send a message to police: "We're the Insane Killers. We even take the time to bring an axe because severing a telephone wire is so important for us."

The Killers are Insane, yes, but they likely had no intention to kill Vermaelen until he threw himself at and pushed one of the Gangsters. They warned him. He continued pushing them away. Vermaelen was also head of security for the Delhaize chain. Those who knew him said he was tough and fearless.

RANSOM

After this attack, an association of supermarkets that included the Delhaize and the Colruyt made an urgent appeal to the public for any information leading to the arrest of the perpetrators. A ransom of 10 million BEF is offered. The following ad immediately appeared in the newspapers:

The murderous Brabant attacks: An appeal to the public

*The Belgium Association of supermarkets and big box stores,
very troubled by the cruel murderous attack against Mr. Freddy*

> *Vermaelen, murdered on the job, during the Friday, October 7*
> *armed robbery at the Beersel Delhaize The Lion supermarket*
>
> *Sends this urgent appeal to the public:*
>
> *A total amount of 10 Million francs*
>
> *Is offered to anyone that offers information leading to*
> *the identification and arrest of the perpetrators of this*
> *unconscionable attack.*[179]

As a reminder, immediately after the Halle Colruyt supermarket attack of March 1983 where the store manager had also been killed, the Colruyt supermarket chain had individually offered up a ransom of 5 million BEF for information that leads to the arrest of the perpetrators. With the latest attacks, the grocery industry is taking the crimes so seriously that the ransom for the arrest of the Insane Killers has been doubled.

Gendarmerie Measures

Between the Aux Trois Canards attack on October 1st and the Beersel supermarket attack on October 7th, the Gendarmerie put in place a secret investigative cell to hunt the Brabant Killers. On October 3rd, Gendarmerie leadership circulates a telex among its high command to announce the creation of the cell designed to bypass the usual investigative structure and methods. It will also supervise supermarket security and coordinate the investigations. To keep it as tight to vest as possible, they don't even tell prosecutors involved in the Brabant Killers' investigation. On October 4th, the Gendarmerie offices are advised by telex and the first national meeting is scheduled to be held on October 5th, led by Commissioner Gilbert. The Delhaize Beersel supermarket attack takes place on October 7th.

Right after the Beersel Delhaize attack, the Mons Gendarmerie finds out that the three early 1983 supermarket hold-ups of Genval, Uccle, and Halle could be linked. Because Claude Dery was the Gendarmerie's official expert, Gilbert gives him a call. Gilbert didn't know about the Ruger from the Mons station. He didn't know anything about Mons contacting Halle. The only thing he knew from Mons was the file of the taxi driver that was found in the trunk in January 1983. The owner of the Ruger— Estiévénart—is in jail, but he's released so he can be watched. On October 10th, Commander Dery, who is in charge of ballistics at the Gendarmerie, informs an agent from the Mons Gendarmerie that there's a match with the Ruger. The first determination is that it was fired during the Insane Killer attack at the Genval Delhaize supermarket in February 1983.

BEERSEL DISCOVERY

Four days after the Beersel attack, an unidentified witness calls to say the Insane Killers abandoned the Golf's backseat in the parking lot during the attack. He was a witness of the attack and attempted to chase them by car when they left. He lost their trail and returned to the Delhaize, where he saw the bench. He says that as a former Volkswagen employee, his prior expertise made him notice that the back-seat pattern is only used with red GTIs. That means that the Volkswagen had to have been a red car that was repainted black. It was a no-brainer for investigators to make the link to the red Golf stolen at the Aux Trois Canards Restaurant in October.

Police go back to the parking lot and, lo and behold, they find the bench from the Golf. The bench is tested and hair found on the bench matches the hair of the restaurant owner's dog. In the immediate aftermath of the Beersel Delhaize supermarket attack of October 7th, investigative crews showed up on site and closed off public access to the premises, including the parking lot. During the whole night, judicial police, Gendarmes, prosecutors, the coroner and forensics experts combed through the whole location. No one ever saw a backseat lying around. Afterwards, the Delhaize cleanup crew never noticed the bench either.

Some speculate that the caller was one of the Insane Killers. During the call, the caller gave details only the Insane Killers would know. Furthermore, the Insane Killers had the bench and dropped it off a couple of days after the attack for the investigators to find. One way or another, we know the Killers dropped off the bench and they must have done it for a very good reason. Throwing away a backseat is not an afterthought. It weighs several hundred pounds and is very awkward to move. The fact they dropped it off, as is, for police to get their hands on, is very unKiller-like.

The Killers were deliberately trying to get the investigators to link the Aux Trois Canards Restaurant murder to the Beersel Supermarket attack. The only debate is whether they try to establish a link when they first got to the parking lot or a couple of days later by dropping off the car's bench and making the anonymous phone call. What most likely happened was that they messed up at the Aux Trois Canards, because their plan was not to kill Van Camp, just to steal his Porsche. When Van Camp resists, the Killers felt compelled to kill him. They just shot him once, not several times at point blank range like many of their other victims. They wanted him out of the way. Afterward, they realize they messed up.

The country knows about the Insane Killers at this point and experts are making forensic links between all the attacks. The only attack not linked forensically is the attack at Aux Trois Canards. At the time, authorities believe the 7.65mm that killed in Nivelles also killed at the Aux Trois Canards, but the Brabant Killers know this is not the case. It's just a question of time before authorities figure it out, which would lead to a separate investigation for the Aux Trois Canards attack. They don't want this for some reason. Is it possible they knew that someone was about to be arrested? Coincidentally, ballistics expert Commander Claude Dery had made the finding just the day before that the Ruger was linked ballistically to the Insane Killers. The only attack the Ruger wouldn't have been indirectly linked to is the Aux Trois Canards murder. If this is what happened, the dead manager and the two injured at the Beersel Delhaize are just casualties of an extremely devious scheme.

GOLF SIGHTINGS

In November 1983, there are a couple sighting of Van Camp's VW Golf in the Namur area. The Namur Region is outside the traditional hunting grounds of the Insane Killers. Oddly, no one removes the "I Love Australia" sticker. It's bizarre that they would give a stolen car a paint job yet not remove the sticker.

A body shop owner sees the Golf, five miles away from Hourpes Forrest. The Golf is repainted and the backseat is removed. A tall, seemingly injured man is sitting in the backseat. The tall man's leg is in a splint.[180]

The Killers are from Ixelles, yet they are trying to be noticed as much as possible in a completely different area of the country, unless they really believe a paint job is enough as camouflage and removing the huge "I Love Australia" sticker is not necessary.

Borains

Only on October 23rd, 1983, does prosecutor Guy Wezel, in charge of the early 1983 supermarket hold-up cases, find out about the Ruger linked to the Insane Killers case. He's floored. Why had he never heard about this gun that just came out of nowhere? The media calls it the gun that 'fell out of the sky.' Wezel finds out that it follows the findings of ballistic expert Commander Claude Dery, establishing a link between bullets shot during the supermarket hold-ups close by the Brussels area and a Ruger that turned up in a marital dispute in the Borinage.

It's the Ruger that was purchased by the Borain Jean-Claude Estiévénart from Michel Cocu in a pub in April 1983. It was then taken away by his estranged wife, De Bruyne. How it ended it in the hands of ballistic expert Claude Dery in Brussels is a story in and of itself. The details are tedious but very important! On May 25th, 1983, De Bruyne hands the Ruger to her social worker who carries it to the local Colfontaine Gendarmerie. She also brings ammo from the Ruger and two license plates that were lying in Estiévénart's car. Why the license plates were also brought is unknown.

On May 26th, Agent Beduwe from the Mons Gendarmerie Station is informed about the Ruger at the Colfontaine station. Beduwe goes to get the Ruger himself. He doesn't remember who told him to go pick up the gun in another Gendarmerie station. De Bruyne later shows up to file an official complaint against her husband with Beduwe present. Beduwe doesn't take the gun right away.

Around May 28th, Beduwe comes back to the Colfontaine station. He picks up the Ruger, the ammo (about a dozen bullets), and the license plates. He drops off everything in his Mons office. Prosecutor Guy Wezel says that De Bruyne was pressured by the Mons Gendarmerie to take Estiévénart's gun and bring it to Colfontaine.[181]

The Mons Gendarmerie check the license plates and find out they were stolen in Enghien, where there had been a hold up in a Casino. At first, the Mons Gendarmerie station seems less interested by the Ruger. It's never registered and sits unnoticed inside a drawer at the station. On July 4th, Officer Beduwe goes on holidays and transfers the weapon to Officer Daniel Choquet. It was well-known at the Mons office that Choquet had an informant in Estiévénart's circle of friends. Choquet is instructed to check if a similar caliber has been fired, and if it had, to get ballistic expertise involved. According to Beduwe: "I give him the gun to continue his research. When I gave him the gun, I had told him that if his research was positive, he had to pass by the Mons substitute to ask for and expertise."[182]

What Beduwe did is unusual for several reasons. There are many other weapons registered at the police registry. Why does something about this one Ruger, in particular, interest him and not all the others? Estiévénart had not been charged for an infraction. And why give it to Choquet? Amory works for Officer Beduwe and also has an informant who has been infiltrating Estiévénart's circle of friends for much longer than Choquet's informant. Informant Mohammed Asmaoui had spied on the Ruger salesman, Cocu and the Ruger buyer, Estiévénart among others. In fact, Amory's informant was spying on Choquet's informant, Kaci Bouaroudj!

Asmaoui was keeping Amory abreast about Bouaroudj's attempts to try to get people to participate in a hold-up near Brussels. The people being asked to participate are in Estiévénart and Cocu's circle of friends. Later

Bouaroudj will give details about the foiled hold-up to a very proud Choquet. But the Mons station already knew all about it. Amory's informant Asmoui had participated in the preparations for the Brussels hold-up: "I did that reconnaissance to inform the Mons BSR, Mister Coulon, and Amory."[183] Furthermore, Officer Choquet, a junior police officer, is only 26 years old. He had been at the station for only 18 months. He only knew small parts of ongoing investigations and was still learning his trade.

After he receives the Ruger, Officer Choquet leaves it in a drawer in his office for a few days. When he comes around to dealing with it, he looks in the Brussels area to see if a .38 Special has ever been shot in other crimes. He sees that one was fired at the Halle Colruyt. It's an Insane Killer attack but he doesn't know it, and neither does anyone else in Belgium. It's just considered a typical failed hold-up at this point. Choquet contacts the Halle Gendarmerie department for more information. On July 10th, the Halle office gives Choquet general characteristics about the fired rounds.[184] He sends the Ruger to fire rounds at the local Judicial Police lab, telling the lab that it regards "a case of robbery concerning Dramaix, J-L, and Estiévénart Jean-Claude." Why Jean-Louis Dramaix's name is mentioned there is unclear. Dramaix will later be linked to the loose network of the Borains.

Two reference shots are made with Estiévénart's Ruger and ammo. One bullet and casing is kept by the lab and one bullet and casing given back to Choquet.

On July 19th, Choquet believes there are similarities with the bullets fired in Halle despite the fact the ammo fired in Halle and at the Judicial Police's Lab are different. On July 20th, Choquet drives down to the Halle Gendarmerie station to request official ballistics expertise. He hands over the Ruger and ammo to ballistic expert Commander Claude Dery. In the meantime, Choquet is informed there are suspected links between the 9 mm that was shot in Halle and the incidents in the supermarkets in Genval and Uccle. So on July 22nd, Choquet asks Dery for additional ballistic comparison for Genval and Uccle. The ballistic expertise requests were never written down in a police report. When he's finished with his tests, Dery returns the Ruger and the bullets back to Choquet. Commander Dery looks at the results and tells the Judicial Police that the results were negative and there is no link with the Estiévénart's Ruger.[185]

On August 14th, it's Choquet's turn to go on vacation. He transfers the Ruger and the ammo back to Beduwe. While Choquet is on holiday, the Ruger is sent back to Halle to be tested. Halle gets the Ruger on August 29th. According to Amory: "I stumbled on the gun and I advised prosecutors that it could have been used in a crime."[186] The fact that Amory is a close friend of Bouhouche, and Dery has worked closely with Bouhouche and is a friend of his, causes ex post facto a huge appearance of a conflict of interest. As Bouhouche is a later suspect in the case, it irreversibly taints the Ruger for a prosecution against anyone else.

When Choquet comes back from vacation on August 31st, he finds out the Ruger is now in Halle with Dery. On October 10th, right after the Delhaize Beersel attack, Dery tells Choquet that the Ruger is a match.[187] The results were negative the first time the Ruger was sent to Dery at the Halle station to be tested. But now, months later, after the Ruger is sent back a second time to Dery, the results change. It's now positive.

Top leadership in Mons only finds out when they receive Dery's October 17th report. Prosecutor Wezel, who was completely in the dark about all of this, finds out later that Francesco Nardella, an acquaintance of Estiévénart, had already had his phone tapped. No one knows who ordered the surveillance or why. Nardela, like Dramaix, will also be considered one of the Borains. It's curious his name pops up in the investigation this early. A crisis task force for the Brabant Region is called on October 17th. Two officers are dispatched from the Mons Gendarmerie: Officer Grandhenri, who knows nothing about the case, and Officer Choquet.

Grandhenri and Choquet are told they have two days to make a list of suspects to be kept under surveillance by the Dyane Swat team. Because Grandhenri knows nothing about the case, Choquet gets help from Amory to draw up the list. There is no police report for any of this; nothing was ever written down. Everything is kept secret.

As for the Ruger, several employees from different police departments will handle the Ruger. Everything is done informally. No records of detention are made. All weapons handling protocols are ignored. No one can even retrace who had what and when. It will take another two months of floating around across the country for the Ruger to be finally deposited in the arms Registry according to standard protocol.

When the list is created, Dyane will begin surveillance of Estiévénart's acquaintance. Usual surveillance protocol is to first take the investigative file to the public prosecutor, who makes a decision on when and how to act. That never happens. The Mons Gendarmerie will participate, as Amory is extremely active in the surveillance.[188] After more than a week of surveillance, a decision is made to raid the homes of the Borains. According to the Mons Gendarmerie, they acted because Dyane couldn't find anything suspicious. An alternate explanation is because Estiévénart had noticed he was being watched.

There is not even a paper trail for the ballistics' expertise request for the Ruger that started all of this! So before they can do the raid, Choquet writes one on October 26th. He must, of course, pre-date it. But he dates it on July 20th, the date of the first request he personally made to Dery that was negative. It's in fact on August 29th, while Choquet was on holidays, that someone else from the Mons Gendarmerie sent it to Dery, leading to the positive test more than a month later. The day after Choquet writes the belated report, on October 27th, the homes of suspects are raided.

On October 29th, Estiévénart is arrested. Amory from Mons participates. The arrest of Estiévénart is a no-brainer because he's the one who owned the Ruger, but then they also detain, inexplicably, the battered and estranged wife of Estiévénart, Josiane Debruyne. Apparently, the fact she's the one who succeeded in getting the gun away from her hard-drinking ex, Estiévénart, didn't bring up red flags they were barking up the wrong tree. Finally, Amory personally arrests Cocu, who had sold the gun to Estiévénart.[189] He had purchased the Ruger legally from a gun shop in 1979. According to the Mons Gendarmerie, Cocu is the ringleader. They don't figure out who had the gun when it was shot; so they arrest everyone.

Cocu is locked up in a cell and interrogated. He was once a local police officer in a small town in the Borinage. Shortly thereafter, his wife became sick and lost her job. The family couldn't live on one salary and went broke. To try to make extra cash, Cocu gets involved in a bank fraud. He's arrested and ends up being kicked out of the police force. He tried applying to the French Foreign Legion but is refused because of heart problems. His life since then has been mostly welfare interspersed with odd jobs. Getting a meaningful job is difficult, as Cocu has a learning disability and failed every year of high school at least once.

Seemingly convinced they have their man, officers use strong-armed tactics to get Cocu to confess that he used the Ruger in Hal and Genval. "They interrogate him for hours at a time."[190] On November 16th, he finally breaks down and gives police the confession they want. According to Cocu, "I wanted them to leave me alone. I was ready to say anything that they wanted to hear. You probably can't imagine how it is, but if you are interrogated day and night, that you're not the same person anymore. You're physically and mentally broken. You hear questions, echoes of questions, and you see the interrogators, the shadows of the interrogators. And the only thing you're thinking of is to sleep."A

Almost as soon as he's finished giving his confession, Cocu retracts everything. This is the first of his many retractions and confessions. Every time he ends up confessing, his interrogators press him for details. How? Who? What? Where? According to Cocu: "I never made up stories. I didn't need to; they would take care of it. They would ask the questions. I would answer by yes or no, and based on that they wrote the Brabant Killers story. But if we read those police reports, it looks like they're listening to me all the time, that I had said all these things uninterrupted."B

A close reading of the confessions highlights the problems with them. First of all, Cocu is just reiterating what the police had in their reports, whether accurate or not. According to his lawyer, Jean-Paul Moerman: "Michel Cocu even confessed to having killed a victim with a caliber 7.65 bullet. The coroner had put that in his report, but it turns out afterwards that he had made a mistake."[191]

Second, Cocu's confessions are often nonsensical—take the police report on his Nivelles Colruyt attack confession as an example. In a nutshell, Cocu confesses he's the driver of a BMW 520. There never was a BMW 520 linked to the attack. Cocu says he is there with his pub friends Vittorio, Baudet, Dramaix, and officer Choquet's informant Bouaroudj, to break into the back of the supermarket. That's five accomplices, which is more than any of the witness accounts. But wait, there's more: Cocu says they also used a Brown Peugeot 604 in the Colruyt's vicinity driven by Nardella, a sixth accomplice. There never was a Peugeot 604 linked to the attack, however.

The only car that was ever driven by the Brabant Killers to get the Colruyt is the Saab Turbo. Who was driving that car? According to Cocu, inside the Saab are four other "very dangerous people." Cocu never gives their names. So that's a grand total of ten armed robbers stealing cooking oil and coffee, and apparently loitering in large numbers in the back of a supermarket. Prosecutor Lacroix, who came to the Borains case at a later date, explains what he had to deal with in terms of confessions: "For the facts of the Nivelles Colruyt, three of the accused made 41 separate confessions that contained blatant inaccuracies."[192]

Furthermore, they contradicted each other.[193]

But details don't matter anymore. Authorities say they have now found the Brabant Insane Killers, all of them. According to Cocu: "They wanted names? OK, I gave them names. Names of acquaintances: from my neighborhood, from the pubs I hung out in. I wanted them to stop. I wanted to sleep."[194] The names dropped by Cocu are a who's who of the poor, the lame, the ill, the uneducated, and the unemployed. None of the people he names speak a proper Belgian French like the Insane Killers; they can only speak in the Walloon slang. (Think Cockney compared to proper English).

Nevertheless, Cocu's confessions lead to the arrests of Baudet, Bouaroudj, Vittorio, and others and they all get the enhanced interrogation treatment. Michel Baudet dropped out of school at 14 and lived at his mother's house; a psychiatrist determines he has a low intellect and is easily influenced. Kacy Bouaroudj never even went to school and doesn't know how to read or write. Adriano Vittorio is sumo-big with a 70 percent physical incapacity. He can't run. He can't do any physical effort. He lives in a trailer park close to the French border. The fact an obese, out-of-shape Brabant Killer with asthma had never turned up before in witness descriptions didn't seem to matter much. He also has a cleft palate. No witnesses have ever described seeing a Brabant Killer with a cleft palate.

The tough interrogation regimen applied to Cocu leads to the same pattern with most other Borains. First, there's a denial and investigators ratchet up the pressure. Then there's a confession and investigators pull back. Finally, there's a retraction. Rinse and repeat. According to Cocu: "…all my confessions came out under threats and a state of total exhaustion." But it never lasted very long: "The next day, when I realized what I had said, I wanted to retract my statements, but they wouldn't listen to me anymore."A Baudet claims he was beaten while his head was covered with a Delhaize bag. Estiévénart claims he was left alone, naked on the ground with his hands tied behind his back for three days.[195] With no toilet breaks, Estiévénart was forced to soil himself.

When Prosecutor Wezel gets to meet the Borains in jail, he's struck by the fact they look "completely dazed." Wezel will complain to superiors that he suspected something was wrong with the interrogation methods.[196]

Altogether, the Borains will make several dozen official confessions and retractions. Aside from the irreparably tainted Ruger and the retracted confessions, officers can't extract a single piece of tangible evidence from anyone. Furthermore, not a single witness of the attacks ever recognized them. Some of the Borains will stay in police custody until 1985; even then they are only released to await trial.

CHAPTER *14*

JEWELRY STORE IN ANDERLUES (DECEMBER 1, 1983)[197]

ON THURSDAY, DECEMBER 1ST AT 6:40 P.M., DARKNESS IS FALLING on the main street in the small southern town of Anderlues. The Szymuzik Jewelry and Clock-Making Shop closes at 7:00 p.m., but the family who owns the business is in their living quarters in the building. It's a typical weeknight and the two daughters, 16-year-old Sylvie and 12-year-old Carine, are upstairs doing their homework. Mother, Maria Krystina Szymuzik, is sleeping on the living room sofa downstairs; the lights are out in the room as she rests. Her husband, Jean Szymuzik, is laboring in his workshop at the back of the building. There is no one in the shop, which will soon be closed and locked for the night.

The shop's front door chime rings as three Insane Killers step into the jewelry shop. They aren't wearing masks or gloves. One of them wears a khaki vest and has very short, blond hair. One of his accomplices wears a green loden-coat, while the other walks with a noticeable limp. The chime wakes Maria Krystina from her slumber in the dark living room, which has a sliding door that opens into the shop. The Insane Killers rip out the surveillance cameras, which transmit the video image to a monitor in the back workshop.

As Maria Krystina opens the sliding door to the shop, she sees the armed men and turns around to run back towards the back of the house.

Unfortunately, she only gets part of the way through the adjacent living room before one of the Killers shoots her. As Maria Krystina crumples on the carpet near the kitchen, she's hit with many more bullets to the upper body and legs. The Killers walk over to her body and finish her off with two more bullets to the head.

In the workshop, at the other end of the building, the jeweler hears the gunshots. Jean grabs an Arminius .38 caliber gun. He opens his shop door, which leads into the kitchen and surprises one of the Killers, who is kneeling on the living room floor over his wife Maria Krystina's body to shoot her again. Jean shoots at the murderous intruder but misses. As one of the Killers takes cover, he screams in French to another, "Shoot! C'mon, shoot!"[198]

Jean is hit by a hail of bullets and drops to the floor. One of the killers walks up beside him, fires two bullets into his head and rips the gun out of the hands of the dead jeweler.

Oddly, the Insane Killers take easily accessible clocks, timepieces, and cheap trinkets. They don't even bother trying to get to the more valuable jewelry by breaking into the display cases. When they take off in the stolen black Golf GTI and drive towards Hourpes Forest, just on the edge of Anderlues, they take the jeweler's .38 caliber gun with them.

Clocks, Ballistics and Close Calls

A common misconception about the Anderlues store in stories about the crime is that it's a typical jewelry store, but it's more accurately described as a clock-making shop that also sells some jewelry. The clocks are featured prominently in the window display in the shop's right window. The owner actually started it as a clockmaking shop and then expanded into jewelry. According to Jean's brother: "We were poor, and my brother repaired clocks and alarms clocks. He got a good reputation and could start his own shop."[199]

While many jewelry or high-end shops limit access to their shops by requiring customers to buzz in for access, the Szymuzik's did not ever restrict access to their store with a buzzer or doorbell. They worried people wouldn't bother to come in if they had to be let in and didn't want their business to slow down.

It's possible that the Brabant Killers didn't intend to kill the Szymuzik's. If Maria Krystina hadn't been sleeping in the darkened living room right off the shop, they could have stolen what they wanted and left before Jean, who was in the workshop, even realized there had been a theft. When the jeweler's wife pops into the store almost immediately, the Insane Killers don't hesitate to murder her so she can't identify them. They are equally ruthless with Jean when he runs over from the workshop with his weapon drawn.

Fifteen rounds in total are shot during the robbery. Ballistic reports show that the Brabant Killers used five different weapons. We can assume they carried two firearms each, just like in Nivelles. They used the caliber .45 ACP that was fired in Nivelles, the 7.65mm gun stolen from the Nivelles police officer that was used at the Aux Trois Canards Restaurant in October, and a .357 Magnum revolver that was used in both the Genval Delhaize hold-up in February and the Nivelles Colruyt attack in September. When they fired the two kill shots into the heads of Maria Krystina and Jean, the Killers use the same .22 LR that they'd already used to kill five other people. Another .38 may also have been used.

Somehow the Killers didn't realize the jeweler's daughters were upstairs—or, if they did, they didn't worry that they'd be witnesses to the double-murder of their parents. Sylvie, the 16-year-old daughter, actually witnessed the murder of her father. After she heard the ruckus when the intruders murdered her mother, Sylvie quietly crept to the top of stairs and looked down just as her father was shot. Horrified, she rushes with her younger sister to hide in the bedrooms upstairs. Their presence goes unnoticed by the madmen on the ground floor.

The two murders were committed for very little. In fact, when investigators arrive, there was so little taken that the first news reports were that nothing had been stolen. Paperwork comparisons had to be made to compare the inventory before and after. The investigation determines, by comparing the inventory list against what's left in the store, that the intruders have only stolen some clocks, timepieces, and other cheap trinkets. Despite having ample time to take whatever they wanted from the shop's merchandise, the Killers didn't take any of the more valuable items. Either they are hasty or they don't know jewelry, as the value of their loot is minimal. The Killers never even tried to take the money from the cash register.[200]

This attack on the small clock and jewelry shop in Anderlues should give investigators evidence that the Borains, who are in jail, are not responsible for the series of violent robberies. Isn't this proof that the Borains aren't the Insane Killers? But, investigators don't see this as evidence that the Borains aren't the Insane Killers. Instead, they see it as proof that the Borains still have other accomplices out there trying to get them out of jail. There is speculation this Anderlues robbery is just part of a plan to give the Borains an alibi. Some investigators even feared more violent attacks were to be expected because so little was taken, reasoning that the deadbeat Borains desperately needed cash. Why, then, would the perpetrators in Anderlues only steal worthless larger items when they had ample time and opportunity to take much smaller, more portable and more lucrative items?

DIAMONDS AND BLOOD MONEY

Because the loot was of so little value, many people speculate that the Anderlues robbery was just a cover because the murder of Szymuzik was actually an assassination. One lead to the Anderlues jewelry store murders is that Szymuzik could have been involved in illegally trafficking gold, jewels, and diamonds through a network that operates between Antwerp and Milan and transited through Switzerland.[201] Jewelers in Belgium were forced to cooperate with the criminal network run by the Italian mob. The investigative theory is that if Szymuzik refused to play by the rules that mobsters might have made an example of him. There is some evidence to back this theory up because Szymuzik had recently felt threatened and had purchased the revolver.[202] If this theory is accurate, it's puzzling why professional hit men would go through the risk of killing a second person, the wife of their target.

WESTLAND NEW POST

In 1990, some claims were made that Westland New Post members could have been responsible for the Anderlues jewelry shop attack, but there has never been any concrete evidence to support this. As the Westland New Post became more well-known and members started coming out of the woodwork, some links between the victims and the Westland New Post group were discovered. For example, one Westland associate had worked as a taxi driver with both the Het Kasteel Inn victim of December 1982 and the taxi driver found murdered in his trunk in the Mons in January 1983. A Westland member did have a flak jacket similar to the ones stolen in his possession, but it looked like he had purchased it legally. In 1989, a Westland member alleges he was asked to write down the license plate of a Volkswagen Golf and give it to another Westland associate. The Far-Right member claimed it's the same number as the one used on the repainted Golf stolen from Aux Trois Canards Restaurant in October 1983. The investigators who pursued these leads came up empty-handed.

HOURPES FOREST

The Insane Killers leave the jewelry in their repainted, stolen VW Golf and drive towards the nearby Hourpes Forest. Here they abandon the Golf and set it on fire. According to some sources, they left a few alarm clocks and costume jewelry wrapped in two bags inside the vehicle.

THE REPAINTED GOLF

They take the Golf to the same place where they dropped off the Golf they stole in Lasnes in June 1983. The back seat of this second Golf had already been removed and left in the Beersel Delhaize parking lot. The license plate on the Golf is a copy of the plate on a Golf parked in Ixelles. We don't know if they had planned to torch the car or if that was an impulsive action.

If it wasn't planned, it's because they felt trapped and feared police units were looking for them. They're not as familiar with the roads here as with the streets in Brabant or in Brussels. There is speculation they were either going to another getaway car or a safe-house nearby.

Secret Training Camp

Marcel Barbier, the Westland New Post member who confessed to the double murder on Pastorale Street from April 1982, claims in 1989 that he was asked by Westland leader Paul Latinus to case the place where the Golf was abandoned in Hourpes Forest one or two years beforehand. According to Barbier, the Hourpes Forest was seen as a potential area for the Westland group to hide weapons and set up a secret camp.

End of the First Wave

The Anderlues attack on the jewelry store closes the First Wave of attacks by the Insane Killers. It will take almost another two years before the Insane Killers strike again. Not a single crime is linked to them during all of 1984 and most of 1985. This period is known as the "pause," a time when the Brabant Killers disappear.

As mentioned previously, the ballistics in the crimes were not completed for quite some time. In January 1983, French Police made the first link between the Maubeuge, France attack in August 1982 and the Wavre Gun Shop attack in September 1982. Some were made in October 1983 because of the widely-publicized Nivelles Colruyt attack. According to

Prosecutor Wezel, it's only in 1984 that everything is linked ballistically.[203]

THREATS

In the ensuing investigations of the Brabant Killers, it's staggering how many threats are proffered. It's not only investigators or prosecutors that are threatened, but also victims and their families, witnesses, and even bystanders. Anyone who can give any worthwhile information to the investigation of the First Wave crimes is threatened. It's systematic and relentless, to the point that ongoing fear becomes the backdrop to the investigation into the Insane Killers.

During the Wavre Gun Shop attack in September 1982, a bystander who witnessed the shootout was threatened that same afternoon. Someone calls him directly at the restaurant where he works as a cook and asks if he owns a green Range Rover.[204] The caller tells him: "*On aura ta peau,*" which means, "we will have your skin."[205] Dekaise is threatened one year after the attack on June 30, 1983, when he is told: "You'll die soon."

Following the Het Kasteel Inn attack in December 1982, the caretaker's son receives death threats. Remember that at this point in time it was a stand-alone crime, not linked to other crimes by ballistics and before there was any sense of there being a series of crimes by a group called the Insane Killers in the press. He's so concerned about the threats, he leaves the country.

Following the Aux Trois Canards Restaurant attack in October 1983, the shooting victim, Van Camp is in the hospital in critical condition and close to death. Although Van Camp is being treated in a hospital not disclosed to the media or public, someone calls the hospital and threatens him less than two hours after the attack. The message is simple and direct: "There is someone there with a bullet in his body…we're coming to kill him." Van Camp died two hours later. When a pub owner starts helping police with their investigation after the attack, she also receives death threats.

Following the Szymuzik jewelry shop attack, Szymuzik's brother was threatened in 1984: "I was told that they would do away with me; it was on the phone." Another time he said: "I was followed in my car during the evening. There was a car that bumped me in back, and they would honk...it happened three times like that. At three different places." The brother adopted Szymuzik's young daughters, who were also fearful they were being threatened. He shared: "One of my nieces was going to school and she said, 'Uncle, I was followed by a car when I went to get on the bus.' She was scared. It was a sort of pressure." Prosecutor Schlicker was also threatened, and so were his wife and children. An envelope was sent to his kids at school with the message: "This time, an envelope, next time, a bomb..."B

These types of threats are tactics commonly used by organized crime organizations, such as the Italian mafia or biker gangs. With these crimes, the threats are particularly terrifying given the speed at which they're made and the access to confidential information, such as the location of victims and witnesses like Van Camp. Are all these people making it up? Could a common criminal gang do this? Maybe it's the Sûreté? How about the Gendarmerie? Who can pull this off?

The threatening messages and terror campaigns successfully intimidate witnesses. Szymuzik's brother even said: "I went a bit too far and I had to take a step back. I touched something I shouldn't have."

Martial Lekeu Speculates on the Identity of the Insane Killers

In December of 1983, Francis V. accuses a Gendarme in the Ardennes of having received bulletproof jackets and arms from the Temse robbery in September 1983 and the Wavre Gun Shop attack. Lekeu, the Gendarme, denies everything but gives his own opinion about the case: "I know who the Killers from the Gang are. I can't prove it, but I have suspicions, very serious suspicions."C

He tells the Wavre Gendarmes that are still taking care of the Wavre Gun Shop attack from 1982: "I believed that the [Brabant Killer murders] could have been perpetrated by a group formed by the Youth Front

and organized by Gendarmes." The Youth Front is the Far-Right organization from which the Westland New Post recruited its most hardcore
members. Unlike the Westland New Post, the Youth Front was a public
organization that had been dismantled after being prosecuted for being
a militia. Several years earlier, Lekeu had been invited to join a Gendarmerie cell in the Youth Front. There were a half dozen Gendarmes in the
cell. At a meeting, Lekeu found out that they had misappropriated documents from the Gendarmerie and were very dangerous. Disgusted, he
became a whistleblower. He believes there is reason to believe the Insane
Killings could be the actions of a Youth Front cell of Gendarmes. Maybe
not the same ones from 1977, but certainly a similar cell.

According to Lekeu: "It's two weeks later that the death threats started, that came from Gendarmes because the terms used were recognizable.
I took them very seriously…A few had been killed [by the Killers] already,
and I got scared."[206] Lekeu claimed that because of the threats against
him, he was forced to leave the Gendarmerie on April 1st, 1984. When
the threats continued, he decided to leave the country and moved to the
United States.

Less than a month after Lekeu's departure to the US, an internal
report by the Info Section of Brussels Gendarmerie circulates. It names
Gendarmes who support Far-Right politics. Even though Bouhouche left
the Gendarmerie a year earlier, he's on the list.

Extortion as Motive

In 1999, businessman Albert Mahieu raises extortion as a possible motive
for the First Wave of Insane Killer attacks. It's significant that three out
of the four supermarkets attacked during the day are from the Delhaize
chain. Is it just a coincidence? Mahieu is involved in a legal battle against
the Assubel Insurance Company. Mahieu, a shareholder, accuses Assubel
board members of fraud. It turns out that some Assubel board members
are also on the board of Delhaize supermarkets or an associated firm.

Mahieu files a complaint against some Delhaize Board Members, alleging that they are involved in a criminal ring that operates fraudulent schemes through Delhaize and Assubel. He specifically names five directors, who sit on the board of both companies, as part of the fraudulent activity.

As part of his complaint, Mahieu alleges that two Delhaize administrators had relationships with madams or prostitutes in the Brussels Red Light District. He focuses more specifically on A., who's the CEO of a US branch of Delhaize. According to Mahieu, A. had a relationship with B. who has run Red Light District brothels since 1978. A.'s relationship with B. could have been at the center of the First Wave Delhaize attacks. More specifically, it may have precipitated the three attacks against Delhaize supermarkets: the attacks in Genval and Uccle in February 1983 and in Beersel in October 1983.

The complaint alleges that A. financed the purchase of eight Red Light District bars, which were managed by B. Her bars were a direct attack on the market shares of the other bars in the District that were run by organized crime, which prompted organized crime to fight back hard. The first step was to get a top Gendarmerie General to blackmail B. That apparently failed as the Delhaize board member, A., used his contacts in the political world to get the Gendarmerie General to back off. That's when they decided to go directly after A.'s fortune, which is of course tied to his role as a key director and shareholder of the Delhaize chain. Organized crime members threatened to attack the Delhaize until A. paid protection money. After A. refuses, the mobsters hired violent hit men to attack the Delhaize supermarkets in Hal, Uccle, and Beersel.

All of the other First Wave attacks were unrelated crimes. Ballistics prove the crimes were committed by the same group of hit men who reused the same weapons. By mixing up everything and attacking random businesses, as well as the Delhaize supermarkets, authorities couldn't figure out what was happening. According to Mahieu, only the people being extorted knew and it's no coincidence that the First Wave Delhaize attacks stopped as soon as A. and his cronies paid up.

PART II:
THE PAUSE (1984)

WATERLOO LION, MUNICIPALITY OF
BRAINE-L'ALLEUD

CHAPTER *15*

BOUHOUCHE GANG EXTORTION

THE BOUHOUCHE GANG IS ALSO INVOLVED IN A SUPERMARKET CHAIN extortion scheme. They create an elaborate scheme that considers all aspects of their nefarious plan. An important step is made in late January 1984, when they find an abandoned building on Buanderie Street in Brussels to use as the place where the extortion ransom can be dropped off. It's a property that enables them to dig into the sewers. They had to find an accurate plan of the sewer system to find this building so close to the underground sewers. This location required minimal digging, which was important because digging takes time, money, and lots of manpower.

Someone using the alias Miguel Lopez Garcia, claiming to be a furniture salesman from Spain, rents the property. He gives a false address and shows the landlord some fake identification, leaving 90,000 BEF in cash (approximately US $2,535) as a guarantee for the lease. To this day no one has uncovered the real identity of this Garcia.

The Gang formulates a plan for how the extortion will work. The Bouhouche Gang has an impressive laundry list of things to figure out for their project. Apparently, Bouhouche had thought it all through. "It was a story worthy of a Hollywood movie," said a person in-the-know, "but to all questions of feasibility he has studied the question and had an answer for everything."

The Bouhouche Gang first considered threatening to burn down supermarkets, but after considering the potential delays as insurance companies investigate, they decided to threaten to bomb them instead.[207] Their plan is to ask the supermarket chain's board members for a large sum of money or they'll bomb individual supermarkets. They also consider threatening food poisoning but perfect their plan for a bombing. They decide to steal explosives that they can hide in large tin cans, which they can leave inside the supermarkets near electricity and gas pipes to create maximum damage. The Bouhouche Gang also decides to detonate explosives during the day for maximum terror. This strategy should ensure that the media reports instill a climate of terror favorable to extorting huge sums of money from the supermarket chain quickly.[208]

To slow down authorities during their escape, they carefully determined the best spot to dig their way to the sewers in the Buanderie building. Ingeniously, they decide to dig at the bottom of the elevator shaft. Once authorities barge in, they'll waste tremendous time figuring out how the Gang got out of the building.

FULL SPEED AHEAD

By 1984, the plan is well underway as Bouhouche began assembling the Gang in 1981 and promised those who joined him 10 million BEF (approximately US $281,690) each from the extortion ransom. Once Bouhouche leaves the Gendarmerie in April 1983, everything can accelerate. He can concentrate all his energies on the extortion project.

The Gang members have ten feet or more to dig from the building to the sewer system, which could take weeks or months. They need manpower and start to assemble a series of people. To complete the escape route, the criminals need a variety of equipment, including steel scissors, chisels, drills, blowtorches, wheelbarrows, and even cylinders of fuel for specialty equipment. They need large cement bags, trowels, spades, shovels, crowbars, hammers, and rolls of plastic bags. Other items they require include high-powered flashlights, buckets for dirt, many pairs of gloves, screwdrivers, goggles, and even sewer worker overalls. They also need a massive dumping ground to accumulate all the debris they pull out of the hole.

To successfully escape, they'll need one or more inflatable, motorized dinghies, plus light and easily maneuverable firearms in case of a firefight with authorities in closely confined quarters. Additionally, they need silencers so people above ground can't use the sound of gunshots to locate where they are in the sewer system. The risk of firefights with authorities is so high that it scares at least one Bouhouche Gang associate away from the project.

The Gang steals a dinghy that is hidden in a shack near Bouhouche's cottage in Knokke on the coast of the North Sea. The message that day is to shoot to kill if they're caught red-handed because any little thing that can lead back to them will jeopardize their scheme; the Bouhouche Gang does not want to leave witnesses under any circumstances.[209]

A convoy leaves Brussels in the evening, meeting up with an accomplice at the outskirts of Knokke. They drive to the beach where the shed storing the dinghy is located and use a machine to scramble police communications. Once on the property, they break down the door of the shed. One acts as armed cover while the others remove the dinghy from the shed and load it up in their Toyota van. The Toyota van is escorted back down to Brussels where it's driven in Box 179 in the Ixelles complex with the dinghy inside.

REFINING THE PLAN

Once the Gang members have the materials they require, it's time to focus on other elements of their plan. They decide that the person dropping off the ransom will be taken as a hostage, which will delay the police intervention as certain protocols must be taken in hostage situations.[210] Because of their intimate knowledge of the Gendarmerie, they are quite aware of Dyane's operating procedures for hostage-taking cases. They'll use this to their advantage to delay the Dyane SWAT team from even entering the building.

They'll then navigate the sewer system in the stolen motorized dinghies, which gives them considerable advantage, considering police officers will be on foot. When they exit in the Senne River, they'll escape in a getaway car that has diplomatic plates, a diplomatic sticker, and a foreign-looking driver. They will also again use equipment to scramble police communications, just as they have in other robberies.[211] Before the authorities realize what has happened, the Bouhouche Gang will be long gone.

Usually, plans like this are underwritten by organized crime because plans of this magnitude cost millions, but the Bouhouche Gang does not deal with the rest of the underworld. They'll need to find the funds to fund the plan on their own. For starters, they need to pay for storage space to warehouse the vehicles and equipment they require—in different locations so they don't attract unwanted attention.

What does the Bouhouche Gang have to do with the Insane Killers? Several times the media have commented that it's extremely suspicious that a Gang is trying to extort a chain of supermarkets while the Brabant Killers seem to focus on supermarkets during their attacks. But unlike the Mahieu extortion allegations, the Bouhouche Gang has yet to make any threats or payment demands. However, there are similarities in the way both groups plan their extortion and, most notably, that both the Bouhouche Gang and the Insane Killers intend to shoot to kill if caught red-handed during their robberies. Two Bouhouche Gang members are on record saying this was a standing order.

BOUHOUCHE

It can be odd to find a Gendarme like Bouhouche who is so deeply involved in serious criminality, but it didn't come out of nowhere. There is evidence that he had sociopathic tendencies when he first entered the force.

When the DEA organized a month-long trip to the US in 1978 for Gendarmes from the Narcotics Division, there was a joint pool of spending money set up. Before long, they realized all their money had disappeared and suspected an inside job. When the team visited Las Vegas, they couldn't help but notice the wads of cash Bouhouche had to spend. While no one was ever able to prove it, other Gendarmes always suspected Bouhouche of the theft.[212]

Later in 1978, Bouhouche steals a gun from the Police Academy, as well as another firearm he sees lying in the police station. He also steals two official police badges from a Gendarmerie officer. He breaks into a car in Ixelles, stealing items inside that include other IDs. By 1979, Bouhouche has already accumulated stolen IDs of all sorts. Some of his work colleagues know he's involved in small criminal infractions. He's also not shy in sharing details about his ideas for bigger criminal schemes with his closest confidants.

A fellow narcotics officer tells of a discussion with Bouhouche: "[At the] End [of] 1979, during a conversation or rather coming in during a shift, I told Bouhouche, Beijer and others that were at his office, that I had just met the fifth richest person in Belgium; that was unbelievable that those types of fortunes could still exist today; that I was stupid to stay at the Gendarmerie when it was possible to make much more taking crumbs off of Billionaires…"[213]

"A few days later, when Bouhouche and I were patrolling [in Ixelles] not far from Louise Avenue where the Billionaire lived, she came up in the conversation…" Bouhouche started asking the Gendarme for details, but: "The questions seemed a bit suspicious and I refused to give him the details he wanted." He adds, "At the time, I started asking myself questions and it dawned on me that, for a police officer, his reactions were kind of bizarre. Two or three days later, Bouhouche suggested we rob the old lady's house. He suggested doing the robbery together because she would have easily opened the door for me. I had even told him she lived alone. At the time, I was not totally sure that Bouhouche was being serious but a few days later when he proposed a plan for the hit, I knew."

PUTTING THE PIECES TOGETHER

In 1979, Bouhouche also told the Gendarme about his scheme to extort money from large department stores: "End 1979 Dany [Bouhouche] suggested that I participate in a racket against supermarkets. The goal was to set them on fire after asking a ransom and then escaping in a zodiac in the Brussels sewer system."[214]

The Bouhouche Gang members need explosives and lots of them. They steal them from abandoned quarries in Southern Belgium, but they're neophytes when it comes to using them. When they steal explosives, Bouhouche Gang members are given a shoot to kill policy if anyone interrupts them during the robbery.

Once they acquire explosives illicitly, the Gang needs someone with knowledge of bomb-making. In June 1981, they trick Sûreté agent Gerard Damseault, who has an engineering background, into giving them recipes to build bombs from his military engineering manual notes. When Bouhouche receives his disciplinary sentence from the Gendarmerie in October 1981, the Gang uses this newly acquired bomb-making knowledge to get back at the Gendarmerie.

The Goffinon bombing by the Bouhouche Gang in October 1981 taught them several valuable lessons for their extortion bombing scheme, primarily the important lesson that they shouldn't purchase equipment or parts that can be traced back to them. The trouble is that they have massive amounts of equipment to acquire. While some items are not easily identifiable and can be purchased in small quantities without arousing suspicion, the easiest way to thwart investigators is to steal what they need.

CHAPTER 16

THE DEATH OF PAUL LATINUS

O N JANUARY 24, 1984, MICHEL LIBERT, THE SECOND IN COMMAND of the radical Westland New Post, is released from jail. Prosecutors can't find any evidence that he was involved in the Pastorale Street double murders of April 1982. They hope to charge him with other infractions. Marcel Barbier and Eric Lammers are still detained for the double murder. Investigators are working to amass evidence for several crimes members of this Far-Right group might have committed, including the double murder on Pastorale Street and stealing NATO classified documents. Authorities are also trying to prove that Westland is a private militia operating illegally.

Libert is furious at Latinus and blames him for the serious legal difficulties that he, Barbier, and Lammers are facing. When Barbier confessed, he believed it was some type of trick by Latinus and he wouldn't end up in jail. Libert takes the lead of an anti-Latinus Westland New Post breakaway faction. They consider Latinus and his remaining supporters as traitors.[215] Lammers says: Latinus "spilled the beans to get out of it, he behaved like a little rat. A kind of despicable snitch, that pushes down his buddies to lift his head a bit more out of the water. That's it. As for me, I was in jail; I only wanted to do one thing falling asleep. Hang him up on a meat hook and to remove all his skin bit by bit."[216]

Ruining His Life

What documents show about the Sûreté's involvement is that the Duck first got along swimmingly with Latinus, then their relationship fell apart in mid-1982—a couple of months after the Pastorale Street double murder. What caused their relationship to unravel is unknown, but Latinus gets progressively more bitter towards the Duck and DG Albert Raes, who is the Duck's mentor at the Sûreté. Latinus seems to feel the Duck got a lot more from their relationship than he did.

Ex post facto, Latinus believes the Duck manipulated him from the beginning when he first started feeding the Duck intelligence in 1979, when he was still at the Youth Front As an informant, Latinus took such a liking to intelligence work that he wanted to be hired by the Sûreté. It's unknown how the Sûreté felt about hiring a Far-Right militant, but they allowed him to apply for the first of two exams. As a nuclear engineer, Latinus easily passed but was then publicly outed by the media in December of 1980 as an extremist following the Laeken murder—the incident when a Youth Front member unloaded his gun on a group of Algerian workers. One died and another was critically wounded. This attack spelled the death knell of the Youth Front. Latinus would later recruit the most hard-core Youth Front members to become part of his underground Westland New Post.

Latinus is now convinced that it was the Duck who planted the stories in the media. He has been quoted as saying, "I suspect that the Sûreté had sent to the *Pour* newspaper a file to sabotage me." The disclosures destroyed the life he had built, even costing him his job. His second Sûreté exam was scheduled a couple of months after the Laeken incident. According to Latinus: "… I understood that a man, the Commissioner for who I had worked before, had sabotaged my application [to the Sûreté]."[217] Feeling the need to start over, Latinus leaves the country.

There's no evidence that Latinus was involved in, or even knew about, the Pastorale double murder before it happened. In fact, some say that when Latinus first found out about the homicides, he just couldn't fathom that members of his group could have done this. While Latinus had advocated violence like arson and beatings, he had not encouraged murder. He makes it seem that he really believes that the Pastorale murders were prompted by the Duck to destroy the Westland. There's no evidence that members directly involved in the Pastorale double murder made any effort to dispel his suspicions.

REVENGE

By 1984, Latinus has alienated a segment of the Westland New Post, destroyed what's left of the movement, and facilitated the incarceration of members on suspected first-degree murder charges. As for the Sûreté, the media and the public have difficulty understanding how it was infiltrating a Far-Right movement that was committing murders. There is no way for the government to easily sweep these incidents under the rug and it's a huge embarrassment.

FINAL SUPPER

Latinus convenes a special meeting of the small group of Westland New Post members who haven't abandoned him. During the discussion, the topic of conversation turns to the Brabant murders. Latinus shares that he suspects that some members in the Westland splinter cell are involved. Everyone in the room knows that those responsible for the Pastorale double murder came from their midst.

As mentioned previously, there's no evidence that Latinus knew about the Pastorale murders before they happened. He suspects that the same group of members responsible for that also participated in the Brabant killings. He specifically suspects Eric Lammers of being involved in the Nivelles Colruyt attack.

According to one member present at the meeting: "[Latinus] shared with us his suspicions… without telling us how he came up with this only by showing us that this person was able to be part of the gang or to tell us he was one of the killers." That member adds, "We had already by the behavior, with what had been shared in the newspapers, some concerns, some intuitions that made us think that it could be Westland members that we knew more or less."

The underlying message Latinus delivers to his Westland supporters is that the movement has been derailed.

THE FINAL CHAPTER

On April 24th, Latinus calls authorities to set up a meeting because he has revelations to share. Two days later, before he can talk to police, Latinus is found hanging in the basement of his home in the Brabant. His cause of death is officially ruled a suicide. However, some prosecutors believe that Latinus was killed. An autopsy determined that the telephone wire that he used to hang himself could barely hold up his weight—a weak yank would have been enough to sever the cord. Furthermore, the distance between the floor and the ceiling seemed too small for an adult man of his size to hang himself; his feet had to have been touching the ground. The case is closed and there will continue to be some question whether Latinus killed himself or was murdered.

While Latinus is gone, suspicions about the Westland New Post's involvement in the Brabant Killings are just starting.

VIELSAM

At 2:00 a.m., in the wee hours of May 13th, 1984, three intruders cut through barbed wire to gain access to a Belgium armory in Vielsam. They fire a salvo from a Thompson submachine gun at the guard on duty that night, a man named Carl Freches. He's hit four times with 45-caliber bullets. The intruders steal a large quantity of arms, including twenty Faul, five Vignerons, a couple of Falo submachine guns, and three Lee Enfield Guns. They load the stolen weapons in a Jeep and a Mercedes and leave. While critically injured, Fresches survives.

This incident gives rise to lots of political finger-pointing in the context of the Cold War. The main suspects have been Far-Left Militants. The left has long suspected NATO or the Americans of being involved. Some, including a superior officer to Fresches, believe the Vielsam attack shows the hallmarks of the Insane Killers—the methods of operation and the cover-up in resulting investigation.

There is still no concrete evidence that the Insane Killers were involved in Vielsam. However, many see it through the lens of the Strategy of the Tension, which is the theory that NATO or the Americans teamed up with the Far-Right to cause terrorist attacks in Western European countries.[218] The idea is that the left would get blamed for the attacks. This would potentially motivate the population to elect a right-wing, strong, law-and-order government. Some attacks from Far-Right groups in Italy and Germany during the last couple of decades of the Cold War were initially blamed on the Left. There is still suspicion that western intelligence agencies armed and funded these Far-Right groups to commit these attacks to manipulate the population. It is also possible that the Insane Killers were part of this Strategy of the Tension.

What we know in terms of Vielsam is that the same night as the attack, a NATO Military war-game exercise, code-named Oesling 84, had been scheduled in the area of the armory. The initial plan was a joint operation that included roughly 36 American Special Forces and soldiers from the Belgian Army. There were also local mercenaries hired to handle logistics. Some critics of how authorities handled the Vielsam attack suspect that it was a live bullet exercise under the guise of a regular war game. Using live bullets would simulate a Warsaw Pact communist attack on Belgium as realistically as possible. Critics also point out that some troops would have used .45 caliber Thompson submachine guns that night. If the Vielsam armory was the intended target, Fresches was just an unfortunate casualty.

As for authorities, they link the stolen weapons to the stock of the French Far-Left terrorist group, Action Directe, which sometimes travels to Belgium to link up with Belgian Far-Left groups. In August 1985, authorities stumble on a Falo gun and Falo submachine gun from the Vielsam armory in a building in Brussels. There are also fingerprints of three Action Directe leaders in the building. In 1987, another Vielsam firearm is found at a farm that was used as an Action Directe safe house.

The Belgian Far-Left militant, Bertrand Sassoye, is also of interest to authorities. Sassoye had started his military service at Vielsam, but deserted in March 1982 and joined the Far-Left underground. There is speculation that Sassoye knew the site and could have been involved. However, no fingerprints ever link him to the attack.

Around the time of the Vielsam attack, the Fighting Communist Cells (CCC) is created as the Belgian counterpart to Action Directe and Sassoye is a founding member. In Belgium, the CCC will be joined to the Insane Killers and regarded as two sides of the same coin. Together, they create chaos and cause serious political ramifications. Many believe the same people are pulling the strings of both groups.

CCC

In October 1984, the windows of a Litton building—where precision-guidance systems for NATO missiles are made—are pulverized by a bomb. Members of the CCC claim responsibility. Their modus operandi is to bomb buildings in order to elicit a huge reaction from the public. They send political tracts to the media with manifestoes. Unlike the Brabant Killers, members of the CCC never kill with premeditation.

In the following days, a bomb goes off on the property of the Man firm and damages the trucks. Then another bomb goes off at the Honeywell building where the electronic materials for the NATO precision-guidance systems are made. The CCC members blow up the building headquarters of three different Right-Wing, Belgian political parties. One building has its whole facade annihilated. Another bomb destroys three floors.

MAMOUTH

With the backdrop of crimes committed by the Brabant Killers and CCC, unrest and impatience are growing in the general population. Whether these attacks are part of a large Strategy of the Tension or not, significant pressure is put on the government to clamp down on the violence. In response, Right-Wing Justice Minister Jean Gol, creates an inter-police agency in September 1984 to combat the CCC. It will use extreme tactics to attain this goal.

On October 19th, 1984, Gol gives the green light to Operation Mammoth, a massive search and seizure among Left-Wing militants. It's all-encompassing, and critics view it as a very heavy-handed response for some property damage. Several mainstream Left-Wing militants are targeted. Even two parliamentary representatives of mainstream Left-Wing parties, the Green Party, and the Socialist Party are subject to a search and seizure at their homes. Left-Wing parties are furious and feel these attacks on their individual freedoms bring little in terms of progress to the CCC investigation, but produce a lot of information on Left-Wing militants for the Right-Wing government. Furthermore, the unrest starts swinging polls in favor of Right-Wing parties.

There are growing accusations that someone is conspiring to make it look like the Far-Left is a legitimate threat to the country's stability. A popular theory among Left-Wing militants who are being targeted is that the American and Belgium soldiers really attacked the Vielsam armory and stole the weapons to give to Far-Left groups or plant on properties linked to them to magnify the peril presented by the Left-Wing. Was the Vielsam attack faked to strengthen the Far-Right government? The Left-Wing folks also bring up the elephant in the room, namely why the power of the state is only used to clamp down on the Left-Wing bombings and not the Brabant Insane Killers?

Senator Roger Lallemand, the Head of the Belgian Parliamentary Inquiry into Gladio, observed: "A type of media terrorism developed here, which used the media to shock the public and political circles. This terrorism could have two sources, the extreme Left or Right. Or, it could be foreign governments and foreign intelligence services. It is a terrorism which aims to destabilize democratic society."[219]

The government tactics to crush the CCC didn't seem to dent its capacity to organize bombings. In November 1984, at the Bierset military base, two communication pylons are blown up. The pylons are very close to where the NATO Mirage 5 planes are posted. In December, NATO pipelines in five different towns are blown up. The pipeline bombings paralyze NATO's fuel supply for three days. In January 1985, the façade of the Allied Military Command's building in Europe is destroyed. Cynics will say that it's peculiar that as soon as the Insane Killers pause their operations, the CCC acts begin. While the Insane Killers are seemingly inactive during all of 1984 and most of 1985, the violence in the country continues, unabated.

CHAPTER 17

DIFFICULTIES FOR THE BOUHOUCHE GANG

B Y APRIL 1984, THE BOUHOUCHE GANG EXTORTION PROJECT IS REally taking shape as they dig the hole under the elevator shaft in their warehouse and steal the items they need to complete their plan. On April 6th, they steal a metallic-gray Renault 18 station wagon in Etterbeek to further their plan. They put a diplomatic plate on it and they will have a foreign looking member of their Gang wait in the car for the others when they exit the Brussels sewers in their dinghy.

Several things work against the Bouhouche Gang's extortion plot. The digging ends up being much more difficult than anticipated with their little amount of manpower. This is problematic because the Bouhouche Gang used a skeletal crew to do the job to ensure secrecy. Removing a sewer grill caused them great trouble.[220] By mid-May, the Bouhouche Gang had managed to only dig a hole that measured a mere two-foot by two-feet and went only six-feet deep under the warehouse's elevator shaft. Project feasibility issues arise and there is a serious disagreement within the Gang.

They're forced to consider abandoning the extremely costly project and Gang members exchange death threats. On May 22nd, the Bouhouche Gang completely abandons their large-scale supermarket extortion project. They've spent all that money, energy, and effort for nothing. Whether it's related to his Gang's extortion project or not, Bouhouche officially leaves the ARI detective agency he used as cover on October 1st, 1984.

JUAN MENDEZ

Bouhouche, who has a gun dealer license, continues collecting and trafficking arms into 1985. He built an impressive gun collection that included many stolen guns. In addition to working out a scheme to steal guns with Juan Mendez, a sales rep for FN in South America and Spain, Bouhouche opens a gun shop in Jette called The Practical Guns Store. Interestingly, Bouhouche still describes his primary occupation as a detective and not a gun dealer. His friend Juan Mendez has also accumulated an impressive arms collection, which he stores in his basement. Although he is only in his thirties and earns a sales rep's modest salary, Mendez's gun collection is valued at 2.3 million BEF (approximately SU $ 65,000), possibly more. His collection includes all kinds of weapons, from self-defence to hunting and even historical weapons.

The weapons Mendez values the most are those that can't be legally purchased, like the HK submachine guns that can only be sold to police forces. In Belgium, only the elite Dyane Gendarmerie SWAT team uses the HK submachine guns—the same special German-made arms the Bouhouche Gang stole when they broke into the Dyane building in January 1982. The Gang couldn't resell them after that theft made national headlines, as there is no way they'd go unnoticed on the black market. Mendez had actively sought to buy one of these elite submachine guns in the past and had even tried to purchase one abroad from a Peruvian Marine Officer several times. When he does finally procure one, it's through Bouhouche and originated from the Dyane robbery. Although Mendez and Bouhouche are friends and have worked together trafficking stolen weapons, this is a weird decision because this particular HK is linked to a major national crime. There are serious consequences for being linked to the Dyane robbery. It means that Mendez knows for sure—if he didn't suspect it before—that his good friend Bouhouche is a major criminal.

Why did Bouhouche transfer the HK from the Dyane robbery to Mendez? Perhaps Bouhouche requires quick access to cash after the extortion plan failed. Mendez would probably have paid Bouhouche a king's ransom for this weapon. Instead of keeping this new acquisition quiet, Mendez shows off the HK to friends, co-workers, arms dealers, and several others. He's not shy and tells people that the only people to ever have this kind of weapon in Belgium were Special Forces in the Dyane Gendarmerie.

COLLECTION

On May 15th, 1985, the Bouhouche Gang breaks into Mendez's home in Overijse. Most items of value are stolen, including his arms collection, which was insured. However, there are so many stolen items that insurance could only pay him a small fraction of the total value. And how do you put a price on items like the contraband HK? Mendez was keenly aware of the rising value of his collection and had already decided to put up an armored door to protect it. He had even scheduled the renovations for May 17th, which was something that Bouhouche knew about. It's likely not a coincidence that the robbery happened only two days before the armored door was supposed to be installed. The break-in happens in broad daylight and the getaway vehicle is parked on the front lawn. The Bouhouche Gang members go to the back of the house where they force open the bottom panel of the kitchen door. They empty the weapons from the basement, which is where most of the arms collection is stored. The thieves also help themselves to a TV, stereo system, VCR, and a computer, as well as miscellaneous items such as jewelry, two walkie-talkies, and a Nikon camera shoulder-strap. A bed linen is also missing and was likely used to carry items through the front door and load them into the vehicle on the lawn.

Mendez's wife gets home at 2:15 p.m. and notices the house has been broken into. She immediately phones Mendez at work. He is extremely shaken and takes the rest of the day off. When he rushes home, Mendez is shocked to see all that the thieves took. However, before he calls the police, Mendez needs to hide some stolen items that the thieves missed.

Mendez calls Bouhouche to help him prepare the house before the police come to investigate. One of the stolen items Mendez needs to hide is a pistol that was hidden under a cabinet. Mendez hands Bouhouche the pistol and he keeps it for the duration of the police visit.

Once all is said and done, Mendez only recovers a fraction of the value of his arms collection. Naturally, he doesn't get the value of the stolen weapons back and he was missing the gun spec documentation and serial numbers for other legally obtained weapons.

Mendez is supposedly a very close friend to Bouhouche. Maybe Bouhouche is such a psychopath that he is able to rob his old friend? Did Bouhouche sell the HK from the Dyane robbery to Mendez to get quick cash, knowing that he'd recover the HK after robbing Mendez's home? Is it possible that Mendez upset the Gang in some way and was now fair game? Is it because the Gang is now desperate for money? Right after committing the robbery, the Bouhouche Gang immediately starts selling off all the untraceable Mendez weapons directly or through agents on the black market and to gun shops.

CRUISE MISSILES

In coordination with NATO, on March 14th, 1985, the Belgium government installs 16 cruise missiles on Belgian soil. There's lots of pushback from the well-organized and popular anti-nuclear movement, including large-scale demonstrations. Roughly 150,000 people take to the streets to demand the removal of the missiles. The Right-Wing government is less popular and could be heading to an electoral defeat.

As if to sabotage the Left's effective, peaceful opposition, the Far-Left begins a new cycle of terrorist attacks. In April, a NATO building is bombed by a movement that calls itself FRAP. In May, the CCC, which is the main Far-Left terrorist group, starts a new bombing campaign of its own. Their first target is to blow up the Belgium Business Federation's (FEB) building.

To accomplish this goal, CCC operators place a bomb in a truck that they park right next to the FEB building. Unlike the ultra-violent, Insane Killers, the CCC always takes precautions to avoid human casualties. They leave the message: "Danger. Booby-trapped vehicle. Advise fellow employees and immediately drive away as far as possible. Absolutely do not touch the vehicle." They also advise authorities directly.

While everyone should be aware of the imminent danger, there's a miscommunication during the emergency response process and the message is never forwarded to first responders. When the firefighters reach the site, they don't know about the booby trap and the bomb goes off when they try to access the truck. Two firefighters are killed on the spot and two others are seriously injured. The CCC becomes public enemy number one as the violence shocks the country. The Right-Wing coalition government orders swift retaliatory law and order measures.

Chapter *18*

Haemers and De Staerke's
New Gangs

Patrick Haemers—the spoiled, rich, good-looking youth who embraced a life of crime—has assembled a crew of competent criminals from the nightclub scene. While the tall, blond Haemers becomes the public face of the Gang, the real brains behind their activities is Philippe L. At over six feet tall and barrel-chested, Philippe L. is also tough-looking. The Gang's dedicated driver is the short, slight, and nervous-looking, Thierry S. The Haemers Gang will be suspects in the Brabant Killings.

The Haemers Gang's niche is armed robberies and they only do big money hits. According to Haemers: "I only rob banks and the post office. They'll never be short in cash."[221] Post offices interested armed robbers in the eighties because they carried wads of negotiable government and employee cheques, plus all pensions would be carried together on fixed dates at regular intervals. For robberies orchestrated on that delivery day, the financial reward could be impressive.

A little more than a month after the Brabant Killers cause the blood-bath in Nivelles in September 1983, the Haemers Gang hits a post office in Herstal. At 6:20 a.m. on November 2, 1983, they enter the building armed and wearing ski masks and gloves. A few dozen people are held at gunpoint.

When the Haemers Gang tries to get an employee to open the safe, they realize they have a big problem. The safe needs to be opened with two keys and the employee with the second key happens to be late that morning. So the Gang waits with their many hostages for another half an hour for the employee with the key. It is worth their patience; the Gang steals a massive 9,480,000 BEF. Haemers boasts about the robbery: "We took twenty-nine hostages for half an hour. No injuries. That's class!"[222]

The Haemers Gang members do careful reconnaissance before their hits: "All the places are scouted for weeks and the itinerary, studied in detail. We determine who shoots first if necessary, who covers, who drives. Each of us has a defined role."[223] They wake up hours before the crack of dawn. At 4:00 a.m., they study truck itineraries. How many post office employees are present? How secure is the truck? Was there a police escort? How many officers were inside? They carefully time their armed robberies to be in and out so fast that they are already far away when the police show up. "Everything was finished in 45 seconds, I always timed the job".[224]

The Haemers Gang is very active in 1985 and on March 1st at 6:00 a.m., they wait to ambush a postal convoy from Louvain. They've spent weeks following and timing the postal truck convoy route a dozen times. The post office has started bulking up security because of the attacks. A Gendarmerie van is now assigned to each post office transport truck. When the convoy makes a stop at the Wilsele Post Office, the truck stops left and the Gendarmerie van stays to its right. The Haemers Gang members arrive in a BMW and shoot twice at the Gendarmerie van, before emptying the truck as they keep the Gendarmes in check with an UZI. They wear ski masks.

When the Haemers Gang starts running low on money, they strike again. On May 20th, they attack a postal truck in Neufville, this time wearing ski masks and driving a Golf Cabriolet. Despite the fact Haemers is high on cocaine, the hit goes off without a glitch and they take off with the huge sum of 10,520,000 BEF (or approximately $ 292,338). Once they are all back in their safe house, they sit on the ground beside a fireplace and carefully sort through each bill to make sure there are no numbered bills. All the bad bills are thrown in the fire.

BAASRODE GANG

On March 13th, 1985, Johnny De Staerke gets a 48-hour pass out of jail. He's been in jail since late 1983, when he was arrested after escaping from the Doornink jail. He's had enough of incarcerated life and never returns to serve the rest of his time. De Staerke connects with ex-cons he met during his time in jail who have agreed to commit armed robberies with him. Johnny De Staerke will be a key suspect in the Brabant Killings. The core members of his new gang are Leopold Van Esbroek, Big Stereo P., and Dominique S.[225]

De Staerke is the last one out of jail. The other three have already started committing armed robberies before De Staerke goes AWOL. The intellectually sharp Dominique S., who's nicknamed "The Computer" by police, plans the hits. While De Staerke was still behind bars, Dominique S. successfully broke into two dozen Delhaize supermarkets at night. He would first visit the supermarket during opening hours and spot where the cigarette counter is located. Come nightfall, Dominique S. would rush in and out of the abandoned Delhaize with cartons of cigarettes and bottles of alcohol. "In five minutes, we could steal 20 boxes each containing 25 cartons."[226] They could easily make 150,000 to 200,000 BEF per break-in. In just two years, Dominique S. steals more than five million BEF worth of cigarettes. Other than a robbery penchant for thieving, Dominique S. has no known vices and runs a second-hand store.

Van Esbroek and Big Stereo are the muscle in the Gang. Like De Staerke, Van Esbroek is a compulsive horse gambler.A He also has an incredibly big mouth and he's a bit of a clown. Van Esbroek has been known to commit frauds, usually non-violent. Big Stereo is a mountain of a man with a mane of blond hair that was first in jail for participating in a series of burglaries with another gang.

De Staerke's combined rap sheet and street cred help make him the face of the Gang, even though he's not the leader per se. According to Van Esbrock, "Johnny organizes nothing, absolutely nothing."[227] However, De Staerke pressures the De Staerke Gang to attempt riskier, big money hits. Their criminal niche becomes armed robbery of post offices in the Dutch-speaking part of the country—but just post office buildings, not armed postal convoy attacks like the Haemers Gang.

The press christens them the Baasrode Gang after the town where they rob a post office on June 26th. They use machine guns, a shotgun, and a hunting rifle in the hold-up, but no shots are fired and they leave with 1.4 million BEF (approximately US $40,000)

CHAPTER 19

WALIBI AMUSEMENT PARK

August 15th is a warm and sunny day in Wavre and the Walibi amusement park is bustling with visitors. Somewhere around 15,000 people cross the gates that day and the cash registers fill up quickly. Security guard Willy Pans is dispatched to make Intergard's third money pick-up from the park's safe and transport the funds to the bank. As Pans makes his way to the amusement park, a dark Honda Quintet rides into the park's back access road, which leads to the back entrance of the park beside a small parking lot for personnel. Three men exit the Honda, sit down, unpack a lunch, and have a picnic.

At 2:15 p.m., Pans reaches the back parking lot for staff. He crosses through the back entrance and picks up 1.3 Million BEF in cash (about $36,620) from the safe. Once Pans returns to the parking lot, one of the picnickers surprises him and fires a bullet that hits his heart and liver. A bullet breaks the back window of another car in the parking lot. Pan crashes down to the ground, where the killer finishes him off with four 9mm bullets to the head. The killer picks up the park's money that Pans was transporting and walks back to the Honda Quintet where the two other picnickers are waiting for him.

A TRIP TO LUXEMBURG

The murder is important for two reasons. First, some have found similarities to the other murders committed by the Insane Killers. A hit like this could have helped finance their Second Wave of attacks. However, it's never been officially included in the list of Insane Killers attacks. Second, this crime has long been suspected of being a Bouhouche Gang attack. However, they never confessed to it and have never been charged for it.

What we do know is that during the summer, prior to the murder of Pans and theft of the park funds, two fake Gendarmes visited the Walibi amusement park in Wavre and asked questions about the park's security.[228] After the robbery, the identity of the fake Gendarmes could never be retraced.[229] The assassin used a rare HK P7 pistol to kill Pan. A similar pistol with the serial number obscured is later discovered at the home of a Bouhouche Gang associate. He claims it was given to him by another Gang associate who refuses to say where he got the gun.

The investigators suspect the gun could have originated from a batch delivered to gun dealer Lorang in the neighboring country of Luxemburg. The Bouhouche Gang members are suspected of purchasing arms there with a false permit to buy foreign arms. Two HKPs were purchased by a Roger Van Vliet, an often-used alias preferred by the Bouhouche Gang in 1984. The Bouhouche Gang even used the alias to rent a box six days before the Walibi amusement park attack. The coordinates of the alias Van Vliet are listed in both the agenda and client databases of a Bouhouche Gang associate. The Bouhouche Gang members also use a forged IDs and a seal stolen from their 1981 Chaumont-Gistoux town hall robbery.

The Bouhouche Gang is very active during this time period and it seems like they really need money. On August 9th, the Bouhouche Gang breaks into the Brussels Courthouse and reach the clerk's office on Level 1. They force the security locks on eight wooden doors, taking the metallic door locks apart with special pliers to reach the court exhibits section. They are probably looking to steal some cash held as evidence, just as they had in 1981. They end up stealing at least one Jaeger-Lecoultre clock and a VCR.

In the Walibi amusement park's front parking lot, authorities find a Renault 4 that was stolen in Brussels in November 1984. The Renault 4 has an antenna on the roof just like the stolen Ford Taunus used by the fake officers from the Bouhouche Gang to kidnap and murder security guard Zwarts at the airport in 1982.[230] It also has false plates pressed using the same mold as the false plates used by the Bouhouche Gang's other crimes.[231] In fact, this Renault 4 also uses the same plate template as a Mercedes 4X4 stolen by the Gang and driven by Bouhouche in 1986. Authorities believe the Renault 4 was intended as a backup car if something went wrong with the Honda Quintet.

The dark Honda Quintet was stolen in Brussels in December 1983. It's later found in a UCL parking lot, in the exact same area as the Woluwe storage units rented by the Bouhouche Gang. The Walibi attack is privately investigated by a Gendarme who is linked to the Bouhouche Gang, but working in another district. He comes up with a far-fetched story concerning a Walibi amusement park employee and sends it to investigators. The murder is still unsolved.

Wavre Investigation

On August 14th, the Wavre Gendarmerie investigators release a fourth report concerning the 1982 Wavre Gun Shop attack. The first report was written a couple of years earlier, before anyone knew the Insane Killers existed. The working theory is that the burglars wanted to steal the silencer prototype because Daniel Dekaise, the gun shop owner, had not respected his side of an international arms deal. They use an open-ended investigative approach and go anywhere their investigation leads them. Most leads they follow are completely unrelated to the Brabant Killers and mainly trace back to the gun shop owner, Dekaise's international arms business.

Their fourth report will have explosive consequences. It's a sloppy report with many inaccuracies that wanders all over the place, attacking politicians and government figures. The Wavre Gun Shop owner, Dekaise is battered in the report as a major suspect, despite originally being treated as a victim after the Insane Killers beat him to a pulp and he ended up in a coma. They write that Dekaise operates in a legal gray zone and much of his business is focused on international deals with the tacit approval of Western Services like the Sûreté, the CIA, or MI6. The report mentions that when Wavre investigators press into his commercial contacts with a warring faction during the Civil War in Lebanon, he says:

"If you know that, I am screwed."[232] It just makes the Investigators push that much harder. Another Gendarmerie officer defends Dekaise: "Do you realize, M. Bihay, if you talk about those cases, you'll have unemployment at the FN and, anyways, those weapons will be supplied by other countries. Why do you want to thwart the higher interests of the State?"[233]

The Wavre Gun Shop investigation has gone so far that the Insane Killers attack has become an afterthought compared to owner Dekaise's alleged involvement in international arms trafficking. Some investigators believe the alleged arms trafficking is more important than the Brabant Killers investigation.

WESTLAND NEW POST

The report also takes the spin from Paul Latinus, the dead leader of the Westland New Post, at face value: the Sûreté is controlled by the KGB. The Sûreté manipulated Westland and they ordered the Pastorale Street double murder through Sûreté's Director, Albert Raes and Commissioner the Duck.

The report also makes several mistakes concerning Westland New Post. It often confuses the Far-Right Movement Youth Front and Westland. It lists six Gendarmes as part of Westland, and they get three names completely wrong. Only one Gendarme was a full member of the Westland: Lucien M. One of the likely sources of the report is Martial Lekeu, the Gendarme who fled to Florida after receiving death threats from other Gendarmes. In December 1983, Lekeu told the same Wavre Gendarme that the Insane Killers crimes were coordinated by a group of Gendarmes. In interviews, Lekeu also confuses Westland with the Youth Front.

DANI BOUHOUCHE

One notable part of the report concerns Dani Bouhouche, but also contains mistakes. It claims Bouhouche is one of the Westland New Post Gendarmes, referring to Westland's membership list, including Bouhouche. But the investigators read Bouhouche while the name on the list is actually Bouche, which is the real name of another known Westland member. They double-up the mistake by claiming Bouhouche's codename at Westland is "Titise." Titise is actually Westland member Bouche's code name. It's not clear if the Wavre investigators had another source linking Bouhouche to Westland other than that membership list.

The reality is there's not a single shred of documented evidence that shows Bouhouche is or was a member of Westland. It's become a popular myth. The only connection is that Bouhouche shoots guns with a friend named Alain W. who became a Westland member. When Alain W. was joining Westland, he asked Bouhouche who was still a Gendarme at the time for some classified Gendarmerie files as initiation. Bouhouche gets an associate who works in the information department of the Gendarmerie to get three files that interested Latinus for Alain W. Through Alain W., Bouhouche becomes acquainted with another Westland member, Eric Lammers.

It's also through Alain W. that the rumor that Bouhouche was the Youth Front's shooting instructor originates. Bouhouche was never a member of the Youth Front, but he knew Alain W. from the gun ranges. Alain W. was a Youth Front member and he would sometimes bring another friend to the gun range with him, where Bouhouche would give them tips. It turns out that Bouhouche had given shooting tips to the Youth Front member the day that the Youth Front member shot Algerian foreign workers in a Laeken pub in December 1981, killing one and critically wounding a second.

However, Bouhouche has never been a card-carrying member of any Far-Right organization. He is not known to have even attended a meeting and Bouhouche was never politically active. That said, there is anecdotal evidence that he had some Far-Right ideas.

Whatever Bouhouche's personal political ideas might be, it's important to know the Bouhouche Gang is an organized crime gang whose purpose is to make money for its members—the Bouhouche Gang has no interest in politics. There's no credible evidence that any other member with the exception of Bouhouche, had Far-Right ideas and there were members from different ethnic backgrounds. Other than money, the only other motive seems to be revenge against the Gendarmerie and people that cross them, such as the bombing attempt against Goffinon's car and the attempted murder at Vernaillen's home in 1981.

The report makes it obvious that the Gendarme don't know about Bouhouche's extensive criminality. The Wavre investigators still don't even suspect that the Bouhouche Gang was responsible for the 1981 attempted murder at Vernaillen's home. However, they dig up some details concerning the 1981 attempted bombing against Goffinon: "Concerning the Peugeot attack, Bouhouche is a friend of the builder or seller of a part of the exploding device in the Peugeot..."[234] And Bouhouche was once suspected of being involved.

FAEZ AL AJJAZ

Another reason some believe that Bouhouche was involved with the Westland New Post is the fact he used a Mazda 626 that was owned by an alleged Westland member named Faez Al Ajjaz for the Vernaillen attack. It's only partially true. The summer before the Vernaillen attack, the leader of Westland, Paul Latinus, met Faez through the editor of a Far-Right anti-communist paper he knew from his Youth Front days. Al Ajjaz is officially the Belgium correspondent for Arabic papers and he is very well-connected with Belgian politicians and ambassadors from Arab countries. He also provides information to Saudi intelligence among others.

Al Ajjaz struck up a personal friendship with the editor. When the editor finds out Latinus is broke and looking for work, he introduces him to Al Ajjaz, who's very wealthy. Latinus, who has no steady stream of income and is living off his mother, begins to get Westland members to do odd jobs for Faez like clean his home, work as his driver or security guard, and do some tech work in his office. There's no evidence that Faez knew of the Westland New Post at the time. He was never a member.

On September 16th, 1981, Al Ajjaz files a stolen car report with police. In the report, he declares his Mazda 626 is stolen and he files a claim with the insurance. What really happened is that Al Ajjaz hid the Mazda in the Ixelles garage complex. His accomplice, mechanic André D., lends the Mazda to a client as a courtesy car.

On September 29th, André D.'s client double-parks the courtesy Mazda while he runs into a shop on Louise Avenue in Ixelles. The key is in the ignition and the motor is running. During that very short time frame, the Bouhouche Gang members seize the opportunity and drive away with the car. André D. is in quite a bind because of course, the stolen Mazda was already declared stolen by his accomplice Al Ajjaz. The car can't be declared stolen a second time. On November 13th, André D. comes clean and tells investigators about the fraud scheme. In 1987, both André D. and Al Ajjaz are found guilty of insurance fraud. In the meantime, the Bouhouche Gang members will use this Mazda 626 to drive to Vernaillen's home to attack him later that year. There's no evidence that Al Ajjaz knew any Bouhouche Gang members.

THE FALLOUT

As Bouhouche is well-connected in Gendarmerie circles, he finds out about the Wavre Gendarmerie report. Bouhouche, who's paranoid about his privacy, is furious when he finds out what's written about him. The three Wavre Gendarmes who outed him will pay for their indiscretion.

Bouhouche also learns that the Wavre Gun Shop owner, Dekaise is getting bruised and battered in the Wavre reports. He also sees the same negative headlines in the papers as everyone else and how the Wavre Investigators have seriously damaged Dekaise's reputation. According to Dekaise: "...my neighbors would ask me what kind of horrible man I was, my contacts in the official markets [police corps and official corps]...were very difficult. It brought me serious problems."[235]

A Bouhouche Gang associate shows up at the gun shop and tells Dekaise he can get the Wavre Investigators off his back. He hands Dekaise a Gendarmerie envelope that holds two stolen revolver barrels, which were stolen by Bouhouche during a search and seizure at another gun shop back when he was still a Gendarme. The Gang then arranges for a Gendarmerie officer to meet Dekaise and get the envelope with the stolen barrels inside. Dekaise tells the officer he was given the envelope by the Wavre investigators. The Gendarmerie officer writes a police report about the stolen barrels that implicates the Wavre team.

When the Gendarmerie hierarchy hears about the Wavre team and the stolen barrels, they pounce without knowing it's a dirty trick by the Bouhouche Gang. The stolen barrels help trigger a disciplinary process against the Wavre investigators, but it barely makes a difference. At this point, the Gendarmerie has already had enough of the Wavre Gendarmes. Aside from going way beyond their mandate of investigating the September 1982 Wavre Gun Shop attack, the report tarnishes the integrity of several public figures. The Wavre Gendarmes have made no friends and their judgment and competence are attacked from all directions.

The three Gendarmes are disciplined. The charge is that they disseminated the report before giving Gendarmerie leadership prior notice of the contents. According to the Gendarmerie hierarchy: "The problem is all the more serious because it's a report where the content is sensitive and that it calls into question in a quite ambiguous way, prominent public figures."[236] The Gendarmerie hierarchy adds that: "A part of the Info is just careless transcriptions, simple gossips or that are unrecorded, unsigned, unverified and not scrutinized that in a consolidated report take a whole new importance."[237] One of the investigators ends up getting a four-day conditional suspension. The other two get administrative transfers.

BAASRODE GANG

During the summer of 1985, Johnny De Staerke's new Baasrode Gang robs the post offices of a dozen towns in Flanders. They go in and out quickly, using a chronometer. Despite De Staerke's violent reputation, no one is ever shot. They also rob a money transport and a hamburger stand in the Greater Brussels area. On August 7th, they use a stolen BMW to rob a post office near Antwerp. Three gangsters enter the post office while the fourth stays in the getaway car. They use machine guns and revolvers and end up stealing 800,000 BEF (approximately US $22,535) from the safe. On September 24th, the Gang members return to rob the same Baasrode post office that made them famous. This time, two gangsters enter the packed post office wearing masks while a third man waits inside the getaway car. They steal 200,000 BEF (approximately US $5,634) from the safe. During the same period, they rob several more post offices in Flanders.

JEEP

On September 10th, Bouhouche and an accomplice drive up to a Mercedes car dealership north of Brussels. Bouhouche hands 10,000 BEF (approximately US $280) to his accomplice, who enters the dealership while Bouhouche waits outside. The accomplice asks to rent a four-wheel-drive Mercedes Jeep in the dealership's lot and fills out the paperwork for the rental company. He uses a stolen ID card and driver's license in the name of Wilfried Gees. The accomplice gives the dealership employee Bouhouche's 10,000 BEF as a deposit for the rental of the Mercedes. He drives away with the Jeep and never returns.

Bouhouche attaches a fake license plate to the Jeep that has a plate number copied from a similar Jeep. The fake plates were pressed with the same template as the plates used for the Bouhouche Gang's stolen Renault 25. Bouhouche throws out the license certificate from the stolen Jeep's registration papers and puts in its place a fake insurance card and certificate of conformity.

They modify the Jeep to allow the use of a police scanner. The specs used are specifically made to match one of the police antennas owned by Bouhouche. In the next few months, Bouhouche and an accomplice will both ride around in the modified Jeep Mercedes. There are similarities with the Ford Taunus they used for their 1982 murder-robbery at the Brussels airport, namely that both have a three-quarters-of-an-inch hole pierced in the roof where radio antennas are usually fixed on Gendarmerie vehicles. The Mercedes Jeep is found in Woluwe-St-Lambert. In the close vicinity of the UCL campus and St-Luc Hospital, which is the area were they usually dump their car when they don't have room in their garage boxes. However, in late September 1985, the Gendarmerie discovers the Renault 18 station wagon stolen in 1984 in the Ixelles storage complex. The car is parked in the immediate vicinity of three storage units rented by the Bouhouche Gang.

Part III:
Second Wave (1985)

Parade in the city of Aalst

CHAPTER 20

STEALING A GOLF IN ERPS KWERPS
(SEPTEMBER 22, 1985)

THE BRABANT INSANE KILLERS WHO HAVE NOT BEEN ACTIVE IN MORE than a year and half, start gathering the things they need for their Second Wave of attacks. Unbeknownst to the public, they're back. They need to find a car to go on another crime spree. Their last Volkwagen Golf had been torched in Hourpes Forest in December 1983.

In the early hours of September 22nd, 1985, a bit after 4:00 a.m., the Insane Killers show up along the fence of the Volkswagen car lot in Erps Kwerps. The lot is monitored electronically by the firm Securitas. The thieves use wire cutters to break through the secure chain-linked fence and gain entry into the lot.

The cars in the lot are not locked and the keys are in the ignition. The thieves move two cars, which gives them a passage to remove a three-door charcoal gray Golf GTI from the lot.

To avoid the next security patrol, they are in and out in five minutes.

CHAPTER 21

DELHAIZE SUPERMARKETS IN BRAINE & OVERIJSE (SEPTEMBER 27, 1985)[238]

On September 27th, at 8:10 p.m., the Insane Killers drive the dark gray Golf to a reserved parking spot for a pizzeria in the town of Braine. Three masked men get out of the car and walk past the pizzeria and down a footpath that leads to the Delhaize parking lot. The Brabant Killers wear dark military jackets; two of the men wear masks of French politicians and carry pump-action shotguns. The Giant carries a submachine gun.

A 12-year-old boy is on his bike, hanging around in the parking lot.[239] The Giant yanks the boy off his bike by the hair and hauls him violently for several feet up to the front door of the supermarket. The Giant keeps pressing a gun into the boy's side and holds him by the collar.[240] Two of the Brabant Killers carry garbage bags.[241]

One of the Killers notices a red van a few yards away with a middle-aged man, Bozidar Djuroski and his 17-year-old son inside. Djuroski is waiting for his wife and daughter, who are buying some alcohol inside the Delhaize.[242] When the father notices one of the Insane Killers getting closer to the van, he screams to his son, "Get down!"A One of the Brabant Killers discharges his weapon through the red van's windshield and the father collapses over his steering wheel. The son is hit in the chest and on the top of his shoulder with buckshot. The critically wounded father dies from his injury later that night. The son loses a lung but survives.[243]

At the Delhaize supermarket doors, a middle-aged shopper named Roger Engelbienne recognizes the young hostage. He firmly tells the armed robbers to let the boy go.A One of the Killers responds with a shotgun blast and says: "That's the lesson for having a big mouth."[244] Hearing the gunshots, some clients try to escape through the back of the store and others hide in the aisles.

The heavily armed men step into the store. The Giant hauls his 12-year-old hostage in one hand and his submachine gun in the other. The two other assailants go without any hesitation straight to the store's vault. The Giant walks over to the cash registers and screams: "Everyone down or I kill you."[245] Most of the shoppers in the vicinity hit the deck. Ghislain Platane, a middle-aged customer who has just finished paying for his groceries, doesn't react fast enough and is mowed down. The customers at the very back scramble for a better hiding spot in the outer reaches of the supermarket.[246]

The Giant, still holding the hair of his boy hostage with a firm grip, calmly threatens the cashiers: "Quick, empty all the cash registers in this bag… Hurry up or I kill this kid."[247] He then systematically moves from one cash register to the other, making sure the cashiers empty the contents of their cash drawers into his brown bag.

In the meantime, the two smaller thieves walk briskly along the aisles towards the office that houses the store's vault. On the way, they cross paths with the store manager who tells the armed men that they can take whatever they want; he'll give it to them. They step in the office and rip out the telephone wires and the manager shows them that most of the money is now in a vault that only security agents can open. One of the masked men is incredulous and angry as the manager is only able to open another smaller vault with some small change and meal checks. The criminals stuff the loot in a very large travel bag with their gloved hands. One of the assailants complains: "Are you kidding! We came for this! Someone's going to pay!"[248] He tears up the checks in front of the manager and says, "We came for nothing!" He shoots the telephone and leaves the office.[249]

The bandits don't hesitate to fire toward any customers who inadvertently call attention to themselves. By the time they exit the office with their loot, the Giant has finished emptying the cash registers with his young hostage in tow. The Giant is very calm, scans the store, and leaves with his accomplices when they walk to the exit. In the parking lot, the Giant lets his hostage go. The 12-year-old boy is terrified by the ordeal but physically unscathed. They leave the store with a total of 776,000 BEF (approximately US $21,829). The dead bodies of three unfortunate victims are left behind.

The Killers walk across the parking lot and back up the footpath that leads to their car parked at the pizzeria. They step back into the Golf and take off with the hatchback still open, speeding toward the town of Overijse.

LOOSE ENDS

Just preceding the Braine attack, a dark Opel is seen parking beside the pizzeria where they later parked. A large middle-aged man with greying sideburns is sitting in the driver's seat looking around. He lingers a bit then leaves. His identity is never established.

OVERIJSE DELHAIZE[250]

Along the 18-mile road between Braine and Overijse, another driver notices an agitated man sitting in the backseat of the dark Golf—not realizing these are the now infamous Insane Killers. The backseat passenger gestures warningly for the man to keep away from the Golf. When the driver draws near the same Golf again, he notices that the passenger in the back seat is now wearing a carnival mask. It takes the Insane Killers fifteen minutes to make it to Overijse.

At 8:27 p.m., the Brabant Killers drive the Golf into the strip mall parking lot in front of the Overijse Delhaize supermarket.[251] The heavily armed assailants park at the far end of the strip mall parking lot. They wear the same masks of French politicians as before, as well as dark fishing hats and the long dark military coats that they wore in Braine. The Killers walk very calmly towards the front doors of the Delhaize supermarket.

A 14-year-old boy named Stephane Notte is in the parking riding his bike. When he notices the masked gunmen, he starts screaming. One of the Killers raises his arm and fires his 12-gauge pump action shotgun at the terrified boy. The child crashes down on the pavement, his lifeless body lying there in a pool of blood. Another one of the Killers grabs Luc Bennekens as a hostage. Bennekens is in the parking lot with four other activists putting up political posters for the upcoming elections.

Another customer, Léon Finné, is heading to the mall's magazine store to buy a newspaper. When Finné realizes what's happening, his reflex is to hurry back to his car because he has a fixed car phone inside. A Killer notices Finné and blasts two shotgun rounds, hitting him in his head and lungs. Finné falls on the pavement right next to his car. The murderer then walks up to Finné, who's lying in a growing pool of blood, flips him over with his boot and finishes him off with another shotgun blast.

Two Insane Killers enter the Delhaize supermarket, while the third stops just outside the doors and acts as a lookout.[252] There are approximately 200 customers inside the Delhaize.[253] The two Killers shoot warning shots as they enter and one of them then screams: "Everyone on the ground! The cash or we kill everyone!" The shoppers near the front of the store all hurry to drop down on their stomachs. The Giant then slowly proceeds to the cash registers, saying: "You! Cashiers! Bring the money!" While the cashiers open the cash registers, he sticks a gun to their throats.

One of the cashiers, Rosa Van Kildonck, has a bit of trouble opening her cash register. It seems stuck, but before she can find a solution, she's fatally shot at point-blank range. The Giant steals 590,000 BEF (approximately US $16,620) from the front cash registers. Jean-Pierre Busiau, a customer near the cash registers, is shot and killed for no apparent reason. The assailants then indiscriminately shoot at other clients in the store. Some shots ricochet off full grocery carts, while others strike in the aisles.

The other Killer in the store makes his way to the office where the supermarket's safe is located. There are three employees in the office. The Killer forces the assistant store manager over to open the safe and hand over the contents, but the assistant manager responds that they don't have access to the main safe—just as happened in Braine L'Alleud.[254] This infuriates the Killer, who only calms down when the employee shows him the money keeping policy document.[255] The Killer destroys the phone with gunshots.

The Insane Killers fire more wild rounds in the store as they exit the front entrance with their hostage Bennekens in tow. One Killer reportedly shouts, "OK. That's it, let's go!" As they leave, they notice a customer parking near the Delhaize who seems oblivious to the situation. When the poor customer realizes he has arrived at an attack on the Delhaize, he tries to flee and the Killers shoot at his car. The man is only slightly injured and survives.

The Killers force the hostage Bennekens across the parking lot where, instead of releasing him, they mow him down with a pump-action shotgun. The dead body of Bennekens crashes down to the pavement.[256] The Insane Killers hop back in the Golf and leave the carnage behind them. A man who tries to write down the Golf's plates and is shot at by the Giant, notices that the Giant has forward-pattern baldness.

Worse Than Ever

The Insane Killers are back with a vengeance, appearing more violent than before in this new evolution. This is the Brabant Killers 2.0 and they have made it very obvious that they are back. They make sure that the police know and that the public and the media are in no doubt they have returned. In an October 3rd Report, the Gendarmerie writes: "There is a very strong similarity with the (Brabant facts of 1983)." They list all the obvious similarities, which are identical to earlier attacks and could have been cut and pasted from the 1983 files. The two most obvious similarities on the list are the use of a Volkswagen Golf and the target being two Delhaize supermarkets. Then there's the recurrent appearance of a Giant. They add destruction of the telephones and other characteristics of their attack strategy.

The Insane Killers built up a brand during their First Wave of crimes, one they're now exploiting for recognition. They're just giving more of what the public and authorities come to expect from them. They attack a Delhaize supermarket because that's what gained notoriety for them—when in reality two out of five times they attacked Colruyt supermarkets. But that image of bandits entering a Delhaize supermarket and firing around the store is what stuck in the public's imagination. The fact they now attack not just one, but two, Delhaize stores in the same night is a dead giveaway. The Brabant Killers even pass by and ignore other supermarkets that are situated along the way between the two Delhaize stores—including a Colruyt supermarket. They attack a Delhaize because they need to attack a Delhaize if that's what everyone expects the Insane Killers to do.

It's the same with the dark Golf. People remember the Insane Killers drove a Golf because of the huge manhunt for a Golf that followed the Beersel Delhaize attack—that's even though they had already committed robberies using a Santana, a Saab, an Allegro, a Porsche, and maybe an Audi. At the very most, only two out of the six cars they used for their First Wave attacks are Golfs. And it could even have been only one Golf, as there are indications the Killers wanted the Porsche and not the Golf when they attacked the restaurant Aux Trois Canards in October 1983. But if you look at newspaper stories from 1983 and 1984, the image of the dark Golf is what the media reported and what stuck in the population's psyche. At some point in later 1983, people driving Golfs were being stopped left and right. The Santana and the Saab were forgotten because they were abandoned right after attacks.

The Gendarmerie list includes perpetrators wearing carnival masks as a recurrent characteristic of the Insane Killers, which is inaccurate. But that's what people remember. Why? Since the Killers became a public phenomenon after the Nivelles Colruyt attack in September 1983, they wore masks two out of the three times—namely at the Aux Trois Canards Restaurant in October 1983 and the Beersel Delhaize in October 1983—they attacked before closing the First Wave. How they hide their faces actually changes from one attack to the next. According to Prosecutor Demanet, "there's a tendency for the perpetrators to not put masks but to wear make-up [wrinkles, wigs, moustaches…]."[257] They'll sometimes wear ski masks and they'll sometimes wear no masks. Until their attack at the Nivelles Colruyt in September 1983, they only wore a mask once. Whatever they do, however, they're very careful not to be identified.

More subtle Insane Killers signatures mentioned on the Gendarmerie list are the destruction of the telephones, and the taking of a hostage. It's true that the Killers systematically cut the phone lines during all their First Wave crimes. It was initially something one of the Killers insisted be done. By the time of the Beersel Delhaize attack, the Killers knew authorities were aware of this strategy. Unlike the other First Wave supermarket attacks, the purpose of the Beersel Delhaize attack of October 1983 seems to have been to establish a forensic link among all of their First Wave crimes, so authorities are looking for one instead of two sets of suspects. It was not for the money. One of the props the Killers used to show it was them is the big axe. Instead of bringing ridiculous firepower like they usually do, they carry a big axe to show investigators that they were going to cut the wires. This leaves no doubt that it was the Insane Killers. Now, during this double attack on the Braine and Overijse Delhaize stores, the Brabant Killers opt for the extra firepower instead of the axe to cut the phone lines. In both locations, after ripping out the phone lines, the Killers shoot the telephones as exclamation point.

EXTREME VIOLENCE ESCALATES

The major difference between the First and the Second Wave of crimes is the violence. The report of the unprovoked cold-blooded murder of their victims is true for the Second Wave. However, it doesn't articulate the escalation of violence in the Second Wave. In the First Wave, a more appropriate description is taken from a late 1983 article in *Het Nieuwsblad*, which notes, "a constant and unusually brutal way of operating and killing."[258] The Insane Killers eliminate witnesses, they shoot towards people hindering them and they also finish off people on the ground. They're ultra-violent criminals.

Now in the Second Wave, the Brabant Killers use extreme violence even when there is not even the slightest threat. Their murders seem contrived and they take any opportunity to kill while keeping the semblance of an armed robbery.

It's only now in the Second Wave that they start killing customers—even customers who offer no resistance, like Ghislain Platane in Braine and Jean-Paul Busiau in Overijse. The Killers also murder their first cashier ever in Overijse—Rosa Van Kildonck, who doesn't manage to open her cash register drawer fast enough. They kill their hostage for the first time ever in Overijse—murdering him even though the hostage obeyed every order during their rampage.

Now they even kill customers in the parking lot—both in Braine and Overijse—before they even enter the stores for their robberies. This is a new, perhaps conscious decision by the Brabant Killers. It's almost as if they need to get some kills out of the way. They were particularly fierce in

Overijse, probably because they felt they hadn't killed enough in Braine. During the First Wave, there were always customers in the parking lot and no one had ever been killed. In some of their First Wave attacks, they just pointed guns threateningly at customers in the parking lots. For example, during the Genval Delhaize robbery in February 1983, the Killers only shoot at a car that could have hindered them. The driver is unhurt.

They now go after children, which also seems to be a conscious decision. In Braine, the Giant grabs a 12-year-old boy by the hair in the parking lot as a hostage. Inside, the Giant tells the cashiers he will kill the boy if they don't hurry. In Overijse, a 14-year-old boy, Stephane Notte, is hanging out in the parking lot and is shot and killed when he screams.

PLAY-ACTING AGGRESSION

Then there seems what could only be described as violent play acting. In Braine, when the Killers get to the vault, there seems to be a forced display of anger, like tearing up the checks and shouting: "Are you kidding! We came for this! Someone's going to pay!" or, "We came for nothing!"[259] In Overijse, right after they enter the store, one of the Killers screams: "We'll kill everyone!" Shortly after this, they shoot and kill both a customer and a cashier. They had previously never killed a single customer during a supermarket raid and now the final tally for the night is four customers killed in the parking area, two customers killed inside and one murdered employee.

In the Gendarmerie's list, they mention, "The attitude of the perpetrators: calm, well organized, military." The First Wave and the Second Wave are actually quite different. The three supermarket attacks in early 1983 had more of a classic hold-up feel, only with more violence. Get in, get the money, get out. The only First Wave supermarket attack that unfolded in such a structured way was the Beersel Delhaize attack in October 1983 when each man walked at a distance and supported the other. In Overijse and Braine they also operate methodically, using much more violence.

At both Braine and Overijse, the Insane Killers fire 9mm bullets with an Ingram submachine gun 9X19mm. They never used the Ingram during the First Wave. The ammo used is FN 9mm Parabellum from 1959. They also use shotgun number one (SG-1) in Braine and in Overijse, and they fire shotgun number two (SG-2) in Overijse. During their drive between the two Delhaize locations, they make a detour. It's very weird considering no one knew they were going to Overijse. They go full speed but don't use the fastest way to get there.

There are some other characteristics of the Brabant Killers not mentioned in the October 3rd report, like the fact that they park far away from the front of the store. In Braine they don't even park in the parking lot and in Overijse, they park at the far reaches of the parking lot. Another characteristic is that they attack supermarkets during weekend nights. As for the Giant, they know he will be linked to them because of his unusual size, but perhaps there's no other choice for them than for him to participate. The Giant has forward-pattern baldness, a massive bodybuilder physique, and he walks with a limp. Then there is the use of shotguns. They didn't use shotguns early in the First Wave; they were only used in Temse, Nivelles, and Beersel. However, after the Nivelles Colruyt attack in September 1983, tactical shotgun sales spiked in Belgium. They could be bought without an ID for 15,000 to 30,000 BEF (or about US $425 to $850).

Special Task Force

Following the Braine and Overijse attacks, there's much unrest in the population and Belgian authorities reinforce police patrols outside supermarkets. A new Brabant Killers Task Force is created on October 1st, 1985. The Task Force has weekly meetings to share intelligence gathered about the Insane Killers. They also take safety measures to protect the population. The Task Force is comprised of a couple dozen officers from Nivelles and Brussels.[260] Mons Gendarmerie officer Christian Amory is not from neither location but still ends up on the Task Force.

One of the decisions taken by the new Task Force is to secure the grounds of a predetermined list of about 50 supermarkets during weekends.[261] Local police and the Gendarmerie patrol all the supermarkets in the country with tactical shotguns. Starting on October 21st, all the Delhaize stores situated close to a highway have snipers on the roofs wearing infrared goggles for night vision. Security varies from one supermarket to the next.

The press visits some supermarkets from the Brussels area to assess their security response measures. The Leuven Delhaize had six Gendarmes on the ground, three snipers on the roof, and three security guards at the door. At the Mechelen Delhaize, no security is spotted. The Overijse Delhaize that was just attacked has five officers in the parking lot and two on the roof. At the Brussels Colryut, four officers are in the parking area and one is on the roof, whereas at the Oudeghem Delhaize, there are 16 Gendarmes with special helmets. At the GB Maxi in Oudeghem, there are three city cops near the cash registers who carry machine guns, tactical shotguns, and radios.[262]

WESTLAND NEW POST

In 1989, former Westland New Post members Michel Libert and Eric Lammers claim that they were asked to case large supermarkets like the Delhaize. They claim this was asked of them in 1981 and 1982 when Sûreté agent, the Duck, was still involved with Westland and Latinus. Both men say they would receive anonymous orders and claim they don't know who was giving the orders, but insist they had to follow the directives. They say they were asked to write down details about the floor plans of various stores.

INSIDE INFORMATION

Agent Amory, is very busy during this time period. Not only is he keeping a close eye on the Borains that are from his own district, he's also part of the Insane Killers Special Task Force in another district and also gets the nod to be the Mons Gendarme in charge of obtaining the floor plans for the local Colruyts and Delhaizes. He's also involved in coordinating snipers and protection and even does rounds as a supermarket sniper. It's around this time that Amory says Bouhouche approached him: "Bouhouche phoned me asking me if surveillances and protections were always organized in large department stores."[263] Bouhouche specifically asks Amory about security and surveillance in the Delhaize stores. Bouhouche wants to know how the snipers are positioned on the roofs of the supermarkets. In October, Amory hands over the confidential Task Force security plans for the Delhaize stores to Bouhouche. He never tells anyone.

THE SUSPECTS

The Haemers Gang attacks a postal vehicle in Casteau-Neufvilles on October 1st. The hold-up is a failure and they make no money from it. Haemers ends up high on the list of suspects for the Casteau-Neufvilles robbery. Authorities organize a stakeout of homes of known Haemers Gang members and execute search and seizures. The only notable find is a shotgun, which is tested to see if it might have been used during the Insane Killer attacks. It's negative. No arrests are made for any other hold-up either.

The Bouhouche Gang is not known to have committed a big hit during this time period; however, Bouhouche shows up at a police station on October 11th and gives police a false statement on behalf of his wife. Bouhouche claims that the Volvo registered in his wife's name disappeared. In fact, Bouhouche faked the robbery because he wants to collect the insurance payout. Bouhouche leaves the Volvo in a public parking area near their Woluwe base, which is where he and his gang usually leave their excess cars. The Volvo is on the UCL University campus very close to where they left the Mazda used to attack the Vernaillen family in 1981.

The insurance company cuts a cheque for 125,000 BEF (or approximately US $3,520) on December 27th, 1985 for the stolen car. Authorities will only find the abandoned Volvo in June 1987. It stayed undetected in the lot for two years. The tires have low pressure, the battery is dead and moss is growing under the vehicle. The license plates have been removed.

As for the Baasrode Gang, they hold up a post office in Malderen-Londerzeel on October 3rd and a post office in Luttre on the 8th. On October 21st, they rob the Ternat Post Office facility. Driver Dominique S. stays in their getaway car, parked right in front of the facility's doors. His three accomplices, all wearing ski masks, enter the facility, jump behind the post office counter, and force an employee to open the safe. Big Stereo is the one who dumps the loot in a briefcase. That's when he hears Dominique S. honking. Dominique S. mistakenly believes he sees a police cruiser. Thinking it's a real alert; Big Stereo, Van Esbroek, and their accomplice scramble out. According to Van Esbroek: "When we heard Dominique S.'s honk, we rushed outside. Stereo P. got away with the briefcase, but it wasn't closed and cash was falling out. A pile of 5,000 BEF bills (worth about US $140 each) fell all over the place. It was all over the place. We were swearing on the way back and had only a few bills to show for it."[264] They blew it and forfeited loot that totaled roughly 1 million BEF (approximately US $28,169).

The bungled Ternat robbery uses the typical Baasrode Gang modus operandi. No shots are fired and no one is hurt. According to Prosecutor De Saeger, "During the series of aggression committed by this gang, shots were fired only at two places."[265] The Baasrode Gang members always use a getaway car with a designated driver. They attack post offices, not supermarkets. On November 2nd, the Baasrode Gang steals a BMW 535i in Zaventem. The BMW is the Baasrode Gang's car of choice for all their armed robberies and their break-ins. On November 6th, Big Stereo P. is arrested for charges unrelated to the Baasrode Gang. By the time Big Stereo is released from jail, the gang will no longer exist.

Jean Bultot

Baasrode Gang member, Leopold Van Esbroek, is arrested in a stolen checks resale sting. Jean Bultot, an acquaintance of Van Esbroek, is also arrested. Bultot, the assistant director of the most important correctional facility in the country, is also charged for fencing stolen video equipment to a friend who runs a store.

It's just the latest mess that Bultot has gotten himself into. Bultot hangs out at the Jonathan Bar, a drinking establishment with a seedy reputation. It's where he meets Francis Dossogne, the leader of the Youth Front whose security and detective firm provides bouncers for the bar. Bultot and Dossogne become good friends. They share Far-Right convictions.

When the Youth Front becomes a target of the government crackdown on private militias, Dossogne is sentenced to three months hard time. He serves it in the jail where Bultot serves as assistant director.

When an amnesty is given to all inmates with less than six months to serve, Dossogne is not included because of the political nature of his infraction. Bultot, who has a big mouth and a larger than life personality, puts up a big fuss on Dossogne's behalf to get him the same treatment as everyone else. He succeeds, but in doing so, Bultot crosses the wrong people in the government. When he applies for jail director positions, he's refused everywhere. Strike one.

Bultot is an active competitive shooter. He makes headlines as the shooting jail director accompanied whit a picture of him firing a gun. Strike two.

Bultot falls into debt and does small favors for some ex-cons. This is when he gets mixed up in the stolen checks resale sting with Van Esbroek. Bultot reacts by sending an open letter to the media claiming that he's the victim of a witch hunt by Justice Minister, Jean Gol. Strike three.

Bultot has succeeded in cultivating a list of powerful enemies in and out of the government. Every agency in the country ends up following him, which is a lose-lose situation for him and for the Baasrode Gang.

Mendez's Suspect

Juan Mendez always stays abreast of the latest news regarding the police investigation into the theft of his arms collection. He believes the police investigation is not progressing fast enough and starts to do his own personal investigation. He visits gun shops and nightclubs asking about arms sales. He puts the message out that he's even ready to buy back his collection at cost from the thieves.

Mendez is shocked when he takes a glance at Bouhouche's gun dealer registry. He notices ammo that he believes could have only come from the robbery of his collection. Mendez keeps quiet but now considers Bouhouche his number one suspect. According to Mendez's brother: "His so-called friend had declared a series of rare ammo, that he held in the same quantities that had been stolen at my brother's."[266] Mendez feels he needs more tangible evidence to prove Bouhouche is involved.

Mendez remembers that Bouhouche is one of the rare people who actually knew the exact date when the armored door was being installed to secure his arms collection. Not only that, but Mendez also remembers an eerie conversation he and his wife had with Bouhouche when Bouhouche said if ever he wanted to break into the Mendez home he could easily push in the bottom of the kitchen door.

By November 1985, Mendez has told friends and acquaintances that he now knows who's responsible for the robbery and says he's about to get his arms collection back soon.

Elections

The October 13th national elections are fast approaching, and given the Braine and Overijse attacks, authorities are prepared with security contingency plans. Their fears of public terror attacks are realized when the CCC blows up the firm Sibelgaz's building on October 8th, shattering 400 windows. On October 12th, the day before the elections, another CCC bomb wipes out the first floor of the Fabrimetal building. The government increases security and on Election Day there are 30,000 cops on patrol to supervise voting.

Early in the election campaign, the major political issue was whether to block NATO from deploying nuclear missiles in Belgium. The installation of 16 cruise missiles in the country brings lots of push back and as many as 150,000 peace protesters take to the streets. Public sentiment seems to embrace feelings of peace and an anti-nuclear stance. Popular favor seems so supportive of these opinions that it is almost a foregone conclusion that Left-Wing political parties will form the new government.

That is until the violence and insecurity caused by the Brabant Killers and the CCC progressively overshadow the issue of nuclearization. The parties on the Right make major headway on a law and order political platform.[267] Opinion polls take a sudden marked Right-turn and when the ballots are counted, it's a huge victory for the Right. The installation of nuclear missiles in Belgium will proceed. A sure thing turns into an absolute rout for the Left. Cynics assert that the violence was just a big manipulation to force the election of a Right-Wing government and to ensure the installation of the nuclear missiles. Did the Belgium government, NATO, or the US incite the violence to sway the vote of the people?

Because Belgium is a proportional representative democracy, not everything is decided on Election Day. It is the day when ballots cast determine where representatives are elected across the country. There are many representatives of Left and Right-Wing parties who are elected. The Belgium system makes it almost impossible for one party to govern as a majority. After the election, party officials negotiate coalitions with other parties to gain a majority. The majority then picks the Prime Minister and the government. This process can take weeks and even months. There's a lot of popular and media pressure for parties to come to an agreement quickly to take the country out of limbo. The parties negotiate by agreeing on a joint political program. An important negotiation issue at this time is determining just what kind of

Right-Wing government could take power in Belgium. How far will it go in law and order measures? How much money will go to security forces? After the first couple of weeks of deliberations, there's still no decision about the Prime Minister and government.

THE SUSPECTS

November brings the death knell of the original Baasrode Gang. Big Stereo is in jail on unrelated charges. Johnny De Staerke had a major disagreement with other Gang members and urinated on their possessions. So the two remaining members scramble to find new partners for various hits. Because Dominique S. is first and foremost a cigarette thief, they concentrate on break-ins instead of hold-ups.

On November 1st, the Bouhouche Gang also becomes active and steals a Renault 25 GTX from a car-leasing firm. They have a key when they steal the car. The investigation determines that a reserve set of keys was kept at Renault headquarters in Ixelles. An employee used this reserve key so journalists could test drive the car. There is evidence this employee had recently interacted with a Bouhouche Gang associate and the key was likely taken then. The Bouhouche Gang members, of course, use the stolen Renault for their criminal activities.

November also becomes a major turning point in the Haemers Gang's history. They are planning a major armed robbery of a postal truck. After their last such robbery, authorities beefed up security again, replacing regular postal trucks with armored trucks, as well as ensuring each postal truck has a police escort. To pull this crime off they now need to obtain an explosive charge that would only blow up the doors of the armored truck. To accomplish this, they contact underworld explosives expert Jean-Claude D.

The Haemers Gang supplies the specifications for the armored truck to Jean-Claude D. According to Haemers: "We had calculated the charge, we searched to find out what kind of armor the truck had. We had read that between the double walls of the truck, there was sand."

Using the specs provided, Jean-Claude D. prepares the right explosive device to blow up the back door with precision.

On November 4th, at 9:00 a.m., the Haemers Gang members drive a BMW up to the postal truck just as it stops in the town of Verviers. After firing UZI rounds on the accompanying Gendarmerie van, three gangsters wearing ski masks step out of the BMW and force the Gendarme out of his van. They tie him up to a traffic sign with his own shackles and then concentrate on breaking into the armored truck. Three postal workers are barricaded inside the truck.

The Haemers Gang members fix one-and-a-half kilos of TNT to the back door of the armored truck. After Philippe L. and Haemers take cover, driver Thierry S. activates a remote control to detonate the explosives attached to the door. The explosion is massive and much bigger than anticipated. The whole back of the truck is pulverized. Two postal employees inside, Henriette Genet and Yves Lambiet, are killed on the spot. The third employee, driver Jean-François Pirlot is also seriously wounded. The Gang made a serious mistake; they believed the truck's armored walls were lined with sand, but it was in fact frigolite. They used the wrong explosive charge.

The criminals immediately realize the extent of the carnage, but somehow still finish the job despite the dead postal workers. Haemers is the one who walks into the truck and removes the bags with a total payout of 7,249,000 BEF (approximately US $204,200). When they return to the Gang's safe house, they realize how badly they messed up. In addition to brutally murdering two postal employees, the UZI they fired is linked to three of their other robberies.

Ultimately, the Verviers hit is the beginning of the end of the Haemers Gang's current composition. Driver Thierry S., who pressed the button to detonate the explosives, feels extreme guilt and drops into a deep depression. Haemers and Philippe L. feel they have no choice but to kick him out of the Gang. A few months later, Thierry S. dies by suicide under suspicious circumstances.

CHAPTER 22

DELHAIZE SUPERMARKET IN AALST
(NOVEMBER 9, 1985)

O N THE AFTERNOON OF NOVEMBER 9TH, 1985, SOME REVELERS IN Houssière Forest[268] find in the remnants of a small fire several wads of partially burnt checks. They were stolen from the twin Braine and Overijse raids—an unmistakable sign that the fire in this large forest south of Brussels was started by the Brabant Insane Killers.[269]

A few minutes before the items are discovered, a white Mercedes with male passengers drives slowly by a group of bystanders in the vicinity of the discovery. In the early evening of the same day, a white Mercedes and a Golf are seen not far from the burned-out fire.[270]

There are also restaurant tickets, cigarette butts, and a carnival mask thrown into the fire, as well as other papers. Handwriting on the papers is legible, with about 20 words that include "stomach, knee, pain center, etc." Some of the items are found in a Jokire bag, which is a shop in Ixelles. All of this reinforces the connection to the Insane Killers, who have established ties to that part of Brussels.

Video remote controls are also recovered at the scene. The brands are Bang & Olufsen, Grundig, Philips, Korting, and Panasonic. There's also an old train ticket for a trip from Brussels to the North Sea Coast of Belgium and a picture of blond hair.A

The Most Hated Man in Belgium

There have been various theories related to this discovery. The simplest answer is that the Insane Killers just tried to burn stuff they no longer needed. But investigators connect some of the discoveries to assistant prison director Jean Bultot, which of course, creates alternative theories. One of these theories is that the Killers planted the evidence to frame the most hated man in Belgium, Bultot.

What does Bultot have to do with any of this? Bultot was arrested with Van Esbroek of the Baasrode Gang in a stolen check sting in early 1985. Given it was for dealing in stolen checks, perhaps he ended up with the Braine and Overijse checks. The burned papers could be from personal notes from a speech given by Jean Bultot in 1984 to the practical shooting and law enforcement community. The notes appear to be written in his secretary's handwriting, but a handwriting expert later determined it wasn't her writing.

Bultot was also accused of fencing video equipment, which would explain the video remote controls. The problem is that the remote controls were from television sets and Bultot didn't steal those. There's an old train ticket for a trip from Brussels to the North Sea Coast of Belgium and Bultot has a girlfriend in Northern Belgium. There's also a picture of blond hair and Bultot has a son with blond hair.

What is more puzzling is how Bultot could be involved in any of this. Remember that Bultot is one of the most wanted men—and most hated. Just as a start, he has two Sûreté paid informants dedicated to spying on his every move.[271] One Sûreté agent infiltrated Bultot's everyday personal life, IRC Antoine D. Like Bultot, Antoine D. is a gun enthusiast and into practical shooting. Bultot is also being followed by other agencies. Which begs the question, how could Bultot have participated in the Insane Killer attacks without detection?

If we look carefully at the items, none of them can definitively be linked to Bultot. They are very circumstantial. Could these items have been mistakenly associated with him? There used to be a fourth theory, that Jean Bultot was actually the one who put the items there. No one seems to seriously believe this anymore.

Prequel-Flanders

That same November 9th, over one hundred miles north of Houssière Forest, the inhabitants of the Dutch-speaking town of Aalst are enjoying Sint-Maartens, the biggest feast day of the year with a big parade in the town's center. The inspiration for North America's Santa Claus, Sint-Nicolas (which is Dutch for Saint Nicholas), is the central attraction of the float. He's accompanied by his trusted sidekick, Zwarte Pete, who has black skin and is a somewhat controversial figure today. Depending on who you ask, Zwarte Pete is either covered in soot after sliding down a chimney or a North African Moor. The children walk the streets with lanterns and sing as they receive pastries and other treats.

In the Aalst central square, it's an unusually warm day. The restaurants and bars have even set tables and chairs out on outdoor terraces. Later that evening, the town is bustling with people partying in the bars and walking the streets. Shoppers still buy their groceries from the local Delhaize supermarket, despite being slightly paranoid about the Insane Killer attacks. However, Aalst is much further north than where the other attacks took place.

Despite the fact the Aalst Delhaize is outside of the high protection area mandated by the Brabant Killers Task Force, the Gendarmerie has implemented some extra security measures. A Gendarmerie team carrying UZI submachine guns and bulletproof vests are supposed to be there until 8:00 p.m. when they are replaced by the local town police to provide reinforced security for the rest of the night.

This supermarket is built differently than any of the other Delhaize stores in Belgium. Notably, it has two entrances. There's an entrance that can be accessed from the sidewalk on the store's street side and a parking lot entrance behind the store. The parking lot is situated at the end of a long car alleyway, which is accessible from a side street. Aside from access to the Delhaize store's back door, the parking lot is a dead end that backs onto a large forest. There's only a grass walking path to cross through the forest.

AALST DELHAIZE[272]

Shortly before 7:30 p.m., the Gendarmerie team in the Aalst Delhaize store unexpectedly ends its patrol and exits the Delhaize's back parking lot. This leaves a half-hour gap in the supermarket's protection until officers from the town police show up at 8:00 p.m.

As soon as the Gendarmes leave in their cruiser, the Insane Killers drive a dark Golf GTI to enter the long alleyway that leads to the back parking lot of the Aalst Delhaize. The alleyway is lined by the back of neighboring stores.

The Brabant Killers park at the far end of the Delhaize parking lot, near the forest and close to the back of a hardware store. At 7:33 p.m., the assailants walk towards the Delhaize while some shoppers are stowing bags of groceries in the trunks of their vehicles. The Killers wear long trench coats and are armed with tactical shotguns and a submachine gun. The Giant wears makeup to darken his face and an afro wig. The two others wear ski masks.

Members of the Van de Steen family have just exited the store's back door. They push their shopping carts filled with groceries into the parking lot. Parents, Gilbert and Marie-Thérèse are heading to their car with their daughter Rebecca, 14, and their son David, 9, when they hear a noise right beside them. When Rebecca suddenly comes face to face with armed attackers, she panics and hides behind her father. She screams: "Don't shoot, that's my dad!"ᴬ One of the Insane Killers guns down the father and daughter and both die on the spot. The Killers then turn toward the mother and shoot her dead. The terrified nine-year-old son, David, runs back into the store as bullets fly around him and shatter a store window. One of the bullets hits a shopper, George De Smet, right in the head. De Smet collapses in front of the door and David has to jump over him to try to find cover.[273]

Two gunmen enter the store's back entrance, walking about ten feet apart. The guy in the back is covering the guy in front of him. The third assailant remains in the parking lot, where he goes on the hunt for other victims as his two accomplices rob the store. Donald Roelandt drives away from the store's parking lot with his 14-year-old son Philip in the back seat. The son dives to the floor just in time as a bullet shatters the car's back window and grazes the father. Roelandt manages to get away despite bleeding from his head wound.

Jan Pasterman is waiting in his car while his kids are shopping in the Delhaize. The Insane Killer walks towards Pasterman, deftly shooting and killing him with five bullets to the head. At the far end of the parking lot, Dirk Nejs is in his BMW with his eight-year-old daugther Elsie Nejs. They are waiting while his wife shops in the supermarket when the Killer walks up to them, shoots and kills Elsie and blows Dirk's head off.[274]

Inside the Delhaize, customers and cashiers have heard the commotion and gunfire from the parking lot. Some run and look for cover, some hide behind the shelves, and others try to leave by the door at the front of the store. When the two Insane Killers enter the automatic doors at the back of the store, the Giant immediately shoots two women who are standing next to each other. This creates more pandemonium in the store.

One Killer stays at the cash registers while the Giant heads straight to the offices. The attacker at the cash registers orders the customers to get down on the floor while he steals alcohol and cigarettes, putting everything in a bag with a postal service logo. When a cashier doesn't hand over money quickly enough for his liking, he doesn't hesitate to use a pump-action shotgun. Another victim murdered in cold blood.

The Giant heads towards the back office. Under his trench coat, the Giant wears a khaki pullover, covered by a blue ski vest that has no collar. He also wears dark pants with front leg pockets and has a belt carrying another pistol and grenades, as well as two knives tied around his neck.

Once at the offices, he finds the assistant manager and orders him in French to open the store safe. The Giant then screams in Dutch, "The money, quick!" The assistant manager empties the contents in the Giant's bag. The Giant also grabs a metal box full of small change before taking the assistant manager hostage and leading him back to the cash registers.

As the Giant returns, a customer dives to shield his daughter and screams, "Get down!" to his wife. The Giant brutally kicks her, but she plays dead. The Giant shoots her in the left shoulder and grabs her by the neck. She screams, "Let me go!"A The assistant manager also says, "Let her go."B The Giant says in Dutch, "Get to the side then."[275] At some point, the assistant manager notices the Giant is distracted and runs away. The Killer chases and shoots at him, but the assistant manager is successful in his escape. One of the Killers shoots and injures a boy who is lying on the ground and makes the mistake of getting noticed by looking up at him. Two other children near the exits are also targets. They both get injured; one is shot in the legs and the other is injured by glass debris.[276]

Marie-Jeanne Mulder is lying on the ground near the glass door of the exit. When the two Insane Killers are leaving by the back door, Mulder makes a movement that opens and closes the automatic doors. This attracts the attention of one of the Insane Killers. She tries to flee on all fours, but he puts his gun to the crack of the doors and shoots her in the throat, killing her on the spot. Her blood seeps all over her ten-year-old nephew Andy Mulder and his six-year-old brother.

The Insane Killers walk away from the store very calmly a few feet apart from each other. The first one carries bags, while the second carries the metal box with the small change. As they exit the store, town police officers arrive at the corner of the street and the alleyway and notice the Killers. Bullets fly everywhere, hitting a metal door, the walls, and the Delhaize sign. The third Killer covers his two accomplices as they cross the parking lot, which is littered with spent casings and shells.

The Insane Killers place the loot in the stolen Golf. They make away with 490,000 BEF in cash (about US $13,803) and 239,000 BEF in checks (about US $6,732) in a white plastic bag that is labeled, "for fresh or frozen vegetables" in blue lettering. The Giant leaves his dark safari hat in the parking lot.

The Brabant Killers wait in the Golf for a couple of minutes with the hatchback still open. The officers at the other end of the alleyway—seemingly the only exit to the road for the Killers—are on foot. Those officers literally stand between the Killers and their escape route. The Killers start to drive forward with the hatchback open, then suddenly switch into reverse. The car speeds up and one of the Killers fires at police from the open hatchback. As the officers move out of the way of fire, the Golf turns onto the street. One police officer shoots a couple of times towards the Golf, but it doesn't stop the Killers. A police van and a Renault R4 arrive and try to give chase, but the Killers are already far ahead and they can't make up the delay. The Golf speeds away at 150 miles an hour, sailing through red lights.

Signature Moves of the Insane Killers

Just as with the attacks in Braine and Overijse, it's clear the Brabant Insane Killers want the public to know they are back in action. They use a Volkswagen Golf and they target a Delhaize supermarket. There's the Giant terrorizing the people shopping and they sever the phone lines and take a hostage. They park far away from the store's doors and attack at night during the weekend.

This time the Giant hides his forward-pattern baldness with an Afro wig and wears makeup to darken his face. He still walks with a limp and never moves quickly, as if he has trouble hurrying up. He is well armed and threatening toward onlookers. His two accomplices wear ski masks with holes only for their eyes and mouths.

Like their other Second Wave attacks, each man covers the one in front. Every movement is done according to a predetermined pattern and each Killer has a specific role to play. While two of them enter the store's back door, walking at a distance of a few feet apart, the third stays outside to cover them. Once they're finished with the hold-up, they walk away from the store very calmly while the third man covers as they cross the parking lot.

Similar to Overijse and Braine—and unlike the First Wave attacks—they use extreme violence without much provocation. They go even further this time and kill more people in the parking lot before the hold-up. They make many victims, including nearly the whole Van de Steen family and George De Smet in the doorway. The third Killer amuses himself outside by hunting more innocent victims in the farther reaches of the parking lot, like Dirk Nijs and his eight-year-old daughter Elsie. Inside, the Killers shoot and kill victims, even those not offering any resistance like the two women taking cover or the slow-moving cashier.

Their violence is chilling and ruthless. The Giant kicks a woman who is lying on the floor and indiscriminately fires at other customers. The Killers even pause to coldly execute a woman who tries to run away, crawling on all fours, and leave her to bleed out all over the two young boys who were with her.

Perhaps most alarming, the Killers specifically target children during this attack in Aalst. Again, this is a conscious decision, but this violence has escalated and there are more juvenile victims. Apparently, their tally in Braine and Overijse was not enough. The Giant grins at nine-year-old David and shoots him in the groin. The other Killer murders eight-year-old Elsie without a second thought. The other youthful victims include 14-year-old Rebecca shot as she cowered behind her father, the ten-year-old boy shot on the ground and the two children shot near the exit.

THE ESCAPE

The Brabant Killers use the same two 12-gauge pump-action shotguns used in Braine and Overijse (SG-1) and (SG-2) with Legia ammunition. They also use the same Ingram Machine Pistol 9X19mm. The ammunition for that is reloaded 9mm Gevelot SFM from 1978. It's clear they want to terrorize the population, but they're not trying to kill as many people as possible. Otherwise, they could have used automatic and semi-automatic weapons with large capacity magazines and fired non-stop on everyone to maximize the number of victims.

At a public inquiry, expert Jan Cappelle notes that: "The attack lasted 13 minutes, while a 'normal' hold-up lasts only three to four minutes."[277] The Delhaize had already removed most of the day's income. The Killers just took a fraction of the day's cash. Unlike their other Delhaize raids, the Killers steal alcohol and cigarettes and put everything in a bag that has a postal service logo. In the parking lot the Giant leaves behind a dark safari hat and it is the same make as one left behind in the Saab after the First Wave attacks. It suggests the hat was left behind deliberately.

Unlike their other targets, this Delhaize supermarket had only one parking exit out an alleyway. If police blocked the exit they were done for because the only other way out is through the forest. Observers are split into two camps as to the viability of an alternative means of escape. According to Jan Cappelle: "The criminals chose to take the entrance that had only one way out; as if they wanted to trap themselves."[278] As for journalist Rene De Witte, he doesn't believe the Brabant Killers were caught in a trap. "They could go through the back, run 200 to 300 yards (on a forest path) along Osbroekpark, and hop in a getaway car."[279]

According to Jan Cappelle: "After the attack, the killers deliberately waited five minutes for the police's arrival and then plowed through the roadblock."[280] This is corroborated by journalist Walter De Bock, who says: "The parking only has one exit, and the evacuation of this trap happened in two phases: the killers first waited three or four minutes in their car and then went on offense by destroying the police's emergency blockade."[281]

The only police officer who really fired at the Killers was seriously outgunned. According to prosecutor De Saeger: "The range of his weapon was less than the distance of 30 to 40 yards between him and the gangsters."[282]

The Aalst Delhaize attack is the last known supermarket attack by the Brabant Insane Killers. There's no consensus why they stopped.

Suspicious Events

According to Prosecutor De Saeger, the "Aalst attack had been well prepared. The layout of the premises and the getaway route had been studied beforehand."[283] This brings us to all the suspicious activities in and around the Delhaize before the attack: It's the investigators' job to separate the wheat from the chaff.

A couple of weeks before the brutal robbery of the Aalst Delhaize store, children playing along a forest path behind the supermarket stumbled on a bag. Inside this bag, they find a tactical shotgun, two revolvers with cartridges, and several ski masks. The arms contained reloaded ammunition. There is no ballistic evidence to link the three weapons and other crimes. The reloaded ammunition and the style of weapons suggest they could belong to the Brabant Killers. They might have hidden them there in the case they were forced to retreat through the forest.

On the evening of Friday, October 31st, a couple jogging around a track near the supermarket notice a very tall man acting suspiciously. He's walking up and down the dead-end street on the side of the forest. The street separates the track and field park with the forest leading to the back of the Delhaize supermarket. A witness described the guy in the street as: "A bear of a man."[284] Like the Giant, he has noticeable forward-pattern baldness. He wore a dark leather vest and boots and appeared to be measuring distances and casing the area.

A light-colored Ford Taunus shows up on that street. The driver has "more of a southern (Italian) appearance. Black hair and a thick moustache."[285] The driver stops and talks with the big man before he disappears into the brush. A third older-looking man with a sharp face comes out of a forest path that connects to the back parking lot of the Aalst Delhaize, which alarms the joggers. The witness confronts the older man by asking something along the line of: "Can I help you?"[286] in Dutch. The man doesn't answer; he just turns around and leaves. When the couple drives away, the three men are all back near the Taunus.

The joggers feel what they saw is so suspicious that they go directly to the police station. When they tell the officer in charge what happened, he immediately contacts motorcycle officers who are near the street. The officers radio back that they indeed see the Taunus and the three men. But before they can do anything the Taunus just drives away. Police don't even write down the plate.

At 9:00 a.m. on the day of the Aalst attack, some Delhaize shoppers notice two suspicious-looking people walking around. At noon, a suspicious Mercedes is seen near the doors. Also at noon, near Brussels, the Gendarmerie is alerted that people are shooting on an abandoned property in the Sint-Stevens-Woluwe area. The police have time to see two cars drive away, a light Ford Taunus and a white Ford Escort with yellow stripes, and determine the suspects were firing 12-gauge Legia and .22 caliber ammo.[287] At 4:00 p.m., a suspicious-looking Mercedes and Audi are seen on Parkland Avenue in front of the Aalst Delhaize. At 6:45 p.m., a Mercedes is seen in the back parking lot.

In the early evening, the local radio station Radio Amigo receives a song request. The caller says it has to be played at 7:15 p.m. sharp or else it's too late. The caller says it's from the Bende van Nijvel (the Dutch name for the Insane Killers) for the Bende van Hoftstade.[288] Hoftstade could be the northern hamlet part of the town of Aalst or Brussels. At 7:15 p.m., in a pub, witnesses see one very large guy with a smaller man. They both speak French which is unusual in this local pub in the middle of Dutch-speaking country.[289] At 7:15 p.m. in Groot-Bijgaarden, a town along the highway between Brussels and Aalst, a suspicious Golf is seen at a Texaco station.[290] At the same Texaco, what looks like a rifle falls out of someone's trench coat to the ground. The suspect picks it up and leaves. At 7:20 p.m., a Mercedes and Golf are seen driving on the highway between Brussels and Aalst near the town of Ternate.

RONQUIÈRES

On the night of November 10th, 1985, two cars back up to the shore of the Brussels-Charleroi canal in the town of Ronquières. It's within walking distance from Houssière Forest. A couple of men step out of the cars, walk to the canal's edge and look around. The name, "Daniel" is heard.[291]

One vehicle is a dark Golf and the other is bigger and light colored; both vehicles have their lights turned off. The men change license plates for each car.[292] A man is seen right along the shore and a bag is seen floating on the water not far from him. A weapons encyclopedia and some gun magazines are later found on shore. The items are suspected of having belonged to the Brabant Insane Killers.

WITNESS STATEMENTS

Two police witness statements are drawn up by the local Soignies Gendarmerie on the incident. The first statement is from the owner of a nearby snack bar, who visited the station after the incident because he's concerned about the Aalst attack. The snack bar owner says that at 12:20 a.m., he was woken up by a running motor and noticed a dark Golf GTI and "two men in military jackets."

The second witness statement is from a witness that officers stumble across when they go to the site to investigate the report from the first witness. This new witness declares that: "It's about 12:20 a.m. to 12:30 a.m....I hear the sound of the closing door of a car. I see two cars. They are stopped and have the lights off. Three people are walking around. One person is on the edge of the water near the cement steps. Shortly thereafter I see in the light a dark bag floating, the size of a garbage bag."[293] The Golf and the light-colored car match the car sightings in Houssière Forest right before the small fire and later in the early evening the day of the Aalst raid. Police believe the second car is a Renault 20 or 30 or a Passat.[294]

Based on these two witness statements, investigators send divers into the water to see if they can find what the suspects have thrown. They don't find anything.

HOUSSIÈRE FORREST

On November 11th, 1985, the charred remains of the Golf GTI stolen at Erps Kwerps are found in Houssière Forrest.[295] The car is torched less than an hour after suspects were seen switching license plates in nearby Ronquières. The backseat and back frame of the Golf are removed.[296] Some used 12-gauge casings are found inside.

GOLFS

After switching their license plates in Ronquières, the Brabant Killers likely drove the stolen Golf directly to the spot and torched it. They left in the light-colored Renault. Some believe the Golf GTI set on fire at Erps Kwerps was not the actual car used in Aalst. They think the Insane Killers would have used a different Golf.

RADIO SCANNERS

The Delhaize Aalst attack strongly suggests the Insane Killers were using radio scanners. Around 7:30 p.m., the Gendarmerie patrol leaves the back parking lot of the supermarket. As soon as the Gendarmerie drives away, the Insane Killers drive the dark Golf GTI from the side street onto the long alleyway leading to the supermarket. This timing suggests the Killers were tipped off by a colleague on site, that they were listening to police frequencies or they just have dumb luck.

After the Aalst attack, the Brabant Killers leave the Delhaize at 7:49 p.m. and turn left, going due south on country highway N405 toward the town of Ninove. Two police vehicles are in pursuit. When the Killers arrive at the first major crossroad, they can either go right towards the new N45 highway or left, which would keep them on the old N405. The new four-lane N45 had only been open to drivers for a very short time. The Killers decide to go left and stay on the old N405 to get to Ninove.

According to Gendarme Luc Boeve, teams are transmitting their new positions: "Meanwhile our radio kept rattling. Team going here, team going there." At 7:50 p.m., the Ninove Gendarmerie is warned over the airwaves that the Insane Killers are speeding toward them in the Golf on the old N405. The Ninove Gendarmerie immediately set up a roadblock along the old N405.

Shortly after the announcement is made over the airwaves, a witness notices a Golf driving with its lights off, speeding at 125 miles an hour. The Golf is making a huge detour back northwest, that takes the Killers all the way back near the major crossroad they had just passed by a few moments ago. Once there, they turn onto the new N45.

In effect, the Killers take the old N405 and as soon as the N405 roadblock is mentioned over the airwaves, they make a huge detour. The Ninove Gendarmerie set up a barricade on the old N405 at about 7:55 p.m. When the Insane Killers double-back, they cross Ninove through the new N45 and speed behind the Ninove Gendarmerie and their roadblock.

For the second time that night, they seem to know the next move of the Gendarmerie. This time it had to have been with a scanner instead of dumb luck. The use of scanners by criminals was a concern of police in the eighties. For example, the Whitey Bulger Gang would listen to police frequencies. Anyone could buy a scanner from a store like Radio Shack and listen to the police. Everything was analog, nothing was coded.

STEREOS REMOVED

There are other indications that the Insane Killers used scanners to run circles around police. Notably, all of the cars abandoned by the Killers had their car stereo removed. Some had the antennas removed.

During the Braine and Overijse double attack, the Gendarmerie put up a roadblock on the N27, the main highway between Nivelles and Brussels. Twenty minutes later, someone at the Gendarmerie calls over orders to take the roadblock down and move it to some small side road. Then a few minutes pass before they take that roadblock down and put it back up on the N27 again. The Brabant Killers slip through, avoiding the roadblock.

These miraculous escapes also happen during the First Wave. During the Wavre attack in September 1982, as soon as the information goes over the airwaves that they're chasing a car with French plates and give the license plate number, the Killers stop, hide, and replace the French plates with Belgian plates that have a different number. After their shootout outside the car in Hoeillart, they take the Groenendael Bridge, which was the only road that was not blocked by police.[297] Later that day, Brussels authorities had put out a general alarm all over the region. However, they called off the alert when they believed suspects in a Jaguar had been detained and all the roadblocks were taken down. The Killers dumped their car on the edge of Brussels and lit it on fire. They had to be pretty sure that the coast was clear to take such a risk.

After leaving the Nivelles Colruyt in September 1983, the Insane Killers take Nivelles Road in Braine-l'Alleud. They're surprised by a police car turning out from Alphonse Allard Avenue. The police car, which was on its way to take part in a roadblock with the Waterloo police, had just been advised of a fleeing Mercedes. No mention is ever made of a Saab. They spot the Mercedes followed by the Saab and give chase.

This is when the Killers stop and ambush the police who are pursuing them. The traditional conclusion is that they might have seen the light of the police far in the distance, so they stopped in an area called the "Diable Amoureux." But it's more complicated than that because the Killers made at least three different decisions. First, they stopped, avoiding the upcoming roadblock. Then they decided to shoot at the oncoming, unmarked car. They didn't do this in Aalst when they were chased by another car. However, the unmarked car in Nivelles was a police car while the one in Aalst was not. Right after they blast the police car, the Killers hold their fire while the next car passes by. That car was white with an orange band. It was not a police car, but it sure looked like one and yet the Killers did not fire at it.

The Killers flee and head toward Nivelles. What is significant is that they abandon the Mercedes, even though it's not damaged and all of their loot is inside. The Mercedes is the only car that had been mentioned over the airwaves before the ambush. The three men all leave in the Saab, which cannot be a coincidence. The Killers always seem to know what the police are thinking and doing.

ROBBERY

Robbery is the simplest motive to explain every single one of the attacks perpetrated by the Insane Killers—even for their more violent Second Wave attacks. Some strongly advocate that the end goal of the Killers was only the cash or valuables they could steal. The purpose of the Braine, Overijse, and Aalst attacks was the money in the coffers. Nothing else. The Insane Killers just happened to kill more people in the process than usual armed robbers.

During a public inquiry, Professor Kellens described the argument in this way: "the methods used in Belgium by the said offenders are simple, even simplistic and tend to gratuitous brutality. This phenomenon is not new and is found in the context of an evolution of crime towards a greater violence." He adds that "it is possible that these criminals, stuck in the spiral of violence, were only simple outlaws; using simple and stupid methods but temporarily effective, the extreme brutality of their operations paralyzing classic police work."[298]

Some of the First Wave attacks lend credence to the argument that the only motive for the Insane Killers was robbery. For example, the three supermarket hold-ups in early 1983 (in Uccle, Halle, and Genval) certainly seemed to be about money. They're comparable to any ultra-violent robberies anywhere: The loot is decent. Shots are fired in panic. Some people are injured. One employee is dead.

The goal of the robberies of the French grocery store in Maubeuge in August 1982 and the Het Kasteel Inn Restaurant in December 1982 appeared to be stealing alcohol. The amounts stolen are also comparable to similar break-ins. The Brabant Killers were surprised twice. It is possible they did many similar break-ins without any complications. A typical break-in barely gets noticed in the press.

Some attacks, for example, the Gang stealing the tools of their trade, are easy to explain. To obtain getaway vehicles, they committed the Aux Trois Canards Restaurant carjacking in October 1983. The goal of both the Wavre Gun Shop attack in September 1982 and the shoplifting of a hunting rifle in Dinant in April 1983 was to get guns. The Temse attack in September 1982 was how the Gang procured flak jackets. While gangsters typically get their guns on the black market, either the Killers had a tinge of amateurism or were very paranoid about getting caught.

The extreme violence does not invalidate the argument that the motive for the attacks was robbery. It can be explained by having one or more psychopaths in the Gang—exemplified by the Mons taxi driver murder. The Killers expected more inside his wallet, but there was little. He was easy prey and one of the psychopaths killed him.

It is more difficult, however, to explain the attacks at the Nivelles Colruyt in September 1983 and the Anderlues jewellery store in December 1983 by robbery alone. We need to accept that three separate criminals completely misjudged the value of items before going on murderous rampages. In Nivelles, instead of targeting typical robbery fare like alcohol and cigarettes, the Killers robbed cooking oil and chocolates. In Anderlues, instead of stealing gold or diamonds, they grabbed cheap alarm clocks and trinkets that are larger and less portable.

HAEMERS GANG

Several Gangs fall in the crosshairs of investigators as suspects involved in the three Second Wave supermarket attacks. Early on, the authorities took a very close look at the Haemers Gang. In 1989, police uncovered items the Haemers Gang members kept in storage at the Appolo Rental Complex. There are lots of weapons, including four revolvers, four submachine guns, and four pistols, as well as a Fal 7.62 rifle and an FN carbine.

Some of the weapons originated from the Mendez robbery, which brought extra heat on the Gang.

The investigation determined that members of the Haemers Gang had purchased the Mendez weapons from a gun dealer who claims he purchased them in September or October 1985 from Bouhouche. A bar manager acted as the middleman between the gun dealer and the Haemers Gang.

Ammunition similar to the type used by the Insane Killers is also found in the storage box, as well as carnival masks very much like the masks used by the Killers in their Overijse and Braine l'Alleud double attack of September 1985. However, in their criminal career, the Haemers Gang members never used carnival masks.[299] If the Gang ever had a Giant, it would have been Haemers himself.

BAASRODE GANG

The Baasrode Gang was another target of the investigation for years. The Golf used during the Second Wave was stolen in Erps Kwerps in September 1985. Gang member Dominic S. has been suspected of stealing a car at the same dealership using the same technique as the Insane killers did. Dominique S. has always denied this. The alleged carjacking happened in the late seventies.[300]

If the Baasrode Gang ever had a Giant, it's Big Stereo. He was linked for a time to both the Braine and Overijse attacks. He was put in a photo line-up in jail and some witnesses believed he was the Giant. Nevertheless, Big Stereo couldn't have been in Aalst as he was in jail. However, there are some who believe that the Aalst attack was designed just to give Big Stereo an alibi.

There are witnesses who notice someone matching Johnny De Staerke's description in Aalst. But De Staerke was only part of the Baasrode Gang for the Braine and Overijse attacks. Shortly after the Overijse hit, is when De Staerke threw a tantrum, went to the garage rented by the Baasrode Gang, and urinated on their stuff before leaving the Gang for good.[301] If De Staerke ever was in Aalst, it wasn't as part of the Baasrode Gang.

Someone who looks like Dominique S. was seen driving a Golf towards Aalst on the night of the attack. However, Dominique S. has a water-tight alibi for that night. Some still find it suspicious that Van Esbroek and Dominique S. left for a vacation to the French Riviera the weekend after Aalst, but unfortunately, it proves nothing.

In the middle of the night of December 5th, 1985, the remaining members of the Baasrode Gang break into a Delhaize in Lokeren. Dominique S. and Van Esbroek are the core members now as both Big Stereo and De Staerke have been gone since October. The supermarket's alarm goes off and authorities are alerted. The duo drives away with 165,000 BEF (approximately US $4,648) worth of cigarettes and wine bottles in a stolen, gray BMW.

On the way back to their safe house, the BMW breaks down, packed with stolen merchandise. Dominique S. and Van Esbroek leave the car in a ditch and flee by foot. At 5:00 a.m. a Gendarmerie patrol finds the abandoned car.

Police scan the vicinity and notice another car in the distance making some light signals, which is suspicious to the officers. The two people in the car confess to being resellers of stolen goods after they are detained and interrogated. The police open the BMW's trunk and find the stolen cigarettes and wine. The resellers drop the names of Baasrode Gang members Van Esbroek and Dominique S.

Police make a search and seizure at the homes of Van Esbroek and Dominique S. When they learn of this, Van Esbroek and Dominique S. leave their safe house, hop in a car, and flee to southern France. It's the second time they've driven there in the past month.

Aside from the stolen cigarettes and wine, authorities find other incriminating evidence in the BMW. They find a dozen 12-gauge Legia cartridges, the same brand used in Aalst by the Insane Killers. They also discover that the Baasrode Gang removed the back seat—similar to the way the Brabant Insane Killers modified their vehicles—and had a built-in system to open the trunk by the back. The license plate is a copy of another BMW's plate. The back lights were intentionally not working. One of their other cars had also been discarded in a way typical of the Killers. According to Prosecutor De Saeger: "After the Gang open fire during an attack in Zellik, the attackers' car was found completely calcinated [torched]. The same scenario was seen in the Aalst attack."[302]

But it's not a slam dunk because there are many differences from the other crimes perpetrated by the Insane Killers. For example, while the Insane Killers always stole the cars with the keys, this stolen BMW was hotwired. None of the other vehicles stolen by the Killers ever had a built-in trunk system. And of course, the car is a BMW and not a Golf.

Contract Theory

Witnesses reported seeing men who looked like both Johnny De Staerke and Philippe Haemers at the Aalst attack. The problem is there is little evidence that any of their other known gang members were there with them. This gave rise to the contract theory—that individual gangsters were contracted to participate in the Second Wave attacks, like mercenaries, by sponsors who would lease their services. There is speculation that the sponsors could be part of the private sector, the government, or a foreign power.

This theory is interesting because it makes it plausible that criminals operate in a unit with soldiers or cops to commit the Second Wave attacks. According to Professor Kellens, this: "does not exclude that some drug addicts were manipulated."[303] This mixing of criminal elements would explain the organized savagery of the Second Wave and the limited leads linking the crimes to other members of the Baasrode or Haemers gangs. It could also mean there could be dozens of Brabant Killers who filled in or were replaced from one attack to the next.

Haemers in Aalst

A couple of leads connect Haemers to Aalst. A Delhaize cashier believes she saw Haemers doing reconnaissance the day of the attack. David Van De Steen, the nine-year-old boy whose whole family was murdered, believes that Haemers is the one who shot him and crippled him for life. He recognized Haemers on TV a few years later and is convinced that Haemers is the Giant.

A couple claimed in 2004 that the night after the Aalst raid they saw someone who looked like Haemers' in Houssière Forest. They were driving and saw two people standing next to a dark Golf. They believe that one of the two men was Haemers. They also reported that there seemed to be someone lying injured or dead on the ground beside the two men. The two men were very agitated when they saw the couple, which scared them enough that they drove away.

The statements from these two new witnesses led to several new theories for investigators. If the Psycho was seriously injured in Aalst by the police officer who shot towards the fleeing Golf, perhaps his two accomplices finished him off and buried him in Houssière Forest. This would explain why Aalst was the last raid by the Insane Killers. However, even though Houssière Forest was dug up, the body of the Psycho has never been found.

Months after Aalst, investigators will check into the alibi for Haemers to exempt him as a suspect. According to Haemers: "Luckily my wife found my alibi, a receipt that showed that on the evening of the attack I had eaten at the restaurant Le Pagalo. I didn't even remember."[304]

De Staerke in Aalst

There were several sightings of someone with De Staerke's likeness in Aalst. A witness interviewed on the Program *Terzake* on the VRT on February 1992 is 80 percent sure to have seen De Staerke exit the Delhaize in a Beige Mercedes just before the attack.A

Several months after the attack, De Staerke's estranged girlfriend made a police statement that she and De Staerke went shopping for groceries at the Aalst Delhaize on the day of the attack. This is critical testimony for investigators. She claims the couple drove up with her son, at some time between 4:00 and 6:00 p.m. She describes how De Staerke scanned the inside of the supermarket and speculates to police that he was giving particular attention to the security measures. She adds that when she watched a broadcast with De Staerke about the Aalst attack, he told her that he had done stuff like that before. When confronted by investigators, De Staerke didn't deny he shopped in Aalst but insisted it was the day before the attack.

A second important testimony for investigators is that at 9:00 p.m. on the night of the Aalst attack, De Staerke dropped off a heavy, blue Samsonite briefcase at a safe house and then left. The safe house is the home of Big Stereo's brother that is located in a suburb of Brussels. Big Stereo's brother never opened the Samsonite to see what was inside. However, he assumed it was weapons because of the weight of the briefcase. It felt like it weighed somewhere between 45 and 65 pounds.

De Staerke returned later to pick up the briefcase and buried it in his yard at home. The next day, De Staerke dug it up and buried it again in another field. It was left there for a while before being dug up and passed to De Staerke's brother Julien. Months afterwards, the briefcase is found at De Staerke's girlfriend's home.

Investigators confront De Staerke about the briefcase story, but he claims there were only diamonds and false IDs inside. Police have the briefcase tested by a forensic lab and traces of gunpowder are found inside. For investigators, this contradicts De Staerke's statement and undermines his credibility. A khaki suit and a bullet holder similar to the ones used by the Killers are found among De Staerke's circle of friends.

A jail mate claimed that De Staerke boasted of killing 28 people. Johnny doesn't deny the statement, but puts it in context: "I never declared it officially but only to a cell mate... Probably to look tough, I don't know. I repeat: I was never an angel but I never killed someone. I swear. I said a bunch of times back then that I shouldn't have said it. But what do you want?"[305] Johnny was never found guilty of murder.

BOUHOUCHE GANG

Some Second Wave leads are linked to the Bouhouche Gang. A security guard who was on duty at the Overijse Delhaize supermarket before the attack said that the only Gendarme he ever saw on site before the attack was a Bouhouche associate. At the time, this associate was stationed in another area of the country. Fifteen minutes before the Aalst attack, witnesses notice two men whispering in French and sipping drinks in the Christoffelken bar not far from the Delhaize. Aalst is in a Dutch-speaking region. The two men reportedly just stared at traffic as it passed by the window.

The first suspicious French speaker was described as a small, thin, clean-shaven man who wears glasses as he drinks water. Three witnesses identify Bouhouche in a photo line-up.[306] The other man is much bigger. Some names have been thrown about but he was not formally identified by any witnesses.

A picture of the Aalst Delhaize is later found in a Bouhouche Gang associate's home. He claims he took the picture when he was working for a client on something unrelated to the brutal crime.

Like the Baasrode and the Haemers Gang, the Bouhouche Gang has a mountain of a man who could be the Giant. He also happens to have an unusual gait due to knee issues when he was younger and later sustaining a bad injury. He had two knee operations, the second in late 1982. In 1983, this man still had a noticeable limp because his knee was still hurting him. Sometimes his knee seized to the point where he wasn't even able to move it.

Other evidence that points to the Bouhouche Gang as the Insane Killers is how they fixed cars. The Mazda 626 they used for the Goffinon attack in 1981 had the radio removed and a slot to hold a listening device. The exact same car radio was found in Bouhouche's own car with the serial number scratched off. The Bouhouche Gang always removed radios from stolen cars. They always stole their cars with keys. So did the Insane Killers. The Bouhouche Gang also had the required listening devices and airwave scramblers in their possession to run circles around authorities.

Delhaize supermarkets

Another popular motive put forward for the Second Wave attacks is extortion, which would explain why Delhaize supermarkets are targeted in particular. It's brought up in Albert Mahieu's legal complaint against

Delhaize administrators in 1999. At that time, Mahieu was involved in a fraud case against Allianz-AGF/Assubel insurance company. A few Assubel directors were also directors for Delhaize-related firms. Mahieu believes this group of directors is involved in a criminal ring, which they operate through both Delhaize and Assubel. He names five directors who were on the board of both companies in his complaint.

The First Wave attacks against the Delhaize supermarkets are related to a dispute over red light district brothels. One of the directors, who financed the brothels, had an affair with the madam of a brothel. The brothels were hurting the mob's market shares, so they attacked the Delhaize supermarkets until the brothels relented. This theory also explains the break after the First Wave of attacks.

The Second Wave of attacks is linked instead to Delhaize's American subsidiaries. Food Giant is a new American subsidiary of Delhaize in America. Food Giant is unionized, and Delhaize fails to restructure it. In February 1985, Supervalu buys Food Giant's warehouse business for $17 Million. It turns out to be a terrible decision for Delhaize and the mob that runs the union is unhappy with the deal, so they contact the Brabant Killers to hit Delhaize again. Finally on February 20, 1986, there's a deal struck between Delhaize, The Lion and Super Valu Stores to own 51% of Food Giant Inc. The attacks stop. Food Giant, which was struggling badly, suddenly prospers.

POLITICAL MOTIVES AND REACTIONS

The Aalst attack is a turning point for the country. On November 10th, 1985, under tremendous pressure from the media, elected officials begin the final talks to name a new government. Starting on November 19th, 740 paratroopers are sent to patrol the streets again. On November 28th, a new Right-Wing government is formed, headed by Wilfried Martens, with security hawk, Jean Gol as his number two man. They agree to a strong law and order program, which is arguably in direct response to the climate of fear created by the violent attacks perpetrated by the Insane

Killers.

On November 30th, US president Ronald Reagan arrives in Brussels for an official visit. To bolster security, 850 Gendarmes and hundreds of police officers are in the streets to assist the 150 secret service and security personnel from the US. That same day, the CCC bombs big NATO supplier Motorola's building and wipes out its computer room. After Reagan departs, the CCC attacks continue unabated. In December 1985, they attack the Bank of America. They also blow up NATO pipelines, spilling 10,000 liters of fuel. They then go after the Central European Operating Agency, which contributes to the care of the pipelines.

On December 16th, the Belgian government makes a major breakthrough. The CCC leader Pierre Carette and his top lieutenants are arrested at a burger joint in the Southern town of Charleroi. The consequences of this arrest are important because capturing the CCC leaders destroys the CCC's ability to effectively continue their bombing campaign against NATO and the US or multinational corporations. The CCC members are indicted for the two deaths of the firefighters who were killed during bomb explosions. The top CCC members are sentenced and serve decades in jail. The movement is dead.

PART IV:
THE SEARCH (1986–)

BRUSSELS–CHARLEROI CANAL,
VILLAGE OF RONQUIÈRES

CHAPTER 23

ASSASSINATION OF JUAN MENDEZ

DECEMBER 1985 IS ALSO THE DEATH KNELL FOR THE BAASRODE Gang. One arrest follows the other as individual members like Johnny De Staerke are chased by authorities. It's just a question of time before they all end up behind bars.

The Haemers Gang holds up a Securitas money transport truck on December 23rd and hits the jackpot. The loot is 17 million BEF (or approximately US $478,870).

As for the Bouhouche Gang, they don't do big hits that December. Instead, a few seemingly innocuous incidents happen, which become more significant in the long run for the Insane Killers case.

On December 5th, FN South American rep Juan Mendez returns to Belgium from a trip to the US. He's now convinced that his supposed friend Bouhouche was behind the robbery of his weapons collection. During the trip, his foreign contacts found him abnormally nervous and agitated, fixated on his stolen arms collection.

On December 6th, French border guards stop an Algerian national as he tries to cross the border with an unregistered GP 9mm. The Algerian has dealings with the Bouhouche Gang. The GP 9mm is part of a deal between the Bouhouche Gang and the Algerian political group MDA to provide them with dozens of unregistered GP 9mm weapons.

Earlier in 1985, the Algerian was visited by contacts involved in Algerian politics. These political militants are members of the MDA, an

Islamist movement of Algerian expats based in Europe. The goal of the MDA is to overthrow the Algerian government and set up an Islamic state. They desperately need weapons. The Algerian linked to the Bouhouche Gang tells the MDA reps visiting Belgium that he has a friend who can broker an arms deal for them.

The broker tells the MDA reps that he has a contact who is a South American Rep at the FN and who could supply them with weapons. The contact is Juan Mendez, who had not yet clued in that his weapon collection was robbed by Bouhouche. The MDA agree to a deal in principle. Shortly thereafter the Algerian and the broker travel to Paris, where the MDA reps are based.

The friend offers a stock of 200 GP 9mm weapons without serial numbers, which he will procure from Mendez—who smuggles them out of the FN through the garbage. The Dutch government is very worried at the time about the large number of FN arms that end up on their black market. The intermediary between the friend and Juan Mendez is Bouhouche. As part of the deal, the MDA reps first get a GP 9mm without a number as a sample. In September 1985, Bouhouche transfers to the Algerian a GP pistol without a serial number as a sample for the arms deal.

The Algerian brought the 9mm to the MDA in Paris to show them as a first sample what kind of merchandise they can expect in the deal. The lynchpin of the massive arms deal is Mendez, who would steal the arms from the FN. The Algerian does tell the border guards that the 9mm originated from Bouhouche, but there is no mention made of a bigger arms deal.

When Mendez is back in Belgium, it is clear there's heat between him and the Bouhouche Gang. He tells acquaintances that, "he would do himself justice." Mendez feels he can't go to the police over this. Either Bouhouche is blackmailing him or he's scared for his physical security.

Before the break-in, Mendez was carelessly showing off the HK submachine gun from the Dyane robbery to several people. There's also some circumstantial evidence that he knew about the Bouhouche Gang's rental of the Buanderie warehouse for the supermarket extortion project. Mendez has also buried large quantities of explosives in his backyard.

Mendez is an important cog in Bouhouche's arms trafficking business as Bouhouche makes some serious money by fencing FN arms stolen by Mendez. Up to 20 percent of Bouhouche's official inventory is weapons stolen by Mendez.

And then there's that huge outstanding arms sale to the MDA. The Bouhouche Gang expects Mendez to produce a large quantity of stolen, unregistered GP 9mms. They have a big problem because Mendez is showing signs that he's had enough of the arms business and he's even taking steps to work in another field altogether. He's looking into going to work in his family's translation business and possibly move to South America.[307] Bouhouche's cash cow would disappear.

Their relationship is tense and awkward. Nevertheless, Mendez negotiates a small arms deal with Bouhouche. Mendez is getting renovations done on his home and badly needs cash. He's ready to sell some of the weapons he has left. On December 30th, Bouhouche visits Mendez to look at the weapons. Mendez offers Bouhouche a GP Inglis pistol, an MP43 caliber 7.92 assault gun, and a 9mm Mannlicher gun. Bouhouche agrees to buy them on short-term credit for 130,000 BEF (approximately US $3,662). He leaves with the three weapons and promises to pay Mendez back quickly.

On January 3rd, 1986, Mendez visits Bouhouche and they spend time allegedly discussing the weapons sale. Mendez wants his money. Bouhouche stalls for time and promises to pay for the purchase by January 7th, 1986.

Assassination

On January 7th, 1986, at 7:40 a.m., Mendez leaves home in his Volkswagen Passat on his way to work in the town of Liege. Mendez usually carpools to work with friend and co-worker Alain Coesens, but Coesens is away on a business trip to South America.

Before driving along the highway, Mendez stops his Passat at the side of the access ramp. It's a long access ramp that's separated from the highway by a long row of trees. There's another car that's parked in front of him and inside the other car is a Bouhouche Gang hit man. Mendez puts his clutch into neutral and pulls the handbrake on.

As the hit man walks up to Mendez's car, Mendez cracks open the door. The assassin pulls out a Browning and shoots two bullets, striking Mendez in the heart. He then sticks the Browning directly in the open door and pulls the trigger twice more, hitting Mendez in his left eye at point blank range. As Mendez's upper body slumps to the right, the shooter fires a sixth bullet behind the victim's left ear. Blood splatters on the inside of the side and front windows and drops of blood drip to the ground through the driver's door. The trench coat Mendez is wearing is drenched with blood.

The killer takes Mendez's car keys but doesn't take the briefcase. He shuts the door and walks away on ground that is lightly covered with snow. The assassin leaves no fingerprints.

Secret Compartment

The murder is an ambush assassination. The bullets fired at Mendez are from a Remington Peters 9mm Para Hollow Point, 115 grains. The Bouhouche Gang is aware that Mendez takes the Namur highway to get to work and that he's not driving to work as usual with his co-worker this day. There are conflicting witness statements about the make of the assassin's car. At least one witness points to a Gendarmerie car.

Mendez had a 9mm FN Browning pistol hidden in a secret chamber over the glove compartment. The murder happens so fast, he never even reached for it.

Fallout

The FN gun manufacturer phones Ms. Mendez to find out why he didn't show up to work. She senses something is very wrong and contacts Bouhouche to find out if he knows where her husband is. He says he doesn't but offers to help. Bouhouche jumps in his car and drives to the Mendez home. Meanwhile, Gendarmes find Mendez's dead body along the highway entrance ramp. The Gendarmerie show up to the Mendez home and one of the trio of Wavre investigators is there. The Wavre investigators had just published the August 1985 report that indicates that Bouhouche is a Far-Right Gendarme. He is quite surprised to see Bouhouche already at Mendez's home.

Gendarmerie investigators find out that Mendez sold three weapons to Bouhouche shortly before the murder and that Bouhouche owes about 100,000 BEF (or approximately US $2,817). When investigators confront Bouhouche about this deal and debt, he denies everything. Bouhouche cooks up a story that it's actually Jean Bultot, the headline-making assistant jail director, who purchased the three weapons from Mendez. Bouhouche says that Mendez wanted to collect from Bultot the day of the murder. Between the time of the murder and Bouhouche showing up at Mendez's home, both Bultot and Bouhouche went to the same movie screening—just not together. Perhaps Bouhouche noticed Bultot present in the audience but Bultot never noticed Bouhouche.

The legal system in Belgium is not accusatory. It's inquisitorial. If a murder suspect blames someone else, the prosecution sometimes needs to verify the validity of the suspect's claim that the other person did it. Investigators determine Bultot had a good alibi at the time of Mendez's murder. Even though both Mendez and Bultot went to gun ranges and participated in shooting competitions, there's no evidence to contradict Bultot's assertion that he had never even met Mendez. However, when authorities first looked at Bultot's possible involvement in the case, one small detail made them spend much more time than necessary on the Bultot lead. When investigators learned that Mendez carried a gun for self-defense hidden in his Passat, they searched the car and couldn't find it.

Why was Mendez's gun important? Because if it's gone, the killer might have taken Mendez's gun from him. A similar gun is found in a clothes basket in Mendez's home and investigators have no evidence that it wasn't the gun from Mendez's car. They need to consider that perhaps the gun was dropped in the clothes basket after the murder, to make it look like Mendez forgot to bring it that day. Or, perhaps that's why he couldn't defend himself. The missing weapon doesn't take Bouhouche off the hook. The police just can't exclude Bultot as a potential accomplice. Maybe Bultot dropped off Mendez's gun to Bouhouche at the screening? Maybe Bouhouche then dropped it in the Mendez's clothing basket when he went over?

These conjectures were made early in the investigation when investigators hadn't discovered the hidden chamber in the Passat's glove compartment. Once they found the gun inside the Passat's hidden chamber with the gun and clips inside, the whole question became moot, but it took a while. Because Bultot was famous for all the wrong reasons, and because authorities suspect some items found in the Houssière Forest before the Aalst attack belonged to him, Bultot is forever tied to the Insane Killers case.

According to Mendez's brother, the reason Mendez never went to police with his suspicions that Bouhouche had stolen his collection and what could have led to his death is, "I think he wanted to make a deal with Bouhouche and had negotiated with him. Something along the lines of: 'Either you bring my weapons back, or I go to the police about the Dyane-weapons robbery or for the Brabant Killer.' Something like that. And Bouhouche didn't have a choice. Mendez started to suspect things related to the Insane Killers."[308]

WAVRE INVESTIGATION

Two investigators who authored the infamous 1985 Gendarmerie report on the Wavre Gun Shop attack of September 1982 are present at Mendez's burial service and notice Bouhouche is also present. Their report on the Insane Killers had mentioned Bouhouche's name. They walk up to Bouhouche and ask him if he would follow them to answer a few questions at the station. When they get to the station, the investigators start with a light topic to break the ice and slowly increase the pressure. Bouhouche surprises them when he says, "Anyways, what you're looking for is the Brabant Killings? Don't bother, there won't be anything more."[309]

Bouhouche's answer to the two investigators has been the subject of much speculation. Why would Bouhouche spontaneously say this to the Wavre investigative team? Bouhouche is not even a target of the Brabant Killers investigation yet. Is Bouhouche suddenly suggesting he had something to do with the Brabant Killings? The comments seem so out of sync that many around the case can't accept that Bouhouche would have ever said this. There are those who believe the two Wavre investigators made it all up. The members of the Wavre investigative team face accusations of incompetence, not dishonesty, because of their 1985 report. The context of Bouhouche's remarks to the Wavre investigators is important. The August 1985 report from the Wavre team had specifically named Bouhouche. It's the first time that a widely read report from the Gendarmerie had ever mentioned Bouhouche and his dubious associations and activities. Other investigators who later work on the case of the Insane Killers first hear of the Bouhouche lead in their Gendarmerie report. Remember that while the report was widely panned, Bouhouche had been very upset by it—so much so that he sent an associate to give the Wavre Gun Shop owner a stolen gun in a Gendarmerie envelope to play a dirty trick on the Wavre team and destroy their reputation.

Bouhouche knows everything the Wavre team wrote about him and realizes they're still looking into the Brabant Killers. During this time, Bouhouche has been claiming that he is trying to solve the mystery of the Brabant Killers to pick up the reward offered by the supermarket association. According to Amory, Bouhouche asked him all the confidential details about the security in the Delhaize supermarkets because he was trying to find the Insane Killers. Is it possible, then, that when he says there won't be anything more that Bouhouche is letting the Wavre team know that he had found out who did it and that he knew their attacks were over? That Bouhouche is not implicating himself? According to his declarations, Bouhouche viewed himself first and foremost as a detective at this time, not a gun dealer.

BOUHOUCHE ARREST

The investigators strongly suspect Mendez was killed by someone he knew. Bouhouche, because he had been very close to Mendez, automatically becomes one of the prime suspects.

The ballistics aspect of the investigation is handed as usual to the ever-present Claude Dery, who notices that the bullets that killed Mendez are illegal rare hollow points. It's the same type as those shot by Bouhouche in the Giannakis Taxi affair back in 1980 when he was still working in the Gendarmerie. Dery had also been charged with the ballistics tests in that case.

Authorities make a search and seizure at Bouhouche's home. They find the three weapons that Mendez sold to Bouhouche in December. They also seize 48 pistols, nine revolvers, and 22 long arms. A weapon known to be stolen from the Mendez collection is found, as is a Nikon camera shoulder strap identical to the one stolen in the Mendez robbery. Bouhouche is now using it on his own personal camera.

They also find a GP 9mm pistol in Bouhouche's home, which experts suspect is the Mendez murder weapon. An expert determines that there has been an attempt to alter the forensic footprint on the gun; both the firing pin and the barrel have been toyed with to hinder identification. They also notably find a box of 50 cartridges of rare Remington, 9 Para-type, semi Jacket Hollow Point, 115 grains that were used to kill Mendez.

A panel of three ballistics experts, including Claude Dery, agrees the gun matches the cartridges found on the Mendez crime scene. The panel finds there exists, "practical certainty that the cartridges and the bullets found on site were shot with the (FN Browning) owned by Bouhouche." Another separate ballistics analysis comes to the same conclusion. Bouhouche is arrested and indicted for complicity of murder on January 26th, 1986.

DE STAERKE ARREST

In March 1986, Johnny De Staerke is finally collared by authorities. He has been a fugitive since he failed to return to jail after leaving on a short-term pass in early 1985. The rest of the Baasrode Gang had already been arrested in late 1985. The Gang gets its day in court in June 1987. Prosecutors charge the gang for about 20 armed robberies and a string of thefts ranging from BMWs and alcohol to cigarettes and videos. De Staerke is found guilty and sentenced to 20 years in jail. The same day as he is sentenced for his role in these crimes, De Staerke is indicted again for the Brabant Killings. He's accused of participating in the Aalst attack.

They indict De Staerke in the Aalst attack for a few reasons: First, his alibi for the night of the Aalst attack is shaky. He gave one story to investigators, and then later he said he didn't remember what he did. Second, the Samsonite briefcase that he dropped off in a safe house the same night as Aalst had traces of gunpowder found in it, even though he'd denied there were ever weapons in the briefcase. Investigators consider that De Staerke was not being forthright. Third, his ex-girlfriend gave a statement that De Staerke had been shopping in the Aalst Delhaize between 4:00 and 6:00 p.m. the day of the attack. Finally, some masks, Legia ammo, a belt, and items found at the home of some of De Staerke's acquaintances are similar to those used by the Insane Killers.

In 1992, using a legal ploy under counsel from his attorney, De Staerke confesses to the Brabant Killings without giving any new details or evidence to back up his confession. De Staerke gambled that authorities didn't have enough to prove their case against him in front of a jury. Because of his confession, authorities were forced to act. That had to either put him in front of a jury or release him. For procedural reasons, the maneuver paved the way to his liberation. There was never even a court hearing on De Staerke's alleged participation in the Insane Killers' attack at the Aalst Delhaize.

Haemers' Arrest

On March 17th, 1986, the Haemers Gang commits its first major armed robbery of the year. They ambush a Securitas money transport in Drogenbos and a witness notices a tall blond man. The amount robbed by the Gang is a gargantuan 27,650,000 BEF (approximately US $778,873). On May 21st, 1986, the Haemers Gang's driver, Thierry S., is found dead with a gun in his hand; he had recently been kicked out of the Haemers Gang. It's ruled a suicide even though he appears to have died under suspicious circumstances. Haemers and Philippe L. find new members to replace Thierry S.

Haemers is finally arrested, but his Gang mounts a successful commando operation to get him out in 1988. Haemers becomes one of the most famous gangsters in Belgium after kidnapping the ex-Prime minister of Belgium, Paul Van Den Boeynants for ransom in 1989. The Haemers Gang kidnaps Van Den Boeynants because they believe he is incredibly rich. To regain his freedom, Van Den Boeynants helps to arrange the ransom money. The Gang members pick up the ransom in Switzerland and flee to Brazil to start new lives. Haemers is tracked down and arrested in Brazil. He's extradited back to Belgium and hangs himself in his cell in 1993. Observers also find the circumstances around his suicide to be suspicious.

In Jail

Bouhouche is now locked up and the Mendez investigators continue accumulating evidence for the trial against him. Bouhouche's friend Christian Amory becomes part of Captain Rousseau's investigation which was investigating Bouhouche. Between late January and June 1986, Amory meets Bouhouche in jail several times in his role as an investigator. And according to Prosecutor Van Lierde, "M. Amory had established during the days close to the death of M. Mendez several internal reports at the Gendarmerie that were only brought to the attention of prosecutors much later."[310]

It starts to dawn on Bouhouche that he's now in a world of trouble and he'll need to concentrate on getting out of the mess he's in. Consequently, he progressively winds down any short-term Bouhouche Gang projects he still had going outside. Other Bouhouche Gang members look at ways to get rid of their stolen arms, explosives, fake documents, and many other items. The explosives and many assets with market value are remnants from the Bouhouche Gang's failed 1984 supermarket racket project. They first try to sell the dynamite sticks and detonators and then look to see if there's a black market for stolen and fake IDs.

At some point in March 1986, according to a source close to the Bouhouche Gang, a Gang affiliate dumped a series of weapons used in major crimes into a canal. If we consider that the Gang had decided to keep the stolen Dyane weapons and the weapons from Mendez's collection, we can conclude the ones that were dumped were quite compromising.

ASSASSINATION PLOT

Bouhouche hatches an elaborate assassination plot against former friend Claude Dery, who is in charge of the ballistic tests. The idea is to make Dery's murder look like a suicide. During this period, the Bouhouche Gang associates regularly meet at the Toucan bar in Nivelles to coordinate and plan. The Gang fabricates a false suicide note from Dery. In it, Dery laments that he deliberately falsified the Bouhouche ballistics test on behalf of the Sûreté. To make it look legit, they obtain a copy of Dery's real signature. Next, they look around for a hit man for the contract. They use a fake ID from their Chaumont-Gistoux robbery of 1981. Hitmen are found, but the price of the contracts for the hit is a sticking point.

When the Dery assassination plot fizzles, they try to steal the evidence for Bouhouche's case from the clerks' office so the case will fall apart. Their first target is the GP 9mm seized because the whole case rested on it, but the opportunity never presents itself. During the summer of 1986, they hatch a jailbreak project. One plan is to slip Bouhouche a handgun and false ID in jail that he can use to escape. Another idea is to get a fake police officer to pick him up from jail with a fake document. Or both. There would be a driver waiting for him outside in a getaway car.

For the escape project, they rent extra space in a storage locker complex and they steal a Passat on December 16th, 1986. The same day they also steal a license plate at the same location from another car. The stolen Passat is stored in the new storage box. Next, the Gang members get a 9mm GP gun from one of the rental units. The gun and false IDs are hidden in a small bucket of spaghetti, which is given to Bouhouche's wife so she can store it in her freezer. The plan is that she can later hand the spaghetti bucket to Bouhouche during a visit to the jail. However, the Gang drops the plan at the last minute.

CHAPTER 24

DISCOVERY IN RONQUIÈRES
(NOVEMBER 1986)

I N NOVEMBER 1986, BAGS OF EVIDENCE LINKED TO THE INSANE KILL-
ers are found by divers in a canal that passes through the town of Ronquières. In police report number 2266, an inventory of what the divers
find is listed: "A grey plastic bag. In this bag are found: ammo, coins, two
spray cans, papers—that included checks clearly originating from the
Delhaize supermarket,- a green metal coffer, bags with the writing Caisse
12." There was also a bag that contained two parts from a bulletproof vest
and a third bag that contained rolls of coins.

There are all kinds of weapon parts. There's a 7.65 mm pistol with the
striker removed and the police seal and registration number obliterated. It's
suspected that it was stolen from the murdered police officer Morue during
the September 1983 Nivelles Colruyt bloodbath. There is the 10-gauge
Centaure duck rifle shoplifted from the Dinant Gun Shop with both ends
sawed-off. It could have been used to butt end the owner of the Wavre Gun
Shop in September 1982. There is a .357 Magnum Revolver similar to the
one that killed the Beersel Delhaize supermarket manager in October 1983.
There is a .38 caliber Arminius that was stolen from the 1983 Anderlues
jewelry shooting. All the identification numbers have been removed.

There are cut-up pieces of many other weapons suspected of having been stolen from the Wavre Gun Shop in September 1982. These

include pieces of a Beretta, an Ingram, and a Ruger. Among the other items found is a black wool trench coat with no sleeves. There is also a bulletproof vest and parts of other bulletproof vests, which are suspected to have been taken from the lot in Temse in September 1983. There is the mini-vault, a cash-drawer, and bags of money taken from the Aalst Delhaize supermarket. Additionally, there is an empty bottle, a Kriko hunting rifle, a knife, a fork, a silicone pistol, a key, and box fragments of Legia ammo.

Missing Shotguns

The notorious pump-action shotguns (SG-1 and SG-2) are not there, however, there are shells suspected of having been shot by each weapon. As a reminder, pump-action shotguns are available anywhere without showing ID. Also missing are the 19X9mm caliber Ingram submachine gun used in Aalst, two 7.65mms used several times by the Killers and the .22 LR they used to finish off so many of their victims.

The key retrieved from the canal is an interesting element with a bizarre, alleged backstory that is leaked during the investigation. Apparently, the key is for Martial Lekeu's old Gendarmerie office from at least two years before. During the second round of public inquiries, it's stated that investigators wondered if the key found in Ronquières was not for Martial Lekeu's caserne in Vaux-Sur-Sûre. Lekeu had been living in Florida since 1984 and had yet to return to Belgium. The odds of Lekeu's key ending up there are close to a statistical impossibility. How was a link ever made to Lekeu? Was it a type of key only used by the Gendarmerie? Why go and check Lekeu's office? Could it have been from another Gendarme's office? Could it have been kept by the Insane Killers to implicate Lekeu at some point in time? Though that would be somewhat pointless, as Lekeu had been in the United States for a while. If it is indeed a key to Lekeu's office, it had to be an item used to implicate Lekeu in the event the Ronquières bags are found. If it's not specifically a Gendarmerie key, how did Lekeu's name come out?

DIVING

The Ronquières find has been a source of speculation ever since. Did the Killers just dump some of their weapons because they wanted to get rid of them? For years that was the official story. Based on the two witness reports from the day after the Aalst attack, it was concluded that the bags had been dumped back in November 1985, right before the Insane Killers' car was torched. Those reports mention that two cars, including a Golf, are seen in Ronquière along the canal. The group is seen removing and replacing license plates. One of the men is seen standing near the shore with what looked like a garbage bag floating not far from him. The bags are found not far from where the bag had been seen floating in the water.

Right after the two witness reports were drawn up, a first investigative team, called the Cellule Info or CI for short, sent a diver to search in the canal but didn't find the bags. Now one year later, a second team called Delta rereads the file and witness reports. They believe that the diving in 1985 was poorly done and decide to send divers to take a second look in the canal. This time they find the bags. Their discovery prompts the CI team to push back, saying they had thoroughly searched the bottom of the canal in that area. The Delta investigators must have been tipped off by someone linked to the Insane Killers. Delta has steadfastly claimed that they came to find the bags just by rereading the two witness statements and the rest of the file.

SCIENCE

Now, a recent report from the INCC, corroborated by another team of experts, finds that the bags could not have been in the water more than one to two months. This finding is based on the state of the papers and coins in the bag. Since then there's been lots of finger pointing between the old CI and Delta investigators. Delta's argument is that the INCC science is bad.

History

We won't get in a scientific debate, but we'll review the history of the discovery to see if it could shed some light on the issue. In late 1985, a CI diver searched for hours in the canal near Ronquières. Depending on who you ask, the diver searched anywhere between two hours and four days. One way or another, CI insists they looked everywhere, thoroughly, the first time around.

By early 1986, the investigation is split into two separate teams: Delta is investigating the Aalst Delhaize attack of November 1985 and the Temse Fabric attack in September 1983 and CI is investigating everything else. As they're looking for the same suspects, their investigations might overlap. There is talk of removing Aalst and Temse and centralizing everything with CI. In the meantime, they need to negotiate who does what and when.

For jurisdictional reasons, Delta also takes care of the whole Baasrode Gang file. As they learn more about the Baasrode Gang, they also try to determine any involvement in the attacks by the Brabant Killers. Delta's working theory is that Johnny De Staerke was present in Aalst in some capacity. Meanwhile, the CI's chief suspects are still the Borains. To bolster Delta's team, they'll recruit an officer who specializes in dealing with informants in drug cases in March 1986.

Also in March, a joint decision is made by CI and Delta, to allow Delta to search all canals across the country for evidence. A list of several canals that should be searched is drawn up. In September 1986, Delta starts searching the canals. They use a boat from Public Works to scan the bottom with a sonar. They start on September 11th, and search the canal each day, for weeks at a time.

The Delta officer who ultimately pointed out the exact spot where the bags were found was the specialist in handling informants. His task at Delta was mostly to accumulate tips from informants. This raised red flags at CI. How is it that the guy whose job it is to work with informants then makes a miraculous discovery that has nothing to do with informants? The only thing we know for sure is the specialist was handed the two witness documents from November 1985 by another agent from CI. The circumstances are hazy.

MOTIVE

If there is manipulation, what could be the motive? Why hand evidence to investigators even if you decide what to give? It's long been speculated that if the Insane Killers dumped the weapons deliberately so investigators would find them, their intention was to link the First and Second Wave attacks. That's inaccurate. If we read newspaper articles from the time period between Aalst and Ronquières, we realize that there never was any doubt that both the First and Second Waves were linked in terms of ballistics and modus operandi. The only thing Ronquières does is reconfirm the ballistic link between both waves.

It's hard to believe that the Insane Killers would have handed everything away to investigators without getting anything in return. Sure, there are hints that the Insane Killers picked and chose very carefully what they put in those bags. Many weapons were sawed into small pieces. Yet they were kept in very good condition; they were well oiled and ready for "daily" use. Why would anyone take the time to chop up perfectly good weapons? Most of the weapons found in Ronquières are suspected of having been used by the Insane Killers because the calibers all match, but there's no certainty because they can't be tested. Furthermore, none of the arms used in the Second Wave are there, just spent casings or cartridges from them. This gives the person who dumped the weapon plausible deniability that he's not one of the Brabant Killers.

After decades, the evidence found at Ronquières has never helped the investigation in any way. How often does such a sizeable discovery of evidence not help a criminal investigation progress at all? The only practical consequence of the discovery is that the Delta investigators, who were focused on the Baasrode Gang and Johnny De Staerke, kept Aalst and Temse. The talk of taking away both the Aalst and the Temse investigations from

Delta and centralizing them with the other investigations at CI is now dead because of Ronquière. The Insane Killers saw some practical benefit in having the investigation stay as is. That's despite the fact CI was still involved in the wild goose chase after the Borains. If indeed it turns out that Johnny De Staerke is not part of the Brabant Killers, perhaps they felt having two separate investigative teams looking for only one set of perpetrators but fighting to justify their own suspects was beneficial to them.

The investigation into the Brabant Insane Killers is full of incidents that could have been caused by manipulations. Several important pieces of evidence disappeared or were destroyed. For example, the entire Mons taxi driver file disappeared during a transfer between Mons and Nivelles and had to be reconstituted using photocopies. Glasses and items with possible DNA disappeared from the Het Kasteel Inn Restaurant murder investigation. The license plate from the Saab used for the Nivelles Colruyt attack disappeared.

Threatening Witnesses

Victims and their families have had a difficult relationship with the investigators in charge of the Brabant Killers, partly because the crimes are still unsolved. At the time the events occurred, in the early to mid-eighties, victim counseling was not very developed and it was very hard for them. Some victims had trouble getting any financial compensation for their losses and many also felt continuously threatened and enveloped with fear. Like witnesses and victims in the First Wave, someone who doesn't want the truth to be known threatens the Second Wave witnesses.

During the Braine Delhaize supermarket attack, the widow of Bozidar Djurovski lost her husband and their son was permanently crippled due to the attack. When she starts getting involved in the case, she receives several anonymous telephone calls that always have the same banging sounds. She feels her line is being tapped for weeks because she can hear a sound on the line. The Monday right after the Aalst attack, a fake Gendarme tries to talk to her son at his school. She starts hiding her name from the press, scared for her life and the life of her son.

Following the Overijse Dehaize supermarket attack, the daughter of victim Léon Finné, who died in the parking lot, receives telephone calls for a couple of months. The last one had a bang sound. She also feels her telephone line is tapped: "As luck would have it, after the facts, my telephone, each time I received a call or I made one, about each 30 or 34 seconds, I would hear a kind of 'bip' in my phone that I did not have before. I am convinced—once again, I cannot give you physical evidence—that we had our phones tapped during at least six months." Each time Finné's daughter or Djurovski's widow did interviews with the media, they started having phone problems. This lasted from September 1985 to at least mid-1986. According to Finné: "After articles in newspapers, I received them two or three times per week, five to eight times each evening."[311]

During the Aalst Delhaize raid, the whole Van de Steen family was almost wiped out. The parents and their 14-year-old daughter were murdered by the Insane Killers. The only survivor is David, their nine-year-old son. His maternal grandfather, Albert Van den Abiel, warns the Gendarmerie he believes it was an inside job. Shortly thereafter, he receives telephone calls: "Continue doing that and the same will happen to you that happened to Vernaillen."[312] Remember that Vernaillen is the Gendarmerie officer who was shot at home with his wife by the Bouhouche Gang in October 1981. At the time of the phone call, the crime is still unsolved. What hit home is that the Vernaillen murder happened in Hekelgem, just a couple of minutes away from Aalst. Both were in Dutch-speaking Flanders and had been widely publicized in the local papers. Furthermore, Vernaillen was hospitalized in Aalst after the attack.

THE TRIALS

On February 2nd, 1987, authorities create a new investigative team to delve into the Insane Killers. The new cell, called CBW, brings together 12 Gendarmerie investigators and 13 members of the Judicial Police. When the Gendarme Christian Amory from Mons finds out about this, he takes steps to be part of the action again. According to Prosecutor La-croix: "Amory had himself proposed to join…"[313] Armory even obtains a reference letter from the commander of the Mons Gendarmerie.

During the new investigative team's first meeting, Amory is present. His job is to verify any alibis offered by suspects. He also takes home—and never brings back—a copy of a Police report from CBW about a typed letter by the Borains, Adriano Vittorio. Sometime after Amory becomes a member of the CBW, Franz Reyners, the head of the Judicial Police suddenly learns that Amory is a very personal close friend of Bouhouche. Reyners uses this compromising information to get Amory kicked off the investigative team.

Amory then sets his sights on the Mendez murder investigation. In March 1987, Amory approaches Mendez case investigator, Rousseau with a suggestion. Amory proposes that he should be the one to inter-rogate Bouhouche because he's a close personal friend and he might get Bouhouche to crack. The Mendez investigators accept his offer to bring that missing climate of confidence during interrogations. It's all in vain as Amory never gets anything worthwhile off Bouhouche.

The Bouhouche Gang makes the decision to get rid of the most sen-sitive weapons still left in their stock: the weapons from the Dyane rob-bery of January 1982 and the Mendez robbery of April 1985. But the Bouhouche Gang has a novel approach; they won't destroy them or oth-erwise get rid of them as typical criminals would with potential evidence. They decide to make money off them.

On March 1st, the Algerian connected to the Bouhouche Gang arms deal with the MDA approaches the French Judicial Police and claims that he has a secret contact selling weapons that "could be" related to the Insane Killers. It's the same police station in which he was detained in December 1985 after being arrested with the MDA gun sample trying to cross the border. At this point, the Algerian national, who's lived the past few years in Belgium, has never gone to Belgian authorities with his information—nor has he ever tried to get the reward promised by the supermarket association. Instead, he drives up to Lille, France to meet a police force that has obviously no jurisdiction on the Brabant Killers murders. He explains he does this because during his 1985 detention, when he spoke with French police about the Aalst incident from the month previous, they listened attentively.

He explains to the French Police that he was asked by a secret contact to fence the stolen weapons he believes could have been used in the Brabant Killers' attacks. He never mentions that the Bouhouche Gang is his secret contact. The secret contact had even provided him with a fake Belgian ID to mask his identity for the transaction. The French authorities obviously inform him that the Belgians are also looking for the Brabant Insane Killers and there is a big reward in Belgium for this kind of evidence. They tell him that there was a reward of 10,000,000 BEF (approximately US $281,690), and suggest he meet the people from the Belgium cell in charge of the Brabant Killings. Apparently, he was the last person in Belgium to have heard about the ransom for information leading to an arrest.

But the trip to France provides benefits for the Bouhouche Gang's agent. Suddenly, he is not just some guy off the streets; he approaches the Belgian authorities as an informant of the French Police. When he meets the Belgian authorities, he reiterates the story about his secret contact who has weapons to sell that "could be" related to the Insane Killers. However, the agent doesn't need to be guaranteed the full 10,000,000 BEF promised by the supermarket association, he's got a deal to propose to the investigators. Asmaoui says he'll get them the weapons for only 4,570,000 BEF (US $128,732)—4,000,000 BEF (US $113,290) for the risk he takes in dealing with the secret contact and the 570,000 BEF (US $15,442) as his cost to buy the weapons. Belgian authorities turn down the deal.

Ex post facto, this deal would have been a win-win-win for everyone. The Bouhouche Gang would have made money off the Dyane and Mendez arms—probably much more than the 570,000 BEF (US $15,442) for the alleged transaction. Their agent would get the balance, which is a big chunk of change and the Belgian authorities couldn't ever cry foul against the agent, because they would have gotten their hands on the Dyane and/or the Mendez arms which would have been an advance in those cases. The agent would have made an honest mistake. He had even kept a Bouhouche Gang associate up to speed during the process.

Belgian authorities never find out who the agent's secret contact was. Referring to a Bouhouche Gang member, prosecutor Morlet said, "The bone that he would hang under the detectives' noses was information over the Insane Killers, a file that every policeman in Belgium wanted to elucidate."[314] No doubt looking for another way to make money off the Dyane and Mendez arms, the Bouhouche Gang gave some limited information to Captain Rousseau about their location in June—not enough details for him to find the weapons, but just enough for them to test him to see if they could get something out of it. Rousseau didn't bite. However, it got him in a little hot water later on, when colleagues found out about the information. In reality, the weapons would have been almost worthless as some Dyane and Mendez weapons had already been found in searches related to Bouhouche.

THE RENTAL NETWORK

On October 26th, 1987, during a search and seizure on a property linked to the Bouhouche Gang, authorities find a diskette full of hidden details about the Ixelles and Woluwe rental networks. It's just a question of processing the evidence and decrypting the contents of the diskette before they learn everything. By November, the Bouhouche Gang knows it's only a question of hours before the Ixelles storage unit, which contains a couple more weapons linked to Dyane and Mendez, is found. They have limited value at this point as stolen Dyane and Mendez collection weapons have already been linked to Bouhouche.

On November 5th, 1987, Officer Goffinon finally finds the Woluwe box, which contains a car. In the trunk of the car, Goffinon finds some Dyane and Mendez weapons. There are also two signaling pistols and a siren light that is also from Dyane.

The Bouhouche Gang members know the jig is up and decide to

damage Goffinon, hoping to derail him, as he's hot on their trail in the Brabant Killers Investigation. What difference does it make if he found a couple more Dyane or Mendez weapons? They'll sacrifice a pawn for a major tactical gain. They'll give up those last weapons, but wipe out Goffinon.

On November 6th, a Gendarme linked to Bouhouche tells the boss of his station that he knows the location and contents of the Ixelles storage unit. The caveat is that the Gendarme is to be treated as a regular confidential informant and his identity is not to be revealed. Someone from the station then calls Goffinon, who is of course in charge of the investigation, and offers the information but keeps the source confidential. Goffinon is told he will only be given the Ixelles storage unit details if he doesn't say he got the information from an informant. Because Goffinon suspects the weapons used by the Insane Killer are inside, he accepts these terms.

That same day, at around 9:00 p.m., Goffinon and an associate go to the Ixelles box rental complex and find Box 179. He sees the three locks and notes that there's a van inside that has no plates. He'll decide to watch the storage unit until November 7th at 2:00 a.m. Later that day, when they still have nothing, Goffinon and his associate decide to enter the box. At 3:00 p.m., they crash the box, but none of the weapons are inside the vehicle. A couple of days later, someone linked to the Bouhouche Gang hands over the weapons to the investigators.

Bouhouche Gang accomplices now claim that they emptied the box after Goffinon found out where they were. Because the Bouhouche Gang is suspected to be the Brabant Killers, the Gendarmerie believes that they might have emptied the Brabant Killers weapons from the storage unit, not just the now-worthless Dyane and Mendez collection arms. And all because of Goffinon's negligence! There is consternation that Goffinon should have gone in right away! Even worse, the accomplice who claims he emptied the storage unit under Goffinon's watch claims he did it all by foot and tramway and made several trips, which reflects poorly on Goffinon's diligence. Over time, the accomplice points out where the weapons were dumped and buried. At least three people tied to Bouhouche exaggerate the contents of the box, as if the Gendarmerie had missed the jackpot.

All of the alleged details make Goffinon look like an incompetent fool. And it gets worse, as part of the deal with the anonymous Gendarme whose boss shared the information about the storage unit location, Goffinon had to promise not to reveal there was an informant and say that it was their own private investigation that led them to the network. So on November 13th, Goffinon pre-dates the interview he did with the landlady to November 6th, knowing that it really happened on the 10th. When it is discovered that he illegally drew up a false police report, Goffinon's reputation is irrevocably damaged. The Bouhouche Gang members have pulled similar tricks on other agents, annoying them a couple of times over the years. They're kryptonite for investigators. Goffinon is booted off the Brabant Insane Killers case.

THE BORAINS

In January 1988, CI prosecutors present their case against the Borains to a judge and jury. As mentioned previously, there are two separate teams prosecuting the Brabant Killers. Delta is prosecuting De Staerke for Aalst, while CI is prosecuting the Borains for some of the First Wave crimes.

The alleged leader of the Borains, Michel Cocu, has been in jail awaiting trial since March 1986. The others were detained a bit later, but they've all been in an out of jail since 1983. And when they're out of jail, they're followed closely. The Borains are charged for some of the First Wave attacks. They're not charged for Maubeuge, Wavre, Beersel, Ohain, Mons, Temse, or Anderlues. They're also not charged for any Second Wave attacks.

Every single one of their few dozen confessions under duress has been retracted. The whole case hangs on the Ruger, which has been tainted every which way. Just before the case was underway, prosecutors received information from a new independent ballistic expert from Germany about the Ruger. The German experts believe the Ruger was never fired during the Insane Killers attacks, which contradicts the prosecutor's original expert. But prosecutors never share this crucial piece of evidence with the Borains' attorneys.

SPAGHETTI GUN

On January 15th, 1988, investigators find the gun that Bouhouche was going to use for the jail escape plan the Gang abandoned—the one hidden in a bucket of frozen spaghetti. It's a composite arm with the number on the barrel scratched off. Authorities determine it was first stolen by Mendez. It's a GP 9mm FN pistol. It was a technique that had been tested out at Dyane in order to smuggle weapons during a case of a hijacking.

Claude Dery does the ballistic tests to compare the GP 9mm with a cartridge known to be fired by the Brabant Killers that was found in Houssière Forest close to the abandoned Golf and the checks. Dery determines that the cartridge had been shot by this GP 9mm. When the court in the Borains case learns of Dery's findings, the trial is suspended. The Borains are released until the court can acquire more details.

The court officials also want to know how the other weapon in the case, the Ruger, wound up in the Mons Gendarmerie. There is also a request for information about how Mons Gendarmerie officers handled the gun. The Judge will say:, "I wonder if the investigation hasn't been deliberately oriented on a false lead."[315] It's the death knell for the Borains case and they're finally released for good.

Investigators go to see Bouhouche in his cell and hand him the initial Spaghetti pistol ballistics report. They threaten to jail Bouhouche's wife if he doesn't confess, so Bouhouche makes a deal with authorities. If they agree to not put his wife in jail, he'll give them another stock of stolen weapons. On February 2nd, 1988, Bouhouche gives the whereabouts of a cache that includes more stolen Dyane arms. It's under an overpass in the northern Brussels suburb of Vilvoorde, wrapped in plastic.

Bouhouche also claims at the same time that there's a logistics cell behind the Brabant killings. Other suspects have also heavily promoted this logistic cell theory, which is very self-serving on their part as it puts a layer of culpability between them and the key elements of the crimes. It's also a clever ploy to complicate the investigation.

Following Tests

After Dery's tests on the Bouhouche GP that was frozen in spaghetti sauce are reviewed, the three experts have very different opinions and can't come to an agreement. Consequently, the GP 9 mm can't be used for a hypothetical Bouhouche Insane Killer trial. Bouhouche is released again to await trial in the Mendez case.

Antwerp

Bouhouche, who is awaiting trial, needs cash. So does his ex-partner at the detective firm ARI, Bob Beijer. Bob Beijer. Ever resourceful, they decide to rob Suleiman Ali, a casino high roller who lives in Antwerp and bets on the big money tables and carries wads of cash to gamble. That night, Suleiman is in the apartment with his son Bassam and brother Said.

Bouhouche and Beijer drive up in a dark Mercedes with a fake Dutch licence plate. Beijer is wearing a wig and carries a pistol and handcuffs. Bouhouche impersonates a telegram delivery man, ringing the bell outside the door of the second floor apartment. When the door opens, Bouhouche and Beijer rush in and find Said, Bassam and Suleiman in the living room

Bouhouche and Beijer take out pistols and scream in English: "Police, don't move!" The three men are ordered to lie down on the ground, but they fight back instead. Said brawls with Bouhouche and they ends up near the stairwell. Meanwhile, Beijer's gun misfires, and Bassam and Suleiman beat Beijer to a pulp. They open a gash on top of his head, break fingers on his right hand, bruise his ribs and leave him unconscious on the ground.

When he gets an opportunity, Bouhouche returns to the living room, where he shoots and kills Suleiman and helps an unsteady Beijer wobble out of the apartment. As they leave, Bouhouche encounters Said, who pleads not to be shot. Bouhouche shoots him in the left eye and leaves the building with Beijer. Bouhouche uses a gun for this crime that he stole more than a decade earlier when he was still in the Gendarmerie academy.[316]

THE BOUHOUCHE TRIAL

Knowing they messed up, both Bouhouche and Beijer flee the country. Unfortunately for them, international authorities help Belgium track them down. Bouhouche is arrested by Spanish police and extradited back to Belgium on December 4th, 1988. Beijer is arrested in Thailand in 1991. Both are released, awaiting trial in 1992.

In 1994, the Bouhouche trial starts. The case is centered on the 1989 Suleiman murder and the 1986 Mendez murder. While putting the case together, prosecutors tacked on other charges, adding the 1982 Zwarts airport robbery murder, the 1981 Goffinon car bomb attack and the 1981 attack against Vernaillen and his wife. Beijer and other Bouhouche acquaintances are also on the stand on various charges. The trial generates a media frenzy, dominating the news.

Bouhouche is found guilty of the Suleiman murder and the attempted murder of Said. He's found guilty of robbery with aggravating circumstances in the Zwarts affair. Additionally, Bouhouche is found guilty of several more minor offenses, like the robbery of Mendez's weapon collection, fencing the stolen Dyane arms, and renting the storage units with false ID. He is sentenced to 20 years of hard labor and is released in September 2000. Bouhouche is acquitted of the Mendez murder, the attempted murder of Vernaillen, and the Zodiac robbery.

As for Beijer, the most serious charge he's found guilty of is aggravated assault in the Suleiman case. He's also found guilty of fencing Mendez's stolen weapon collection and the Dyane arms. Bouhouche's other acquaintances get off completely.

During the 1994 trial, a previously undiscovered cache of Bouhouche Gang weapons is found in an undergrowth of forest on a private property in Villers-la-Ville. There are bags filled with weapons, explosives, and documents—the explosives are the ones that had been stolen to use in the failed extortion racket.

Back in 1987, the Bouhouche Gang tried to trade the Villers-la-Ville disclosure for something from investigators. An associate had emphasized the disclosure they could share might involve something dangerous for the very young children. Investigators didn't bite and no deal was struck. The young children still live on the property and are 10 years old at the time of the discovery.

The cache includes weapons from the Dyane and Mendez. There are also a few dozen ID documents coming from Chaumont-Gistoux and other Brabant Wallon towns. In addition to stolen and fake license plates, there are also dynamite sticks, two dozen detonators, and one grenade.

Bouhouche dies in a forestry-related accident in 2007. He was living in France in an old house without electricity or water and it appears he was trying to cut down a tree. The chainsaw broke, he stumbled and the tree fell on his head, killing him on the spot. His body is incinerated without an autopsy.

CHAPTER 25

TERRORISM AND GLADIO

WHILE EARLY INVESTIGATORS CONCENTRATED ON ROBBERY AS A MOtive, by the late eighties, investigators begin to consider terror more seriously. After all, terror swayed the Belgium election of 1985 and kept power away from the Left political parties. This, in turn, kept Belgium strongly aligned with NATO and the Western powers, ensured the nuclear missiles placed in Belgium stayed there and resulted in the election of a law and order government. Whether the motive was truly terror or robbery, the Brabant Insane Killer attacks had an undeniable political impact. Before the Killers began their campaign of violence and terrorized the nation, the Right was heading towards a historical defeat. Their terrifying crimes brought violence and insecurity as the number one issue of the 1985 election campaign. Obviously, the Insane Killers weren't fully responsible for the insecurity. The Far-Left group CCC also played a role, but in the end, a Right-Wing law and order government was elected and that had real everyday consequences for the population. More than 7.5 billion BEF (about US $210 million) are invested in new security measures. The Gendarmerie gets 10,000 new weapons with better firepower and 1,000 new cars.[317]

Which begs the question: Did Western intelligence services create the Brabant Killers and orchestrate the crime spree that terrorized Belgians? The fact four people linked to the Brabant Killers case moved to Florida around the time of the killings, three of whom were Gendarmes, arouses real suspicions in Belgian. Some top police chiefs and prosecutors believed some Western intelligence services were involved.

If we put any value in the threats victims received, the participation of someone on the inside has to be considered. Some of those threats go beyond just looking for the name of a suspect in the phone book and making a call. If the lines were tapped, agencies in Belgium with the capabilities to tap phones need to be considered.

There were plenty of threats during the Brabant Killers' investigations. Some of the threats made against the victims are quite elaborate. It suggests that a simple criminal would have difficulties pulling them off without help from law enforcement or the Sûreté. For example, the grandfather of the nine-year-old boy that had the rest of his family wiped out decided to mount his own private investigation on the Brabant Insane Killers. On December 28th, 1985, he gets a request in the mail to pay a fine for an unpaid parking ticket, but it's not for his car. The car that had been ticketed has the same plate number and the same color—metal blue—as his own Mercedes 300 D. However, the car that was really ticketed was a BMW 520. Even eerier is the fact that the car was parked on Flagey Square in Ixelles, the epicenter of the Brabant Killers' activities. Chillingly, the taxi driver, who was murdered by the Insane Killers in January 1983, was picked up by one of the Insane Killers at that very spot. And, of course, the Insane Killers were notorious for using false plates of similar looking cars. According to the grandfather's nephew Hugo: "The family sees it as a kind of signal from the attackers… A kind of warning: we know where you are, shut up!"[318]

Ten years later, during the second inquiry on the Insane Killers, the same thing happens to this bereaved grandfather. He receives another fine for an unpaid parking ticket in the mail, only this time it's for a gray metallic Peugeot with the right license plate number. This time the car had been ticketed in Antwerp, but he hadn't been to Antwerp for the past decade. He considers the message to be, "We still know where you are!"[319]

Early investigators generally brushed off these claims. They're in a Catch-22. If they accept that the threats are real, the Insane Killers are more than just street thugs, which contradicts their working theory and would open up a can of worms. Instead, investigators did their best to explain away all the threats as either the imagination of the victims or other personal issues they had.

Gladio

Were the Insane Killers the Belgium version of the "Years of Lead" attackers that perpetrated the terrorist violence that shook up Europe in the eighties? Notorious examples of this violence include the Oktoberfest attack in Germany in 1980 and the Bologna Bombing in Italy in 1981. These attacks have been blamed on NATO, the US, and the intelligence agencies of other European countries. Who is responsible for these attacks is still under debate. To determine whether the Brabant Insane Killers were part of this phenomenon, we need to get a bit technical to determine how it would have worked out.

We now know that many of these "Year of Lead" attacks were caused by Far-Right extremist groups. But unlike the typical Far-Left attacks, these groups never claimed responsibility for their actions. Which led the terrorized population to wonder if the terrorist attacks were the responsibility of Communist groups? And if so, were these groups sponsored by the Soviet Union? The Insane Killer attacks also seemed like terrorism, but no groups ever claimed responsibilities for those either.

After the Second World War, America and Britain stationed secret troops in each country in Europe, and called them "stay-behind" armies. They kept operating until 1989, the year that brought the fall of the Berlin Wall and communism in Russia. During those years, they were so secret that each country's leader and ministers didn't know anything of their activities. These stay-behind armies coordinated with NATO's top leadership. Their initial purpose was to organize armed resistance in the case of the occupation of Europe by the Soviet Union. But during the time when these armies were waiting in vain for an invasion by the Soviet Union, some of them are suspected to have been used to commit terror attacks.

In Italy, the Italian intelligence service is accused of aiding and abetting Far-Right groups linked to the stay-behind armies with support from the Americans and covering for them during investigations following their terrorist attacks. At first, the attacks were blamed on the Italian Communists. There was a major scandal in Italy when details surfaced of the ambiguous roles of the Western intelligence agencies in the Year of Lead attacks.

If there was a secret stay-behind army in Belgium, were the Insane Killers part of it? Did they get help from the stay-behind army? There was a public inquiry into the matter but the two point-men for the stay-behind armies—Albert Raes, head of the Sûreté, and his army counterpart—refused to give the names of the agents in the stay-behind cells. So we don't know if the men suspected of being the Brabant Insane Killers were stay-behind agents.

WESTLAND NEW POST

The neo-Nazi movement Westland New Post has been suspected of having been a tool the Western powers or an international cabal of VIPs could have used to pursue their interests. They have also been accused of being involved in the Insane Killers' attacks. To understand the roles Westland could have played in regards to the Insane Killers, we need to delve into the nature and the history of the underground group.

Not only did the Westland New Post steal NATO classified documents and spy on Left Wing groups, two members were also charged in the double murder on Pastoral Street and Marcel Barbier was found guilty. In the public eye, the Westland is a group of dangerous extremists. It wouldn't be a major shock if the Insane Killers came from their midst.

The leads tying them to the Brabant Killings are not contemporaneous to the events. But some Westland members had privately suspected other members of being involved at the time. The links started coming out around 1989 when investigators began to invest more time and energy on terrorism and the Far-Right.

The message from some old members was that they were asked to case supermarkets in 1981 and 1982, and some of those supermarkets were later attacked by the Insane Killers. For example, Westland member Eric Lammers says, "Later on I realize that the Colryut, Delhaize that we're casing, it's exactly what was attacked later by the Brabant Killers."

Arguably, even if they weren't the Brabant Killers, the Westland could have been part of the larger network doing dirty work for the Sûreté and other Western intelligence groups. One line of investigation explored targeted assassinations as a motive of the Brabant Insane Killers. There is some speculation that the victims of the Brabant Killers are only anonymous to a casual observer when really the attacks were intended to cover up targeted assassinations. Some say that many of the victims knew too much about orgies by VIPs that involved minor children. Consequently, a cabal of powerful people wanted to shut them up for good.

The Westland New Post was just one tool of this cabal and they may or may not have been the private hit men who came to be known as the Brabant Insane Killers.

These VIP orgies came to be known through the Pinon affair, which will be forever intertwined with the Brabant Insane Killers mystery. To understand why VIP's would have any interest in using unsavory neo-Nazi groups like Westland to do their dirty jobs, we need to explain the Pinon Affair.

THE PINON AFFAIR

To explain the Pinon Affair and how it relates to the Brabant Insane Killers, we need to go back to the late seventies. In March 1979, psychiatrist Doctor Pinon files divorce proceedings against his homemaker wife. These divorce proceedings launch the Pinon Affair, which takes on national proportions.[320]

The Pinon Affair is a play in two acts. Pinon Act 1 is the actual divorce case, which largely concerns the payment of alimony and custody of the Pinon's children. The court initially grants Ms. Pinon custody of their daughter and gives the father access rights.

However, before the final judgment, Ms. Pinon's father is involved in an aggravated assault incident. When the court finds out, it determines the grandfather could be a danger to his grandchildren and opens up a separate Youth Protection File case. The child custody file is transferred to Judge Z. in Youth Protection and the Court issues an interim order to place the children in foster care until final custody issues are settled. The Court also orders the couple to meet privately for a last-ditch effort at reconciliation.

During this court-mandated discussion, Ms. Pinon allegedly shares with her estranged husband that she's had an affair, which is important as adultery has serious consequences in divorce cases in Belgium at the time. When Dr. Pinon prods his wife further, she confesses she's actually had numerous affairs and participated in orgies with several men and women. Ms. Pinon even gives her husband the names of six of her lovers, three of whom are other doctors. Among those named are a Dr. X., who hosted the orgies, and the Duck, the Sûreté agent who is handling Paul Latinus. At the time, the Westland New Post didn't exist, but Latinus was involved in the Far-Right Youth Front movement.

Ms. Pinon allegedly then confessed to her husband that some of the orgy participants were underage. Even if this is true, "underage" could mean different things as the age of majority in Belgium is over 18 years old, but the age of sexual consent is 16. An underaged 17-year-old can legally consent to have sex with an adult, but if Ms. Pinon means under the age of consent that will have huge consequences on the couple's legal proceedings. Because there is no recording of the couple's conversation, it's unclear what Ms. Pinon meant by "underage." While feigning compassion, Dr. Pinon hires a detective to get more evidence for the ongoing divorce case.

Dr. Pinon's detective gets the following elements on tape: "I had orgies with Dr. X, I did it and I didn't like it, and I told him and I had discussions with you...." When Dr. Pinon listens to the recording, he's underwhelmed. He's adamant that Ms. Pinon talked about minors during their reconciliation meeting, but he never succeeds in getting the recorded evidence to back up his claim. The Judicial Police officer who later listens to the tapes states: "It doesn't appear in the text of the taped conversation between (Dr. Pinon) and his wife (Ms. Pinon) (…) that children would be mixed up with eventual parties between the people that are mentioned above."

Nevertheless, the Judicial Police sets up surveillance around Dr. X's residence, where the orgies are allegedly happening. No evidence of illegal activities is ever found in their investigation. The Judicial Police decide not to pursue the matter further and close the file. Dr. Pinon writes a letter to the Youth Court Judge regarding the contents of the tapes, but it doesn't move the case further.

Then, suddenly police reopen the case. First, Dr. Pinon tells police he's been the victim of a series of break-ins. He tells them he suspects the thieves are looking for files or cassettes concerning the alleged orgies. Then, a second incident piques the interest of police: A woman rumored to be Dr. X's lover kills herself in a downtown Holiday Inn. Police decide there's enough to investigate if real crimes related to these orgies are being covered up. Despite their more in-depth investigation, however, they come up empty handed again. In March 1980, the police again close the file on the matter.

Fast forward to 1981, when Act 2 of the Pinon Affair begins and this is when it gets national attention. At this point, the divorce proceedings are proceeding at a snail's pace and the children are still in foster care. Dr. Pinon decides to take the law in his own hands and embarks on his own private investigation to prove the allegations. When his private investigation is complete, Dr. Pinon puts the results of his findings in a letter to his lawyer, which is then forwarded to various Belgian media outlets.

In the letter, Dr. Pinon alleges that Judge Z.'s car was spotted parked overnight at Dr. X's home where the orgies are held. Judge Z. is the Youth Court judge handling the Pinon children's custody issues. Dr. Pinon also heard that the national leader of the Gendarmerie participates in the orgies. The involvement of these high-level officials is, he says, why the orgies stay covered up. Dr. Pinon also alleges, "A few weeks later, I overheard from a conversation at the College of Physicians, that many people are involved. It seems that even Prince Y. was a participant."

The fact Dr. Pinon's letter is mostly hearsay is problematic for the Belgian media and they don't publish his allegations. But Pinon keeps an ongoing communication with the Left-Wing *Pour* newspaper editors, who are known for not shying away from controversial stories. Still, there's not enough evidence to publish Dr. Pinon's story until Dr. Pinon contacts the *Pour*'s editor with tangible evidence to back up his allegations. Dr. Pinon has found Ms. W., who says she has direct knowledge of the important people who participated in the orgies, namely Prince Y., the Gendarmerie General, and Judge Z. and Dr. X.

Dr. Pinon recently met Ms. W., who is also in the midst of a custody battle. When they shared their divorce stories, Dr. Pinon told her about the VIP orgies. That's when Ms. W. replied that she is aware of the orgies, and even knows other famous people that participated: one former Prime Minister, one influential Minister, and a popular real estate magnate. She had found out that the woman who is said to have committed suicide while staying at the Holiday Inn did not kill herself; her car was sabotaged. Furthermore, Ms. W. says two other minors who participated in the orgies have also killed themselves. Even worse, she has heard that Dr. Pinon's Youth Court Judge, Judge Z., provided the minors for the orgies.

THE *POUR* NEWSPAPER

Pinon presents himself at the *Pour* with Ms. W. There they meet with the Editor in Chief, Jean-Claude Garot, who records the meeting. Ms. W. begins by listing all the big names involved in the orgies. Garot doesn't care much about Judge Z. or Dr. X. but listens intently when he hears the names of the ex-prime minister and Prince Y. Ms. W. then explains that the orgies are usually held at a famous golf course and there are approximately 30 participants. The minors are brought in by Youth Court Judge Z., who also happens to be in charge of the Pinon custody issues. Judge Z. is also now dating Ms. Pinon, despite the fact he was presiding over her case.

Regarding the minors, Ms. W. says, "Some even died, it's the truth!" She alleges that some minors killed themselves because, "They were sucked in the system if you want, and they fell in love." She adds, "There's one from Nivelles that put a bullet through his head" because he fell in love with a woman who participated in the orgies. He was only 15-years-old and it happened when he had to stop seeing her because: "Well, it's finished you can't see her anymore and he shot himself—he had found some stability and then they take it away from him."

According to Ms. W., "a second one hanged himself" when Judge Z. yanked him away from the group when he started getting feelings for one of the participants. She added that, "they built some self-confidence, in a woman, and the next day, bang, he went too far, the end!" Ms. W. relates that she found out about the murder and two suicides when she overheard a conversation about the cover-up: "Because Prince Y. is in the story, he's aware of everything (whispers) and he asks that everyone keeps their mouth shut." Prince Y. tells Judge Z. that he's protected, and nothing will ever happen to him.

After the discussion with Ms. W., the *Pour* newspaper feels they have a big scoop and enough evidence to go to forward with it. The fact that a Prince and big names in the political and business world are involved is political dynamite. They begin to put everything together before going to press with the story. The story of the VIP involvement leaks out to Right-Wing circles. Frantic calls are made to the newspaper begging them not to publish the story. There are rumors of big money payments offered to *Pour* to cover up the story, but the editor is undeterred. They'll be going to print with the story.

THE ARSON

Late at night on July 4th, 1981, six motorcycle riders drive up to the building that houses the printing presses and publishing department of the *Pour* newspaper. There's no security guard. The bikers easily break in and make their way to the second floor, where they throw a first Molotov cocktail. The fire's flashpoint starts there. They then throw some more Molotov cocktails at several other places in the building. The bikers run back to their motorcycles and take off as a massive fire erupts in the building. Despite the best efforts of the firefighters, the building is a total loss by the next morning.

Authorities open up an investigation and the culprits are quickly tracked down—mostly Far-Right militants from the Youth Front, which was already on life support since the Laeken attack in December 1980. The biker who recruited the team of arsonists was a close associate of Latinus back when he was still a member of the Youth Front. The biker's accomplices are supporters of the Youth Front's defunct hardcore cell. Unbeknownst to the public, the lead biker has just followed Latinus into the newly formed Westland New Post. They all get sentences ranging from three to five years. The Left-Wing *Pour* newspaper was already precarious financially and is forced out business for good. The Publisher Garot leaves the country and starts a new life in America.

Despite the fact that he is not charged, there is some evidence that Paul Latinus—in his capacity as leader of Westland—was on the ground that day. Latinus is familiar with the head operator who led the team of bikers as he was a new member of his new underground movement. Latinus is alsa suspected of having been the mastermind behind the *Pour* arson. As leader of the hardcore wing back in his Youth Front days, Latinus had never shied away from arson.

The night of the arson, the biker gang members met and departed for their task from a Far-Right watering hole called De Pomp Pub in the western part of Brussels. There are rampant rumors that the Sûreté has agents of influence there. Bruno Van Deuren, the suspect who confessed several times to being involved on some level in the Wavre Gun Shop attack by the Insane Killers in September 1982, claims that all the stolen weapons from the gun shop were hidden at De Pomp Pub.

The motive for the *Pour* newspaper's arson is still debated today. A common explanation is that the arson was related to the paper's intention to publish Dr. Pinon's claims about the VIP orgies with minors. Publishing these allegations could have crushed the Belgium post-war establishment, which has strong links with the Christian Democrats. It's the height of the Cold War; damaging the Christian Democrats, the Right, and the Monarchy could set the stage for the Left to take power. The Pinon story was an existential threat to the State and the *Pour* newspaper had to be torched. The newly-founded Westland New Post could be manipulated to do the job. And the Duck is even suspected to have been present during these alleged orgies, so he might have a personal interest in preventing the *Pour* from coming out with the story. The powerful cabal of VIPs needed to act. Could the Brabant Killings, just like the *Pour* firebombing, be one of the methods the cabal use to protect their interests?

REVENGE

However, the cabal of VIPs are not the only ones to have a motive for the arson of the *Pour*. It could have been a case of revenge by Paul Latinus. *Pour* is the Left-Wing newspaper that made the disclosures about Latinus, the Youth Front and the Laeken murder in early December 1980. Latinus was employed at the time in the office of the Christian Democratic labor minister. He believed he was on the verge of being admitted into the Sûreté as he had passed the first of his two exams to get in. A few short weeks later, Latinus is being investigated in the Laeken murder case because he knew the perpetrator. He loses his job and his name is all over the papers. Latinus feels he has no choice but to leave the country, realizing he will probably never be able to follow his dream of becoming a Sûreté agent.

Latinus insists that all new members do something illegal to enter the Westland. All the army members were asked to steal NATO documents. However, Alain W., who's not part of the army, suggests that Latinus can get copies of files from the Gendarmerie. At this time Bouhouche, Alain W.'s friend from the gun range, is still working in the Gendarmerie, so Latinus brings him special requests. One of the three files he asks for is the recent *Pour* arson file. Bouhouche has an associate working in the right department to get him the file. In July 1982, the Sûreté receives information that Latinus tried to use the police reports from the *Pour* file he received from Alain W. to damage the reputation of the editor-in-chief Garot. Apparently, Latinus feels torching Garot's newspaper is insufficient revenge for what the *Pour* newspaper did to him. But if the VIP cabal didn't call the hit on the *Pour* and it was instead Latinus, it weakens the argument that there's a cabal out there willing to use any means necessary to silence whistleblowers, of which the Brabant Killings are a part.

Empty Shell

To gauge how serious is the claim that the Westland New Post was involved in the Brabant Killings, we need to have a closer look at Westland's history. Since the late eighties, some Westland New Post members strongly promoted the idea that a nameless, faceless powerful Western elite manipulated Westland to do their dirty deeds. They allege that this Western elite worked in coordination with the Belgium Sûreté to organize their own team of criminal operators and the Duck was their point man inside Westland.

There are three key figures who actively promote this theory: Libert, who was accused of organizing the theft of classified NATO documents; Barbier, who spent years in jail for the Pastorale Street double murder; and Lammers , who was accused, but not found guilty, of the Pastorale Street double murder—and who was convicted of another money-related double murder a few years later. These men also suggest the same Western sponsors planned the Brabant Killings. However, this theory is different from what Latinus confessed before his death and to what police reports and statements by Westland lead us to believe.

Before his death, Latinus told the media that the Belgian Sûreté was running Westland, but it was on behalf of the KGB and not the West. According to him, the Pastorale Double Murder was a KGB operation. Further, Latinus said in 1981 th DIA, the American Military Intelligence agency had given him the mission to unmask the Sûreté because it was run by the KGB.

At no time did he mention an elite Western entity ran the show.

If we look at police reports, Westland was active from early 1981 to late 1983. Latinus had been a paid informant of the Sûreté since 1979, which was two years before Westland was created. He spied on Left-Wing movements, first using Youth Front members and then Westland members. He would pass any information he gleaned to the Duck. Latinus founded Westland and under his direction, it grew to about twenty to thirty members.

Many Westland members were acquaintances of Latinus when he led a sub-group of the Youth Front, which included the most hardcore members. Other Westland members were Michel Libert's acquaintances from the communication division of the army. When recruiting new members for Westland, Latinus insinuated that his relationship with the Duck was a sign that the Sûreté and the Belgium state were supportive of the group; they were an anti-communist organization just doing what the government couldn't legally do itself.

Latinus asks the Duck to give Westland members a course on how to do surveillance and case a property. The Duck accepts and gives a course at Marcel Barbier's apartment; this is beneficial for him as he can expect to receive better quality information from Latinus' group. A couple of months later, the Duck gives Westland members a practical exercise where they have to case a real property and spy on a real person. The Pastorale Street double murder of February 1982 happens during the time the Duck was involved with Westland. In mid-1982, Latinus and the Duck sever their relationship.

The period of time when the Duck leaves Westland corresponds with when Latinus loses interest in his group. At this point, Latinus has money trouble and really uses Westland as a tool to make money. For example, Latinus gets Westland associates to infiltrate drug rings or arms trafficking organizations so they can sell their findings to any agency that wants to buy it. From this point on, Westland as a Far-Right underground organization only exists as an empty shell run by Michel Libert. He's the only person who still seems to take Westland seriously. While Latinus can't be bothered with the political side anymore, Libert has plans for several interconnected departments. Unfortunately, Libert's plans never amount to much more than a paper existence.

Latinus has little success selling his information and his precarious financial situation goes from bad to worse. After the *Pour* newspaper outed him in December 1981, in a series of headlines that not only linked him to the Youth Front, but suggested he might be linked to the Laeken murder, his life is stuck in a rut. Once the *Pour* newspaper suffers his wrath, he turns his anger towards the Duck and Sûreté Director, Albert Raes. Latinus is paranoid and believes they were the sources behind the *Pour* newspaper's headlines. He feels they need to pay.

Latinus has a three-step revenge plan. First, he outs Westland by thrusting them into the public eye. He doesn't care about Westland any longer and is well aware that shining a light on it will destroy the movement. Getting back at the Sûreté is even more important! Step two is to make Westland look bigger and scarier than it ever was, so unpalatable that it shocks the public! To accomplish this, Latinus will disclose the Pastorale Street double murders committed by Westland members. Step three is to show the public that the Sûreté was involved in the whole thing from the beginning. And not just working with them, he intends to make it look like the Sûreté was running the show.

Latinus believes this will fatally damage the reputation of the Sûreté and become a major embarrassment for the Belgian government. He also knows this kind of revelation will also ruin the careers of the Duck and Albert Raes—and they'll hopefully end up going to jail for conspiracy to murder.

Then the 1983 incident happened, when Marcel Barbier got drunk, had an argument with his brother, and shot at people in the street. When the police got involved, the secret of the existence of Westland was revealed to the public before even Latinus could successfully leak it through the press.[321] Some people believe Barbier made a scene just to get the police involved. Whatever the case may be, Latinus jumped on the opportunity to take his revenge. He moves to step two of his plan and links Westland to the gruesome Pastorale Street double murder. Latinus accuses Barbier and Eric Lammers of being involved and even gets Barbier to confess. The public is very disturbed and disgusted.

Latinus then leaks to the media that the Sûreté was actively involved with Westland in April 1982 when the Pastorale Street double murders were committed. The public finds out three Westland members had even been paid informants for the Sûreté, including Latinus and his top lieutenant, Libert. Furthermore, at least three Sûreté agents had regular contact with Westland. Aside from the Duck, the code names of the other agents are the Dog and the Rabbit. But even more damaging for the Sûreté is the disclosure that the Duck, a management-level agent, had been a card-carrying member of the Westland under his real name who even gave private surveillance lessons to these dangerous extremists. The public is horrified to learn that the Duck's training of extremists included at least one practical exercise on the ground tailing a real, live target. During the time span the Duck was giving the courses, Westland committed the Pastorale Street double murder.

Latinus is able to convince members to play along with his allegations because he sells the self-destruction of the Westland New Post as an anti-communist crusade. This is when Latinus discloses that Westland's reason for existence has been to smoke out the KGB spies from the Sûreté: Director Albert Raes and the Duck. But the media and public couldn't care less about his KGB stories; what upsets most Belgians is that the Sûreté was infiltrating a Far-Right movement that was committing murders and stealing classified NATO intelligence. This revelation seriously tarnishes the image of the Sûreté. It's an embarrassment for the Minister of Justice, Jean Gol, who is responsible for the Sûreté. Director Albert Raes ends up getting a lateral transfer to another position inside the Justice Ministry. The Duck gets a short suspension. Neither is charged with a crime nor does any jail time. These consequences fall very short of what Latinus had hoped would annihilate his foes.

THE PASTORALE STREET DOUBLE MURDER

The Pastorale Street double murder of February 1982 is crucial because it is so brutal, so heinous, that it makes Westland look truly evil. It also gives credence to the claim that Westland members were capable of committing the equally terrifying Brabant Killings. Much confusion has existed concerning the motive for the double murder. In February 1982, Westland members were asked to meet Libert, who told them they had to case the area of the Pastorale Street apartment. Libert tells them that a man and woman living in the second-floor apartment of the non-descript residential building are Soviet spies. Westland members follow these orders and case the neighborhood, take notes, and report their findings to Libert, who's heavily involved in the coordination of the operation. On February 19, 1982, at 8:30 p.m., a car drives up to the exact Pastorale Street apartment that had just been cased earlier that month. Two men exit the car and enter the building's front door. The men barge into the second-floor apartment where they shoot the couple and slit their throats.

When the Pastorale Street attack is linked to Westland in the media more than a year after, the focus is on how terrible the crime is and that extremists committed it. While members had been told the victims were KGB members, it was obvious they were not. The public is not given much more information. Because Westland members were forced to commit crimes as an initiation into the group, many assumed this terrible crime was one of those instances. It seems plausible that new members were given random people to kill. What bolsters this explanation is the fact that some Westland members were involved in pagan practices, and in this instance, the two victims were asked to kneel in front of each other before they were shot and had their throats slit. It looked like some kind of ritual. In reality, the Pastorale Street murders had nothing to do with politics or Westland per se. The couple are not Soviet spies, as the Westland members were told; the motive was actually personal. The victim Vander Meulen was the ex-husband of Barbier's girlfriend. While Libert was the de facto number two in Westland, Barbier was in theory of equal rank in the movement. So Barbier definitely had enough clout to get members to spy on the couple. It's Libert who suggested Barbier tell the Westland members the Soviet spy story so they would do as they were asked.

Barbier's girlfriend was involved in a messy custody fight for her children. Her ex, the victim Vander Meulen, wanted to get the kids from her. The ex-husband had threatened her, saying that he would tell the Courts that she was working as a waitress in Brussels' Red Light District, which could have had very serious consequences for the custody issue. Not only that, but Barbier's girlfriend was entitled to a big insurance payout if her ex-husband died. Police briefly interrogate Barbier after the murder, but can't find any links to him.

We don't know if the decision to kill Vander Meulen and his new girlfriend was made before or after the WNP members cased their property. Perhaps Barbier just wanted to just spy on his ex, or maybe something they found when casing the apartment was the cause of the murder. Some of the members who cased the Pastorale Street property never made the connection to the brutal murder that was committed there a few days later. There's no evidence that Sûreté agent the Duck was ever aware of the surveillance or the murder before Westland's connection to it was leaked in the papers. It's possible that Latinus was not aware when it happened, but he was certainly advised soon after. Latinus was reportedly quite upset about Westland's involvement.

LIFE AFTER WESTLAND

The Pastorale Street double murders still hang like an albatross around the necks of the Westland members. What they've done is frowned upon by general society, but if the murders were non-political (because murdering KGB spies would have been different than an ex-husband) the Far-Right peers are also disgusted. The Westland splinter cell responsible for the murder try to fight for their honor, but everyone knows the Pastorale Street murders were their misguided crime. Their line of defense for committing the Pastorale Street murders—legally and in media interviews—is that they were victims of the system. They claim that an elite group of powerful, secret plutocrats manipulated them and sponsored the crimes with the helping hand of the Sûreté.

For Libert, Westland was never just a small organization with two dozen members that quickly ran out of steam, it was a far-reaching secret conspiracy that stretched across Europe. From what we can tell, Libert confuses the very real contacts Latinus uses during his attempts to make money with these mysterious sponsors. The contacts only knew that this guy, Paul Latinus, wanted to sell them his private investigative services. They likely had never heard of the Westland New Post or thought it was probably just some type of detective or security firm. The fact Latinus unsuccessfully pitches the Sûreté, the Gendarmerie, other police forces, and businesses is seen as proof that Westland was being supported by these powerful people. Libert, Barbier, and Lammers also say they were just pawns without free will in the hands of this powerful cabal; they, like the other members, have to blindly follow the directives issued by this distant elite group. They were just cogs in the system forced to commit these murders and crimes.

Like Latinus, Libert, Barbier, and Lammers promote the image of a scarier Westland New Post—and they say it was all coordinated by the Sûreté, which considered this acceptable. There are alleged plans to kidnap the head of the state media. There's a secret trial held in absentia for Youth Front's leader Dossogne; his sentence is the death penalty, which was, of course, never enforced. Latinus knows that the more toxic the WNP appears, the worse it becomes for the Duck and the Sûreté. After Latinus dies, the other three go much further than him in promoting this. They blame everything they can think of as being committed by the WNP, including the crimes of the Brabant Insane Killers.

According to Lammers, "I always had the feeling, and even more than a feeling to have been conditioned, trained, prepared to commit that type of thing. And for a reason x or y, I was not used and looking back. I'm sure now that if at the time they would have order to commit those attacks. I probably would have been obligated and compelled forced in a non-enthusiastic way to do it. I would have done it." The splinter cell WNP members start talking about the Insane Killers after

Barbier is sentenced to life in 1987 for the Pastorale Street double murder. They accuse Westland of many crimes, some of which we know for a fact they never committed. They claim to be responsible for crimes like the Goffinon bombing, the Vernaillen home attack, the Zwarts airport murder, and the Dyane robbery, all crimes for which the Bouhouche Gang was charged, found guilty, or confessed to. For example, Lammers claims the Dyane robbery was just a Westland initiation for a new member. The Insane Killer story is just one of these stories in a long list of crimes.

Lammers also uses this opportunity to settle old scores. He accuses the members from the faction that stayed loyal to Latinus, of being the Brabant Killers. For example, he says of one Latinus ally, "I knew him from the Youth Front… He came to advise me that we prepared some work and that were doing surveillances things like that. And finally that work we didn't do it and later on I realize that the Colryut, Delhaize that we're casing, it's exactly that that was attacked later by the (Brabant Killers)." The Latinus ally claims he has never cased department stores.

If the Insane Killers were part of Westland they would not have come from those who allied themselves with Latinus. They don't fit the profile. The Westland killers would have been in the more violent faction that included Barbier and Lammers—and we also know they were in jail for the First Wave and the whole Second Wave. Barbier is detained for the Pastoral Street murders. Lammers is released but quickly picked up again in April 1985 for the armed robbery of a truck full of Marlboro cigarettes, as well as the robbery of valuable paintings and diamonds. He stays in jail until 1988.

TARGETED ASSASSINATIONS

The theory holding that Westland members firebombed the *Pour* on behalf of a powerful cabal of VIPs has variations. One of these is that the cabal sponsored the Brabant Killers using hitmen. The hitmen don't necessarily need to come from the Westland New Post, the cabal has many tools at its disposal. The reason the cabal had to cause the Brabant Killings is that they were being blackmailed by people that have incriminating evidence about crimes against children that they committed.

The Brabant Killers' victims are only indiscriminate for a casual observer. Anyone looking at them more closely will realize that the Brabant Insane Killer attacks covered up targeted assassinations. The Brabant Killers went after specific, predetermined victims during their attacks. The victims had in common that they all knew too much about the VIP orgies with children.

It's similar to the Pinon Affair and the VIPs involved might be the same or not. Videocassettes had been made of the sex parties. But this theory holds that the victims were terminated by the cabal of powerful people that hired a group of hitmen to finish off the witnesses. These hired murderers came to be known as the Brabant Killers.

When the backgrounds of individual victims are investigated, rumors start flying. For instance, taxi driver Costa Angelou, who was murdered in January 1983, allegedly owned a copy of the orgy tape. Similarly, two others alleged to have a copy of the cassette are Het Kasteel Inn caretaker, Jose Van Den Eynde, murdered in December 1982, and Jacques Van Camp, from the Aux Trois Canards Restaurant, who was murdered in October 1983. If the cassettes were blackmail material against the cabal, this explains the murders because the cabal had to clean up the problem by silencing those who could bring them down.

The notorious Nivelles attack from September 1983 was also purported to be motivated by copies of the videocassette. Some believe the murdered couple, Mr. Fourez and Ms. Dewit, who were shot as they filled their car's gas tank, had been targeted specifically. They were lured from the highway to make it look like they just stopped there for gas, but Ms. Dewit was the personal assistant of a notary who had a copy of the cassette. The notary, who had been blackmailing the VIPs, was paid

144,000,000 Francs (or approximately US $4 million) to return the cassette and keep his mouth quiet. However, Dewit and her husband had kept a copy for themselves. They had to be killed.

As for Officer Morue, who was shot and killed in the back of the Colruyt supermarket that same night, the Killers knew he would be responding to the alarm. They had access to his work schedule. They wanted him also dead because he had a file on the hitmen. They timed their attack in such a way that it only appears like a failed nighttime break-in.

The motive is much the same for the Second Wave attacks. The real target during the Braine and Overijse Double attack is victim Leon Finné, who is ultimately shot down in the Overijse parking lot. Finne was a banker by trade and a money man behind these sex parties. The cabal got Finne in one of two ways: Either Finné was lured to the strip mall or Finné was killed before and dumped on the parking lot.

The problem is that the much-talked-about cassette has, to this day, never been found.

Martial Lekeu

Aside from the Westland New Post there's a second nefarious underground cell that came to be suspected of being the Brabant Killers. In this case, the whistleblower is the ex-Gendarme Martial Lekeu who moved to Florida in 1984 because he feared for his life in Belgium. He had also been accused himself of being involved in the Brabant Killings.

After the Temse fabric attack of September 1983, Vincent L. and Francis V. allegedly drove to Lekeu's home to bring him bulletproof vests from the Temse fabric attack and weapons from the Wavre Gun Shop attack of September 1982. Francis V.'s allegations bring attention to Lekeu for the first time in the Brabant Killers case. One of the police sketches in the Temse attack kind of looks like Lekeu, plus his alibi was not great. Lekeu denies everything and finds the accusations silly.

After Francis V.'s accusations, Lekeu meets with the Brabant Killers investigators and blames the Brabant Killings on a secret cell of Far-Right Gendarmes. Soon after making the accusations of his own, Lekeu allegedly starts receiving death threats against his family from Gendarmes. He claims the threats are so personal he has no choice but to leave the country. He ends up in Florida in 1984.

Florida as destination is peculiar as four suspects related to the Insane Killers will end up there. This bolsters the suspicion that the Americans had a hand in the Insane Killers and helped the men immigrate. Lekeu left Belgium in 1984 and lived in Florida until his death.

In 1989, Lekeu hears that investigators assigned to the file are looking for him. He phones the Belgium press from America and starts repeating all the same accusations he made about Far-Right Gendarmes having been responsible for the Brabant Killings. He says this is what led him to leave Belgium for good and move to America. While talking to the press, Lekeu still sees himself as a whistleblower, but the press and the investigators only see him as a suspect. So when Lekeu denounces the Gendarmerie and the Far-Right, he comes off as also implicating himself. And Lekeu talks a lot…and the more he talked to denounce others, the more Lekeu seemed suspicious and the more the Brabant Killers started looking like a wide-ranging international conspiracy.

The takeaway message reported in Belgium is that Lekeu is in Florida hiding from Belgian justice. However, However, Lekeu insists he's just hiding from the Far-Right Gendarmes that threaten to kill him and his family. Prosecutors working on the Brabant Insane Killers case fly to America. They meet Lekeu in Atlanta at the offices of the Consulate General of Belgium. They question him about all of his explosive declarations in the Insane Killer case. He confirms again he left for America when he felt threatened by the Gendarmerie, but it had nothing to do with the Francis V. accusations.

The G Group

When Lekeu first blamed the Gendarmerie and the Far Right in December 1983, he was no doubt thinking back to an experience he had had earlier in his career. While he worked as a Brussels narcotics detective in the seventies, Lekeu was invited to join a secretive Far-Right group of Gendarmes affiliated to the Youth Front. The Group was called G Group—G of course standing for Gendarmerie. They had code names like G1, G2, G3; the leader was G1, a Gendarme who works at the (Gendarmerie's) Central Office of Intelligence.

The Group was new and Lekeu was present at the inaugural meeting. He receives the codename G5. The meeting is mostly about Far-Right political themes, but Lekeu is very disturbed by what he discovers. It included black and white photos of suspects arrested during left-wing protests and classified files taken from the Gendarmerie headquarters. He also believes the G Group members he meets are dangerous and wouldn't shrink away from violent crimes.

Lekeu tells Gendarmerie brass about G Group. After the Group's second meeting, the Gendarmerie opens up a discreet internal review. Head office disbands the movement after confronting participants about the rule against being involved in politics. Lekeu is extremely upset the Gendarmerie does not come down on them harder. Nothing seems to be done to punish the mishandling of classified information. According to Lekeu, this was because the Brussels Gendarmerie was infected with Far-Right ideas. The G Group only learns years later that Lekeu was the informant who snitched on them.

When Lekeu first hears about the Brabant Insane Killers attacking the Nivelles Colruyut in September 1983 and the Beersel Delhaize in October 1983, he has flashbacks to the Far-Right Gendarmes of the G Group—despite that the cell was dissolved in the seventies and he's had no contact with them since that time. He's convinced that whoever the current members of that Gendarmerie cell must be the Killers. During his public statements in 1989, Lekeu uses interchangeably the Youth Front and the Westland Youth Front; it's one and the same for him. He gives authorities the names of Gendarmes he believes were part of the cell during the Brabant Killings. In December 1983, he had given this same information to the Wavre Gendarmerie which made the notorious 1985 report. They make the same mistakes in the report as Lekeu does, confusing the Youth Front and the Westland New Post. Lekeu is thus probably a key source of the Wavre Gendarmerie report as it concerns the Far Right Gendarmes and the Insane Killers. The Report is the first public uttering linking Bouhouche to the Insane Killers. It makes the mistake to include Bouhouche in the list of Far Right Gendarmes. Lekeu says he's received death threats from some unknow Gendarmes after he talked to the Wavre Gendarmerie. He's so spooked he feels the need to leave Belgium.

CONFUSION

So when Belgian justice and the media come calling in 1989, Lekeu is still denouncing the Far-Right Gendarmes that he snitched on in the late seventies and he believes are the same ones that came after him after he talked in December 1983. Lekeu still sees himself as a whistleblower and not a suspect. This gave rise to lots of confusion, because when Lekeu talks about the Americans, he means that they're helping him against the Far-Right Gendarmerie. However, everyone in Belgium who listens to Lekeu or reads his quotes in print, sees a Brabant Killer suspect claiming he has links with Americans. This distorted interaction between Lekeu and the media continues until his death in 1997

After he snitched to the Gendarmerie and became disillusioned, he turns to his American friends. When Lekeu worked with the Narcotics Division of the Gendarmerie, he met Frank Eaton, who was the head of the DEA in Belgium: He was in contact with him since 1974-1975. For investigators, when Lekeu talks about being linked to the DEA, they read CIA.

The Americans did not exfiltrate Lekeu because he was an undercover operative, they helped him get to the States to protect him from the Gendarmes he felt threatened him. To make it to the States, he met Americans in Paris and obtained a visa. He left for the US on August 22, 1984, with the rest of his family. He landed in Miami, because Frank

Eaton from the DEA was there to meet him.

Once he arrives in the US, Lekeu claims he immediately took a false identity—not to flee Belgian justice, but to save his skin from the Gendarmes who are threatening him. Frank Eaton and the DEA contact helped with his American immigration papers. He was immediately offered two jobs; one was to work for the J. Gordon Liddy firm—the same Liddy who went to jail for the Watergate scandal. After doing some private detective work, Lekeu uses his narcotics department background to work undercover in Florida. He is a witness in subsequent high-profile drug cases. In 1997, he passes away from cancer in Florida.

CHAPTER 26

THE GENDARMERIE

THE LINK BETWEEN THE SEVENTIES G GROUP AND THE BRABANT KILL-ings is tenuous at best. Nevertheless the fact that Lekeu was threatened by unknown Gendarmes after he denounced them in 1983, can't be ignored. As we finish writing this book, in the fall of 2018, new allegations against unknown Gendarmes are made public. In November 1986 on the day when weapons and items were found in Ronquières, a witness claims that three unknown Gendarmes asked a diver to get them a bag at a spot in the canal. Once the diver pulled out a burlap bag, they left with it in a beige car. This all happened a couple of hours before the official discovery of the bags. These Gendarmes were never identified. It adds credence that the miraculous Ronquières discovery was manipulated.

We'll now look at the Gendarmerie as its own separate category because some leads implicate them. But not as part of Far-Right politics, but just as Gendarmes. It's not one and the same. Most Gendarmes are law and order types but it doesn't automatically make them Far Right extremists.

PATROL AGREEMENT

Before the Aalst supermarket massacre in November 1985, there was an agreement made between the Gendarmerie and the local police. The Gendarmerie had the responsibility to keep guard till 8:00 p.m. Then the local police took over at 8:00 p.m. But on the night the Brabant Killers attacked, the Gendarmerie left about half an hour before the closing time, which left no one there to guard the supermarket. Almost at the exact same moment as the Gendarmerie leave the parking area, the Insane Killers turn into the alleyway that takes them to the Delhaize's back parking lot.

The Gendarmerie patrol unexpectedly ended their patrol at the Delhaize and left the store, and just then the Brabant Insane Killers slipped in at exactly the right time.[322] As previously discussed, the Brabant Killers could have accomplished this feat by listening to the Gendarmerie frequencies on a police scanner—or because someone with a walkie-talkie sends them the all clear. But there's more here.

The traditional explanation the public has received is that none of the Aalst supermarkets were permanently supervised. There was just a police cruiser making the rounds. Consequently, the Gendarmerie patrol would visit the Delhaize, then go to the Colruyt, and then to the Aldi. But that explanation has been more and more challenged, and Gendarmes aware about the situation claim it didn't happen that way.

It just so happens that the prior six weeks the Gendarmerie had stayed at the Aalst Delhaize until 8:00 p.m. If the Insane Killers had picked any weekend before that, they couldn't have gone in. And if they tried on one or more weekends and noticed the police was still there, they wouldn't gear up again on the slight chance the Gendarmerie would leave. The agreement was never to travel from one supermarket to the next, but to stay until closure at 8:00 p.m. They would have needed inside information to know it wasn't happening that way that night.

Now, there are two explanations given to explain why the Gendarmerie left the supermarket early. First, there happened to be a Gendarmerie party that night and many Gendarmes were there. The Gendarmes had left early for the party, imagining that nothing could have ever happened. The second explanation is that the Gendarmerie patrol received a call from the head office telling them to leave their post. The Killers had inside information from the Gendarmerie or hit an incredible stroke of luck.

EMERGENCY ROADBLOCK

After they left the Aalst supermarket going due south, the Killers successfully execute a maneuver that makes them avoid a Gendarmerie roadblock. Then a bit later, investigators lose all trace of the Brabant Killers. There are sightings that they might have ended up in Houssières Forest, but they aren't strong enough to be sure. There is never irrefutable evidence about where the Insane Killers went that night.

If they decided to drive back to their hideout, it would have meant they had to drive through the town of Halle, which is the gateway to southern Brussels. However, the Halle police had set up an emergency roadblock to block the main thoroughfare. It was an automatic plan put in place after each violent hold up; every police officer or Gendarme would go to a designated place to establish police roadblocks.

Right before the time the Brabant Killers would have needed to drive through Halle, the Halle Gendarmes officers got a message to lift the roadblock over their radio. Now the Killers had just murdered nine people that night, 17 in their two last nights of work. The Gendarmerie is in a wild car chase after the Brabant Killers, going due South—and that could very well be going through Halle. But at that exact time, they're told to lift the roadblock over the radio with the accompanying code word "Gudule." The order was to not apply the standard alert procedures; "Gudule" is an internal radio code, essentially saying the order was coming from Gendarmerie Central. A more common code would have been "Dara," which is another way of saying that a message is coming from the local Gendarmerie station.[323]

Another bizarre incident that happened that night is that the same Halle Gendarmerie station received a bomb alert at 7:00 p.m., 30 minutes before the Killers hit in Aalst. The call happened at a time when authorities took bombing threats very seriously because the CCC had still not been dismantled. The Halle Gendarmes spent three hours looking for the bomb, which diverted crucial manpower. It turned out to be a false alert. If the Brabant Killers had any interest in going to their hideout that night, no one would have been available to block them.

WILD GOOSE CHASE

The November 1983 night of the Delhaize Beersel attack also points to inner knowledge of the Gendarmerie. In fact, the Gendarmerie received criticism in the news because of their slow response. What was very upsetting is that the Gendarmerie station is very close to the Delhaize store. Even so, the wife of a victim reached the supermarket before the Gendarmerie even showed up!A

According to Frans Reyniers, who led the Judicial Police, the Brabant Killers successfully lured the one and only Gendarme officer who happened to be working that night away. According to the Gendarme who worked that night: "What I know for sure, is that the perpetrators of [the Delhaize manager] Vermaelen's murder must have known us on their thumb. They had to know that only one of us was on guard that evening, and it was me. I was called away at that exact moment because of a very urgent telephone. I had to immediately go to the Colruyt..."B The very urgent telephone call was a fake.

The Colruyt supermarket had recently set up a tip line to receive anonymous information because one of their employees had been killed by the Brabant Killers in March 1983. To be able to talk on that tip line, you had to physically be in the Colruyt. According to the Gendarme who responded to the call: "They had an informant on the line that wanted to discuss the Brabant Killers and wanted to speak immediately to someone from the Gendarmerie. When I returned to the station I heard a radio communication that an attack had happened at the Beersel Delhaize..."324

DISTRICTS

In September 1985, during the Insane Killers' double supermarket attacks in Braine-L'Alleud and then in Overijse, the perpetrators display bizarre driving behavior. When leaving the Delhaize in Braine, they drive full speed towards the Delhaize in the town of Overijse. To go in a straight line from Braine to Overijse, you leave the French language administrative region of Wallonia and you cross over to the Dutch Language Flanders administrative region. And you also change Gendarmerie police districts. Braine is part of the Nivelles District, while Overijse is part of the Leuven District. The Insane Killers don't drive in a straight line between both towns, which they should have done. They make an obvious detour that helps them avoid the Wavre Gendarmerie District. The Brabant Killers have seemingly been tipped off that there is a secret cooperative agreement between the Nivelles and Wavre District Gendarmerie Forces.

SWAT TECHNIQUES

After the Aalst attack in November 1985, Arsène Pint, the founder of Dyane—the Gendarmerie's elite swat unit—phones the current Dyane director. Pint says: "Damn it, I only hope our guys didn't do this."[325]

Dyane takes care of all the most dangerous SWAT missions in the country, but because Belgium is small, the same dozen guys do 100 percent of all SWAT operations everywhere in the country. The job is so demanding that, on average, a Dyane SWAT team member has a shelf-life of only 10 years. The Dyane members learn specific techniques—some of which Pint suspects the Brabant Killers used.

According to Pint, ordinary gangsters don't use the same highly-specialized tactics as those used by the Brabant Killers during the attack at the Delhaize supermarket in Aalst. He remarks, "In Aalst, they shot everywhere with their riot guns, and in the meantime the others slipped inside. That looked a lot like a tactic that we call Fort Chabrol." In Dyane lingo, a Fort Chabrol is a technique used by a SWAT team when confronting an entrenched shooter.

Another Dyane officer describes the technique: "As an officer, I needed to direct one of the three teams during the intervention. The more experienced had to go in by the front door and go immediately to the stairs on the left. I had to go in with my men by the back door, 'cleanup' the first floor, and then meet the first team on the second floor. The third stayed outside in back as reinforcement."[326] The only difference in Aalst was that instead of three units, the Brabant Killers had three assailants and each assailant took on the role of each individual unit.

Furthermore, the weapons used by the Brabant Insane Killers are similar to those issued to elite anti-terrorist units. In the eighties, the submachine gun was the rage and so were 12-gauge shotguns. Handguns and assault rifles were just starting to gain back popularity among SWAT teams in the late eighties. When he saw the ammo used by the Brabant Killers, he was surprised: "We also used those in the Dyane group."A

It seems more likely than coincidence that the Brabant Killers used two 12-Gauge pump-action shotguns and the same brands of ammo and magazine as Belgium's elite anti-terrorism unit for swat operations. Not only did the Killers use the same weapons, they also moved in the same coordinated fashion as the SWAT team. The Killers would clear a zone, using a decent pace to get to the furthestmost point. In other words, the Brabant Killers moved like professionals—unlike typical gangsters who rush in and spray bullets indiscriminately, the Killers didn't move faster than they can shoot. They used economy of motion and moved to gain ground. They calmly and systematically cleared areas.

The strategy the Killers used demonstrated some training and experience. They would park far from the door, either in a far corner of the parking area or outside of the parking lot completely. They would walk at a short distance from one another, covering for each other. Then they would meet up at the front door. The first to arrive waited for the last to arrive. Then they used one of two techniques: In Braine in September 1985 and Beersel in October 1983, two of them reached the door of the office, while the third man cleared out the store. Any obvious threats are eliminated right away (Vermaelen in Beersel and Engelbienne in Braine). The first man enters the office, the second man stays back at the office door to clear out the room. Once they've met their objective, the two then make their way back to the supermarket's front doors, where the third man meets them. They cover each other's retreat in the parking area and make their way to the escape vehicle.

In Overijse in September 1985 and Aalst in December 1985, the Killers reach the supermarket's front door as they did in the other attacks. However, the last man stays back at the store entrance and exit, to cover their backs and clear the parking lot. Only one of the men goes to the office while the other man covers him and heads to the cash registers. The explanation is logical; Overijse is their second attack of the night and police are all out in their cruisers and Aalst is their highest risk operation ever—the whole country of Belgium is on alert. Aalst is the first time an attack happens at a location in the dead center of a town. They are not on their home turf as it's in the center of Dutch-speaking Flanders. The risk of having a confrontation in the parking area was higher in those cases, so they took additional precautions.

The founder Pint asked the current Dyane chief to check if some of his guys weren't involved in the Aalst Delhaize raid: "When I returned home, I immediately called General Bernaert: "General, I have this gut feeling that I can't get rid of. I want an investigation into everything that has to do with the Dyane Group." Bernaert's research into Pint's concerns lasted one whole weekend. On the Monday after Aalst, Bernaert called Pint back and said: "The research is negative... All the staff have been screened, all alibis examined."A They did this investigation all manually so that no one would notice anything on the computer that would tip anyone off. They didn't want the staff thinking that their generals are suspecting that they played a role in the Aalst attack. There has never been confirmation of whether they investigated past members of Dyane, which would be sensible as some suspects in the Brabant Killers attacks had once been part of it. Even in 1995, Pint couldn't shake his suspicions that someone at the Gendarmerie was involved.

The Killers certainly fit the profile of trained law enforcement in many of their actions. While not specifically a habit of SWAT teams, the way the Killers parked during their supermarket attacks is significant. While armed robbers commonly park right in front of the locations they intend to rob, the Killers never parked right in front of the supermarket doors and they always left the front clear. It's typical for many police units around the world to use this strategy when they make an intervention, instinctually or deliberately. According to one police officer: "Never park your squad car in front of the address you're sent to, no matter how routine the assignment sounds. They call this parking spot the 'kill zone' because it immediately puts you in harm's way... So don't be lazy. Park half a block down and scope out the scene"[327]

According to police expert Lode van Outrive: "The Insane Killers were quite familiar with the functioning of the Belgium police."[328] In Ronquières near Houssière Forest, the Brabant Killers got rid of a book on bullets used by police forces. Other than a firearms historian, who would have any interest in a book like that but a police officer? Also of interest are magazines found in Houssière Forest in November 1985. The magazine covers included titles such as *The Uzi used in the police, Manufrance: the new police shot gun* and *Colt Agent* with the image of police badges. All but one had police-related covers.

Consider, too, the scraps of papers found after the Wavre Gun Shop robbery in September 1982. The text on the bits of paper likely refers to a nighttime break-in at a dealership that happened a few days before the Wavre Robbery. The papers mention a meeting point and plans to meet "beside the police station." What kind of gangsters would make appointments right next to a police station? Would anyone else other than a police officer ever use a police station as a meeting spot if they wanted to go unnoticed?

Some Gendarmes and investigators have suspected that the investigations into the crimes of the Brabant Insane Killers were sabotaged from the inside. Gendarmerie officer Bernard Sartillot, who was shot by the Insane Killers during the 1982 Wavre Gun Shop attack, said: "I'm convinced that there was collusion in the investigation with the killers, I'll never say otherwise. When you ask me how it's possible that people made 28 victims and were never caught, I answer that to ask the question, is already to answer it."[329] During the first public inquiry, Prosecutor Poelman said there was treachery in the investigation into the Killers: "People implicated in investigative tasks deliberately informed the Killers about the ongoing investigation."[330] Further, he said, "We know that [some officers] cheated at certain moments ... Why wouldn't they have cheated more?"[331] According to prosecutor Van Lierde: "Among the people charged are several [ex-] gendarmes, that knew the investigative procedures…and of interrogation and use them to criminal ends in order to trick investigators."[332] Van Lierde was so concerned about the issue that he wrote a letter on August 2, 1987, seeking to exclude the Gendarmerie from the investigation.[333]

CHAPTER 27

PUTTING A TRIAL TOGETHER

THERE HAVE BEEN A COUPLE OF ALLEGED CONFESSIONS OF BRABANT Killers in the past couple of years. The families of the victims get their hopes up. Everything usually rests on one guy who sees a benefit out of confessing. Often the confessions are second-hand as the people alleged to have confessed are either dead or deny it. No physical evidence ever come up to bolster the statements. The witness profiles don't match up with the Insane Killers. It generated some short-term excitement about the case in the media. The result is more disillusionment among all those involved. It really always comes back down to the gangs mentioned in this book as the usual suspects: in particular the Haemers Gang, the Baasrode Gang, and the Bouhouche Gang.

COURT CASES

Ultimately, the goal is to get one of these suspected gangs before the courts. Or hope for the miracle of having another gang falling from the sky with a smoking gun!

We can look back to the lessons learned from two instances when suspects were charged. Once against the Borains Gang and once against Johnny De Staerke from the Baasrode Gang. Why wasn't a conviction secured?

When the Borains were charged, the state had no independent witness—other than another Borain—who could place any of the Borains Gang members at any crime scene. Their whole case rested on contradictory and nonsensical confessions that were obtained using enhanced interrogation tactics. The case was predicated on the fact the Brabant Killers were not too swift and were ready to risk anything to steal a buck. Despite all the hours spent working to get these allegedly low-intellect witnesses who had confessed to bring any shred of additional evidence forward were unsuccessful. The investigators were aware of the weakness of the Borains fitting the Brabant Killer profiles as they only ended up charging them for mostly minor crimes from the First Wave and no crimes in the Second Wave. In the end, the whole case rested on a gun that had zero value as the ballistic examinations were all contradictory. A pair of close acquaintants of Bouhouche, also suspects in the case, could have access to the gun during the investigation—a terminal flaw for a piece of evidence.

Then there was the case against Johnny De Staerke from the Baasrode Gang that never ended up seeing a courtroom. Here, again, it's very probable that the whole case was prompted by a manipulation on the part of the Insane Killers. The De Staerke lead rested on eyewitness statements regarding one single attack. As a reminder, De Staerke was in jail for most of the First Wave attacks, but some Aalst witnesses believe he looks like someone they saw earlier the day of or in the days preceding the attack in and around the Delhaize.

They indict De Staerke in the Aalst attack for the main reason that his ex-girlfriend gave a statement that he had been shopping in the Aalst Delhaize between 4:00 and 6:00 p.m. on the day of attack. He says it was the day before. Both statement were taken a long time after the attack.

There is no physical evidence. There are Legia ammo, masks, a belt and items found at the home of some of De Staerke's acquaintances that are similar to those used by the Insane Killers. If the look or brand of items was an important factor, you could find the same or more with the Haemers or the Bouhouche Gang. There is zero credible physical evidence.

Then De Staerke provided a shaky alibi when he was asked for one, months after the Aalst attack. He gave one story to investigators, and then later said he didn't remember what he did.

The Samsonite briefcase that he dropped off in a safe house the same night as Aalst had traces of gunpowder, even though he'd denied there were ever weapons in the briefcase. Investigators are suspicious that De Staerke is not being forthright. To be clear, even if it is gunpowder, it doesn't prove anything other than that De Staerke has credibility issues.

It was paper thin evidence. The investigators probably indicted De Staerke because they believed he could give them more, but more never came. Nor did other sources ever contribute evidence or testimony that could be used to bring a case against Johnny De Staerke or the Baasrode Gang.

Contract theory

To explain the presence of De Staerke operating alone in Aalst, without the rest of his Gang, we need to assume some other group got him to work with the Insane Killers on their final massacre. Which begs the question: How would this make any sense? One theory built over the years is the contract theory, which has also been applied to Patrick Haemers of the Haemers Gang. He would have been hired personally to do the job. Although Haemers was never charged, the slim evidence linking him to Aalst is about similar to what there is for De Staerke. A victim who saw Haemers years later on television believed he was the man who shot him. When Haemers was asked months after Aalst for an alibi, he came up with a restaurant bill, which some considered as suspicious as if he hadn't ever had an alibi because it was too perfect. Just as with De Staerke, Legia cartridges and masks were found in a Haemers Gang box.

The contract theory is often used to prove that terrorism motivated the killings. Some sponsor would have mixed Special Forces with gangsters who knew how to do hold-ups and knew the lay of the land to pull off attacks to scare the population. The goal was ostensibly to influence the elections, affect the presence of NATO missiles in Belgium, to give more firepower to the Gendarmerie or all of the above. In the fall of 1985, the general public know barely anything about Patrick Haemers or Johnny De Staerke. Belgians were aware that there was a gang called the Baasrode Gang that committed a series of armed robberies, but left no victims. They're also aware of another gang, still unnamed, that had their first victims the week of the Aalst Delhaize attack in November 1985, when they used a bomb that was too big for their intended objective, the back door of an armored postal truck. To anyone not acquainted intimately with his activities at the time of Aalst, Haemers is a farcical armed robber who went to jail for the poorly conceived Deerlijk Bank attack. And De Staerke has been a fugitive from the law since 1985 and he was not publicly known to be a hold-up specialist.

Even if outsiders wanted to recruit a bandit from either or those gangs, would they really have gone for Haemers or De Staerke?! Why go for the junkie or the hothead? Why not Dominique S. or Philippe L., who were the brains in the outfits? The theory goes because they wanted real killers, but Dominique S., Haemers, De Staerke and Philippe L. have all been accused for the same number of shooting murders in their criminal careers. That is to say, none. Not one murder victim killed with a gunshot. While there's a bit more in the Haemers Gang and the Baasrode Gang leads than all these recent dubious second-hand confessions, the cases have not moved an inch in years in terms of evidence. There is not much for investigators to go on…

THE RIGHT SUSPECTS

To bring a case to trial, you need to develop the right suspect. A couple of important characteristics that have been brought forward about the Brabant Killers were that they included police officers and practical shooters. We find that is almost certainly the case, which automatically excludes the Baasrode Gang and the Haemers Gang. If there were police officers among the Brabant Killers, that explains why during their four major shootouts with police, the Killers always come out on top, un-scathed, while officers end up killed or wounded. The Brabant Killers know the police have limited firepower at the time. They know who and what they're up against. They also know the Gendarmerie's rules of engagement and they often anticipate their arrival. If they do a sloppy job, they can always fix anything on the back end as they participate in the investigations and have access to the files.

It would explain why the Killers seemed more than quite aware of the police's radio communications and intervention plans. We don't exclude that there were institutional problems or human errors made. However, we are now convinced that there was internal sabotage in the Gendarmerie that leads us to where we are. Upon reviewing all the information available, we clearly see cover ups and conspiracies at an investigative level. While we don't exclude that it could have gone higher in the hierarchy, there's no evidence of that. As we've seen in similar cases where police investigators were mixed up with organized crime, that's all that's needed to completely mess up all the investigations. Consider notorious American cases like those involving Louis Eppolito and Steven Carracappa, the NYPD detectives who worked for the mob, and John Connolly, the FBI detective who helped cover up for Whitey Bulger's Winter Hill Gang.

The Brabant Insane Killers weren't your typical Gangsters who just pick up a gun for a hold up and would miss more times than not when shooting at a target a couple of feet away. The Killers definitely had interest in guns and ammunition and some were skilled marksmen or practical shooters.

In Soignes Forest in October 1982, evidence of involvement in practical shooting was found among items abandoned by the Insane Killers.[334] In Houssières Forest and Ronquières, there were gun magazines and books found. And the fact the Killers used reloaded bullets suggests people who shoot a lot.

The only suspected gang that fits the bill on both counts is the Bouhouche Gang, which is very top-heavy with Gendarmes. At the very least there were two active practical shooters in the gang.

We've discarded completely the theory that the Brabant Killers had a logistics wing or sponsors. Everything they did could be explained without it, and there's no evidence that there were ties to such outside entities. It seems clear that the Brabant Killers are a gang whose members went out in the field themselves and killed 28 people.

But there's so much we don't know about the Bouhouche Gang. Everyone knows about Philippe De Staerke's alibi in Aalst, about Patrick Haemers' alibi in Aalst and even Martial Lekeu's alibi in Temse. Unlike these other suspects, the key Bouhouche Gang members were not in jail or out of the country during major parts of the Brabant Killings. And some, individually, were members of police forces. What are their service records? How many times were they on one of their shifts working? There must be records of this? It's not public knowledge. For example, did any of the top members have an alibi for the night of the double raid in Braine and Overijse? We don't know. Do they have alibis, other than themselves, for each of those attacks? Is there evidence that absolutely exonerates them as suspects? We don't know.

BOXES FOR STOLEN CARS

We do know about the Bouhouche Gang's criminal activities. Could these activities have given them an alibi of sorts? The Bouhouche Gang rented a network of apartments and car boxes to house stolen vehicles. We know a fair amount about the details of this network. Here we'll focus in on the car boxes only.[335]

The Bouhouche Gang would steal vehicles to use them for their own criminal activities, not resale. They rented boxes to store their stolen vehicles. When they did not have enough boxes, the Gang was forced to park their cars in the streets and parking lots outside of their Ixelles or Woluwe rental complex bases. It left them vulnerable to discovery by authorities. Law enforcement seized the exposed vehicles a few times.

As for the Brabant Killers, their vehicles were abandoned and torched. They never left their vehicles in the street, having a good hiding place for their vehicles. Like the Haemers, Baasrode or Bouhouche Gangs they probably rented a garage box to hide them. Because the Brabant Killers only possessed one car at a time, we believe that they only rented one box. They immediately get rid of a vehicle when they steal another one. In fact, the one and only occasion that they had two vehicles—a dark Golf and an Audi—at one time was between February 22 and March 3, 1983.[336] Limited storage space forced the Killers to park their Audi in the street where it was found by authorities in Ixelles on March 3, 1983.

Knowing what we know of the Bouhouche Gang, did they have the logistics apparatus to run the Insane Killers's operations in addition to their own? If they did not, it was a defence they would have surely used. The Bouhouche Gang had two main rental complex centers—Ixelles and Woluwe. During the second half of 1985, they developed a third center in another part of Brussels called Anderlecht.

The Bouhouche Gang started renting vehicle garage boxes out of pressing need. Starting in 1981, they had a box for every stolen vehicle. They first rented a box in the Ixelles complex on September 11, 1981. Days after, on September 28, 1981 they stole a Mazda 626. On October 7, 1981, they stole a Toyota HiAce van which was crucial to transport the heavy equipment needed for their extortion project. In both cases, the stolen vehicles were crimes of opportunity since each car was double parked on Louise Avenue with the keys inside.

Despite the ease of access, the Bouhouche Gang faced the dilemma of having two vehicles but only one safe box to store them. Out of necessity, the Gang parked the extra stolen vehicles on the street outside of their Ixelles or Woluwe rentals. Unfortunately for the Gang, their Mazda 626 is seized by the authorities on October 28, 1981.

The same thing happened when the gang stole another car. Around January 1, 1982, they stole an unmarked, green Mazda car with weapons inside from Dyane headquarters. They emptied the contents but parked the stolen Mazda outside their Ixelles base. Like the previous stolen car, the authorities found it on January 4, 1982.

Between February 23 and 26, 1982, they stole a white Ford Taunus that they later disguised as a police vehicle to commit crimes. Learning from their previous mistakes, they immediately rented a garage box at their Woluwe Base on March 20. They now had two boxes for their two vehicles.

On May 10th, 1982, the Insane Killers stole a Volkswagen Santana and hid it in a garage. Meanwhile, on June 1, 1983, the Bouhouche Gang rented a third box despite the fact that they were only known to possess two vehicles—the HiAce and the Taunus. The use of this box overlaps with the duration of the Brabant Killers First Wave, the Bouhouche Gang left the contents of this extra box suspiciously unaccounted for.

On September 30, 1982, the Brabant Killers torched and abandoned their Volkswagen Santana. The Brabant Killers did not have a vehicle from October 1982 to January 1983. During this period, they committed two crimes. One took place in a taxi, for which they did not need a vehicle, and one involved an alcohol robbery where they murdered the caretaker at the Het Kasteel Inn in Beersel. Witness statements pointed to a vehicle of which the size and brand is debated. However, the witnesses agreed that the vehicle was white. Coincidentally, the Bouhouche Gang only possessed two known vehicles during this period—both white.

In early 1983, the Bouhouche Gang still rented three boxes—one for each of their two cars, and the third with unaccounted for contents. Meanwhile on January 28, 1983, the Brabant Killers stole a Peugeot, and shortly after on February 14, they stole a Volkswagen Golf as well. They immediately disposed of the Peugeot the next day, proving that they only had one secure garage space. On Februrary 22, the Killers stole an Audi 100—the only time they had a second car. The authorities recovered the Audi in the street in Ixelles just a few days later on March 3.

The Bouhouche Gang meanwhile replaced their two Woluwe vehicle boxes for two vehicle boxes in Ixelles on July 10, 1983. The lease for both boxes in Ixelles started on July 10th, 1983. They abruptly cancelled the lease on the two boxes in Woluwe on July 20, 1983. Despite the opportunity to get rid of the unaccounted-for box, they maintained all three of their boxes in Ixelles.

On June 7, 1983, the Brabant Killers abandoned and torched their Volkswagen Golf. They immediately replaced it by stealing a Saab on June 9, which they kept through the summer until the car broke down after the Nivelles Colruyt attack on September 20. On October 1st, 1983, they replaced it with the red Volkswagen Golf from the Aux Trois Canards Restaurant that they repainted black. They later abandoned and torched that car on December 1st, 1983, bringing the Brabant Killers' first wave to an end.

That December 1983, the Bouhouche Gang finally filled the third box that had been unaccounted for, since more than a year.[337] They stole a Honda Quintet that they used for their Walibi amusement park hit of August 1985.[338]

After their first wave, the Brabant Killers were inactive for more than a year and half and did not have a vehicle. During this period, the Bouhouche Gang busily dug at their Buanderie Street warehouse site for their extortion plan.

Their plan required a big car to flee from the sewers' exit. On April 5, 1984 they stole a Renault 18 station wagon for that purpose. They affixed a diplomatic corps marking on it. This new vehicle posed a problem because they now had four vehicles and three boxes. Prioritizing their other vehicles, they parked the white Taunus outside their Woluwe base which was later found by law enforcement on June 6, 1984.

With the loss of the Taunus, the Bouhouche Gang returned to stasis with three vehicles in three boxes. On November 21, 1984, they stole a Renault 4 that they ultimately used for the Walibi hit. This addition gave them one excess car. Because the Bouhouche Gang had just given up the Buanderie extortion project, they probably left the Renault 18 station wagon that was tied to the project outside during the next couple of months.

In the week before their Walibi amusement park hit of August 15, 1985, they rented two other boxes—one rented in Anderlecht on August

9, and the other rented in Woluwe on August 14. The leases for two of their Ixelles boxes expired only on November 1. However, they seem to have abandoned the two old boxes since they soon started parking cars outside of boxes again.

The question remains, why did they abandon those two Ixelles boxes and not their other Ixelles box? They rented the Ixelles box they kept by phone and mail under the alias Castaldo in 1981, while they rented the other two Ixelles boxes in July 1983 using the alias Bremer. The two boxes rented in 1983 housed the two cars used to commit the Walibi murder of August 15. After the Walibi attack, they never returned to retrieve the Renault 4 that they used as a backup vehicle. Instead, they drove five miles to their Woluwe base where they had rented one vehicle box the day before. Despite the available secure space, they chose not to immediately store the car in the box. As a result, the authorities found the vehicle within hours of the hit. Trying to reuse the two boxes that they used to store the two cars for the murders proved now difficult and dangerous.

With all of the lease and vehicle changes, the Bouhouche Gang still had three boxes left in Woluwe, Ixelles, and Anderlecht for their two remaining vehicles—the Renault 18 with the diplomatic corps markings and the Toyota HiAce van. Because they had one available secure space, they stole a Mercedes Jeep on September 10, 1985.

Meanwhile, the Brabant Killers stole their first car since 1983, choosing a Volkswagen Golf from Erps Kwerps as their Second Wave vehicle. Unlike during the Brabant Killers' First Wave, the Bouhouche Gang accounted for all their rented boxes. However, seven days after the Erps Kwerps robbery and one day after Braine-and-Overijse Brabant Killers double attack, authorities found their Renault 18, which theoretically should have a place in one their three boxes, outside of a box in the Ixelles Complex on September 28, 1985. This suggests they possessed an unaccounted-for third car.

The flux of vehicles within their network of securely rented garage boxes indicates that the Bouhouche Gang had the logistical capability to complete both their known criminal operations and the Brabant Killers crimes. Like their alibis, little has leaked out on this issue. Did they ever explain these coincidences? Accounts could exist to explain these discrepancies, but none have leaked out of the investigations.

CHAPTER 28

EVIDENCE

NOT MUCH FORENSIC EVIDENCE EXISTS IN THE CASE IN GENERAL. There was the Ruger implicating the Borains and there was the spaghetti gun implicating Bouhouche that was found when he was locked up, but both needed to be excluded. There has, of course, never been any DNA evidence linked to a known suspect. The only other forensic evidence against the Bouhouche Gang and the most critical piece of evidence in the whole case is the Saab Turbo license plate.

It's a false license plate, which was pressed using the same matrix as the one used by the Bouhouche Gang. Both matrices had a quirk that was linked to the L'Autac firm's mold. In fact, a few false plates pressed using the same L'Autac mold used for the Brabant Killers' Saab had been used for the Bouhouche Gang's other crimes.[339] The Renault 4 plates used for the Walibi amusement park murder in August 1985 and the Mercedes 4X4 stolen by the Gang a few weeks later also use the same L'Autac mold. Authorities believe the Renault 4 was intended as a backup car during the Walibi hit if something went wrong with the Honda Quintet.

But the clincher is that both the Brabant Killers and the Bouhouche Gang used the same technique to artificially age the plates. According to an expertise from the Judicial Police the Saab's false plate found the morning following the Nivelles Colruyt attack that ended with three murdered and three wounded, was aged artificially using the same method as the false plates used by two other cars of the Bouhouche Gang, the Renault

25 and the 4X4.[340] The Saab plate was kept in the Nivelles Court Registry. Unfortunately, this critical piece of evidence disappeared into thin air in the early years of the investigation.[341]

However, perhaps just as damning as the plate for the Bouhouche Gang is the fact that three Gendarmes who were eyewitnesses positively identified perpetrators as people they knew personally—and that's two of the rare moments the Brabant Killers had little face covers or makeup. During the Wavre Gun Shop attack in September 1982, they were identified because they had started to remove their makeup and wigs to blend in before being fortuitously surprised by a Gendarmerie car. They were also identified because their faces were seen during the shootout at the Diable Amoureux after the Colruyt Nivelles break-in in September 1983.

At face value, the forensics behind the license plates plus three police officers identifying personal acquaintances is plenty enough to get people convicted for murder. However, this didn't happen. Are there problems with this evidence not known by the general public? One credible eyewitness that the jury believes is usually enough to put someone away for murder.

WHAT IF?

If the Bouhouche Gang is involved there are major consequences. It would mean that at least two friends of Bouhouche—as Gendarmes— have perfectly valid excuses to have DNA and fingerprints on the evidence without being the Killers. For example, investigators took turns putting on a hat from the Brabant Killers that was used at the Aalst Delhaize supermarket.[342] They had lots of direct access to the evidence. They could have removed the evidence on the scene or replaced the evidence stored during the years of investigations. The law enforcement officials linked to Bouhouche had a particular knack for being involved in the investigations of their own crimes. It took years of frustration before the Goffinon bombing, the Vernaillen attack and the Zaventem airport heist were solved.

Even the fact they're among the major suspects is a big problem for the investigation. If an investigation ever charges anyone else but the Bouhouche Gang going forward, any competent defense lawyer will bring up the fact that the Bouhouche Gang had their fingers in every aspect of the investigation. They had direct contact with the pieces of evidence needed to convict the Brabant Killers for years! The evidence is irrevocably tainted for everyone else. Unless prosecutors come up with a foolproof confession with new suspects and avoid a trial, it's impossible to imagine how they'd ever get a conviction. It would be like the Borains all over again, except with the knowledge that the Bouhouche Gang could have spent years compromising the very evidence the prosecution needs to use to convict the accused.

Motive

The motives traditionally used to explain the Bouhouche Gang's participation have been problematic. Their prior attacks are too complex to justify the straight robbery motive label like the Borains. It's usually some form of wanting to embarrass authorities or show that the Gendarmerie was helpless like the Dyane robbery of January 1982. Perhaps they were Far-Right militants? Perhaps embarrassing authorities in Belgium to make the population react was done on behalf of an agency sponsor? It's a twist on the terrorism motive. But just like the simple robbery motive, the terrorism motive is less than obvious. Forcing a terrorism motive on all the facts is extremely difficult.

Of course, that doesn't stop the authorities from bringing a case against the Bouhouche Gang without a motive. They've been identified on the crime scenes with the murder weapons by people they know. The witnesses just happen to be police officers. And before it disappeared, the Saab license plate was the only piece of forensic evidence linked to any suspect that wasn't debunked. But as we've seen in prior research, uncovering a motive helps with the clearance rate of cold cases.

What is the Bouhouche Gang? As mentioned, the Gang was founded by Bouhouche. We chose not to name the members of the Gang. Some were not accused of violent crimes unlike key members of the other gangs. What we can say is that Bouhouche is a central figure in the Gang and it's top heavy with members who've worked in law enforcement. They also had strong contacts inside the Gendarmerie that might have been manipulated by the Gang. Bouhouche's friends are a motley crew of police officers, criminals and murderers, but most of his friends did not know the extent of his criminal activities; even his most hardcore criminal friends. Most of his friends have nothing to do with his Gang and they should all be presumed innocent. Perhaps authorities will share the identities of the Bouhouche Gang members if they ever build up a case against them. Among them are the Psycho, the Old Man and the Giant.

We'll review all the facts in the case and we'll pin down the reason the Insane Killers committed a particular crime and why they killed a particular person. We'll also match them with the story of our main suspects, the Bouhouche Gang. We'll unpack and dissect, piece by piece the motivations of the Bouhouche Gang in committing the Brabant Killings. We've also done this same exercise of figuring how each of the other suspects mentioned in this book fit in with the facts. It showed that weak evidence linking them to the Brabant Killings isn't the only problem, they just don't fit at all. Because of this, we won't include the details here; they can be gleaned by readers from the rest of the book. The Bouhouche Gang is the only lead that makes any sense and can explain everything.

CHAPTER 29

WITH ARMS, WITH HATE,
WITH VIOLENCE

RIGHT BEFORE THE BRABANT KILLERS STARTED THEIR CRIMINAL CA-
reer, the Bouhouche Gang had already started theirs. The main,
all-consuming focus for their criminal activities was their plan to extort
supermarkets.

One acquaintance of Bouhouche familiar with the plan said that
Bouhouche was already talking about his scheme to extort money from
supermarkets in the late seventies: "End [of] 1979 Dany [Bouhouche]
suggested that I participate in a racket against supermarkets. The goal
was to set them on fire after asking a ransom and then escaping in a
zodiac in the Brussels sewer system."343 All the First Wave crimes of the
Brabant Killers were perpetuated in the process of accomplishing this
very goal.

The Bouhouche Gang was trying to put together their ambitious
extortion plan, a variation based on the French "Heist of the Century."
The "Heist of the Century" was a famous crime led by Albert Spaggiari in
1979 when he and his team of bandits dug a tunnel from the town sewers
to break into a bank building. The loot they stole was enormous and their
exploit became something of legend. When French authorities got into
the vault room, they found this slogan painted on the walls: "Without
arms, without hate, without violence." The Bouhouche Gang conceived

their own version of the tunnel robbery; instead of digging a tunnel from the sewers to reach the money, they planned to dig a tunnel from the building with the money to the sewers.

Given that their murderous criminal career included murdering Francis Zwarts, Willy Pans and Juan Mendez and shooting the Vernaillen family in their own home in cold blood, their version of the motto, however, would be completely antithetical to Spaggiari's. It would have to be: "With arms, with hate, with violence."

The Bouhouche Gang first planned to extort a chain of supermarkets and there are indications they were considering GB Inno's, a chain the Brabant Killers never attacked. When the supermarket company's directors put together the ransom, it would be carried to the Buanderie building, which would have an escape tunnel to the sewers. If the supermarket chain did not comply with the Gang's demands, they would blow up the chain's supermarket stores one by one until the chain complied. They also considered poisoning food on the shelves as an alternative or as an additional deterrent.

There are four phases to the extortion project: the Funding Phase (stealing the money required), the Equipment Phase, the Digging Phase and the Extortion Phase. The first three phases match a specific period of the attacks by the Brabant Killers. They never make it to the Extortion Phase where they would start extorting Supermarket Directors. Unlike the "Heist of the Century," which was funded by organized crime, the Bouhouche Gang had to come up with all the money themselves. Given the massive amounts of materials, equipment and related expenses they face, the costs are astronomical.

The Brabant Killers' first known armed robbery in 1982 had the purpose to get a car to commit break-ins to steal alcohol, the Santana they end up with fits the bill. The robbery happens within walking distance from their workplace. They could just finish their shifts and meet up afterwards. It's also not far from Flagey Place in Ixelles nearby the Ixelles complex where they rent their boxes.

Early on, the Bouhouche Gang funded their extortion project by steal-ing alcohol, for example during the Maubeuge Grocery robbery in August 1982 and the break-in at the Het Kasteel Inn Restaurant in December 1982. There may have been other break-ins during this period that went undetect-ed; we only know of these because they ended up engaged in bloody confron-tations. Lots of money is needed for their project, which means many bottles of alcohol need to be stolen and it's inevitable that it goes wrong sometimes. As for the weird location of Maubeuge, France, one of the Bouhouche Gang members grew up and lived just across the border in the Borinage, so he would have been very familiar with Maubeuge.

They also funded their project by stealing from two valuable trans-porters during the Mechelen robbery in July 1982 and the Zaventem Heist in October 1982; they impersonated Gendarmes to pull off the hits. To be able to organize their hits the Brabant Killers stole weap-ons. The Wavre Gun shop attack of September 1982 got them what they needed. The calibers used in the following attacks confirmed it.

During the chase that followed, one of the Gendarmes in the un-marked Renault who chased the Insane Killers in the stolen Santana between the gun shop and the Hoeillart intersection believed he could identify the perpetrator in the back seat. Officer Campine has always claimed the suspect in the back seat was a Gendarme colleague of his and part of the Bouhouche Gang.

The Bouhouche Gang used scanners to listen to police radio frequen-cies. One of their scanners included the frequency list of all the codes for the Gendarmerie, the Judicial Police and for local security firms. They had specialty trade documentation on Gendarmerie style antennas, as well as a tubular antenna and three police-grade antennas in their posses-sion. There is anecdotal evidence that for a while, the Gendarmerie car chasing them could not get on the radio waves. The Bouhouche Gang has acknowledged they used radio airwave scramblers in their cars.

They also used at least three submachine guns for the Zwarts road-block the following month, which are the same weapons Gendarmes typically use to man roadblocks. Submachine guns and handguns are, unlike rifles and shotguns, useful for the Bouhouche Gang's extortion project. Submachine guns are easy to handle, high-capacity weapons in case there's a shootout in the sewers.

They dumped some items in the Soigne Forest in October 1982. There's no evidence the things were planted; it was simply sloppiness on their part. One of the places where they've dropped off items had been the same place where they had emptied items from a truck they stole. In the items that belong to one of the Bouhouche Gang, there is a map marked with an X at this spot.

They then get involved in the investigations to mess them up, and even get access to the evidence to destroy, contaminate or replace it. Until late 1987, the Bouhouche Gang had their fingers in every Insane Killers file. They probably also had some indirect help from contacts on the inside of the Gendarmerie from then on.

They meddled with a variety of investigations, like choosing the Gendarmerie district of Mons to investigate a murder that happened in South Brussels in January 1983. They just dropped off the taxi and the car in the middle of the Mons district. Or, when they investigate their own case, they throw out evidence—like the Het Kasteel Inn. DNA evidence of two Gang members was left on glasses and cups at the Het Kasteel Inn, but the evidence disappeared. One of the Bouhouche Gang members was on site as part of the investigation. The same thing happened with investigations into the Bouhouche Gang attacks such as the Goffinon bombing and Vernaillen attack.

In early 1983, they switched from the more intensive crimes of stealing bottles of alcohol for the black market to holding up supermarkets. Because stealing bottles of alcohol is only mildly profitable, and there's always a risk of being caught on the resale, they graduate to holding up supermarkets. The Wavre Gun Shot attack of September 1982 provides them with enough firepower for armed robberies. The Genval and Uccle Delhaize armed robberies of February 1983, as well as the armed robbery at the Halle Colruyt of March 1983, give them the funds to they require to continue funding their extortion scheme.

During this period their plan was to attack supermarkets they knew in the Southern Ring around Brussels. The Bouhouche Gang installed a radio-communication antenna on an apartment's terrace in 1983, which allowed them to keep radio contact sustained during these Brussels area hold ups.

They don't go after Delhaize supermarkets in particular. While two of their three first attacks in the spring of 1983 had been a Delhaize and the other a Colruyt, it could have been the other way around. They attack in the evenings just before closing time because they all had 9 to 5 jobs. They lived in different cities and this is when they could meet.

Because they had to steal cars that had keys for them to use, it was mostly targets of opportunity. One of these is victim Genevieve Van Lindt, who managed a printing company in Ixelles not far from the boxes (storage units) and was a professional contact of a close friend to Bouhouche. When the Bouhouche Gang ended up with an extra car, they had to torch it or park one on the road in Ixelles or Woluwe where their storage box complex was located. The cars were sometimes picked up by authorities, but they were careful not to leave incriminating fingerprints.

When the Killers robbed a supermarket, they were known to indiscriminately grab a hostage. It seems to have started during this period of their first three supermarket robberies when they stumbled on someone walking right in front of them and they spontaneously grabbed them. It doesn't seem to have been some grand plan on their part.

All three Killers always proceeded to the store; they never left anyone behind in the getaway car. This is a police officer reflex: they're taught or learn not to park in the kill zone. Furthermore, when they had no choice to park near the Wavre Gun Shop because it was surrounded by tight, one-way streets they were forced to move a police van to get their car out.

Ballistics

The Wavre attack in September 1982 was designed for them to avoid situations where they are forced to use their limited weapons, except things went wrong, and they were forced to do just that. It's at this point they start looking for marks to take the fall for them. The Bouhouche Gang members get their law authority sources to do independent research into criminals who fit the bill. Starting in early 1983, they accelerate their searches. The Maubeuge results come in that Wavre and Maubeuge are a forensic match; because of their access to police information, the Bouhouche Gang members get this information right away.

They also reuse weapons such as using their 22LR likely with a silencer in Mons in January after they used it in December at the Het Kasteel Inn. It's more important to use what they need to not get caught immediately. They know that at that specific time in Belgium, the wheels of the ballistic testing moved extremely slowly. Furthermore, they knew they could have a hand in manipulating ballistic testing results.

It's during this late winter of 1983, that they zone in on the Borains as scapegoats. Ballistics links suddenly become a positive instead of a negative. Once all the attacks are linked to the Brabant Killers, there's only the need to implicate a single set of perpetrators. The trail implicating the Borains was manufactured from A to Z by the Brabant Killers—just like the Rebozo Four trial to protect the mob in Boston in the seventies, assisted by second-hand contacts in the FBI who had a vested interest in keeping Rebozo out. Here in Belgium there's no need to have second-hand contacts as the Brabant Killers have the luxury of being directly involved in the Gendarmerie investigation at different levels.

When the Bouhouche Gang has the Borains as their mark, it doesn't matter which weapons they use anymore. Their blunders can all be linked up and blamed on the Borains so the authorities only end up going after one set of perpetrators. They use whatever arms they need to do the job and they can unleash their psychopathic urges. They slowly let the trail to the Borains marinate, ready to be activated by their proxies at the right moment.

EQUIPMENT PHASE

Spring 1983 is the start of the Equipment Phase for the Bouhouche Gang. They have accumulated enough money to live off and rent or purchase what they need as they gather all the pieces of equipment they need to steal for their supermarket extortion plan. It's better to steal things so they can't be traced back to them when they pull off their own version of the Heist of the century and all police in Europe are after them. The Gang has a grocery list of items to rob that includes bullet-proof-vests, a blowtorch, bomb containers, alarms and more. They don't need to hold up supermarkets or steal alcohol anymore. Bouhouche can leave the Gendarmerie, using the money-losing venture of the ARI detective firm as cover for his criminal activities.

The robberies during this phase target critical equipment or items for the extortion plan. The total monetary value of their crimes is negligible, as the items are not stolen for resale. The nighttime break-in on May 27th, 1983 is for a blow-torch and tanks. A blowtorch is staple fare for any big money heist that involves digging holes and piercing through layers of materials.

One of the Brabant Killers' claims to fame is the ridiculously small financial gain. The birth of this legend starts because of the blunders during this period when they needed clean objects for their extortion projects and had no hesitation to kill to get them in Temse, Nivelles and Anderlues. Up to this point, the loot the Killers went after seemed quite normal and comparable to typical break-ins or hold-ups. They stole seven bulletproof vests from the Temse fabric in September 1983, oil and big bags of coffee from the Nivelles Colruyt in September 1983, alarm clocks from the Anderlues jeweler store in December 1983. In all three of those robberies, they made no effort to go for the cash or safe.

All they need is a fast car to drive them anywhere in Belgium to get the specific items required for their extortion scheme. Any new car with speed and horsepower will do because they got rid of their last Golf, which linked them to supermarket robberies committed in February and March 1983. They steal a Saab in June 1983. Unlike the other First Wave cars used only briefly by the Insane Killers, they drive the stolen Saab Turbo several hundred kilometers.

The great majority of their early break-ins are not particularly violent, but, like during their string of break-ins to steal alcohol in 1982, statistically, some break-ins are bound to go wrong. That's exactly what happens in Temse, Nivelles and Anderlues, when they encounter unwelcome surprises. Regular criminals will leave a witness behind and risk being identified and they'll also try to escape when confronted by the Gendarmerie. Not the Insane Killers; they'll fix a problem by killing themselves out of it.

This is the known modus operandi of the Bouhouche Gang. When they stole explosives in the quarries or the dinghy, they were ruthless and decided potential witnesses were expendable and they would shoot to kill. No witnesses are to be left, even if the items stolen are cheap and the monetary value divided among participants is insignificant.

Why would they give a shoot to kill order when they're only stealing small, inexpensive items like alarm clocks or metal tins? Because value is in the eye of the beholder. A clean, untraceable item is worth a lot more to the Killers than the same item for anyone else. Even if the flak jackets in Temse were new models, they weren't worth a lot of money. To make sense out of the insanity of killing over small gains, the legend of the state-of-the-art bulletproof vest is born. No one ever mentioned the inconsequential value of the state-of-the-art vests. Why would anyone shoot to kill a couple and fire directly at windows of a residential neighborhood to hit onlookers? Like Spaggiari with his "Heist of the Century," the Brabant Killers needed to obtain the stuff they needed by any means possible as long as it was stolen and untraceable. The black market is not an option if they want to remain untraceable; they need to do it themselves.

The Brabant Killers desired the tanks of oil and big bags of coffee they stole from the Colruyt Nivelles so much that they went back into the store to rob them after they murdered a couple just passing by to fill up their car with gas. Not only that, they take several minutes in the store to get what they want. Why? The tanks of oil were very important for them because they could use those large tin cans as bomb receptacles. Five cans of 50-liters of peanut oil and five cans of 50-liter of corn oil make great pressure-cooker type bombs that can easily be slipped into a grocery store. Cans of oil have long been a staple of terrorist groups to hide IEDs made of dynamite sticks, as have large bags of coffee. The 45 kilo bags of coffee were ideal for hiding IEDs. As for five boxes of chocolates, they were probably stolen to be used for poisoning. The benefit of using sweets for poison is that the sweetly aromatic chocolates disguise the smell of poison, depending on the poison used.

The blowtorch and tanks were initially stolen for use on the extortion project. When the need arose to break in a supermarket, they couldn't just force the back door like restaurants. Unlike the Baasrode Gang, which could have done this with their eyes closed, they had zero experience in this type of crime. They improvised and used the blowtorch.

The Bouhouche Gang used equipment stolen for their extortion project for other unrelated crimes that they suddenly needed to commit. When they found out that because of the fallout of Bouhouche's disciplinary problems with the Gendarmerie that they needed to punish Goffinon, they already had stolen explosives for their extortion project on hand. The Gang could use these materials to make the IED they used to attack Goffinon in October 1981.

The ambush technique against the Colruyt Nivelles that followed seems very much like the technique a Bouhouche-led commando had devised in case where they were caught red-handed. It was related to the robbery of a dinghy that happened not too long before the Nivelles attack. A friend of Bouhouche, well aware of the dinghy robbery, when asked by a journalist if the police interception plan used during the dinghy robbery was the same as the one in Nivelles, answered: "It was something like that."[344] According to time markers given by Bouhouche Gang members, the dinghy robbery attack could have happened mere days or weeks before Nivelles.

They had to use guns if they were caught red-handed during the robbery.[345] If during the operation they were arrested by the police, according to a person aware of the Bouhouche Gang's thinking in the matter says their car, "had to take the police in a sandwich, and that meant shooting them in the back." A dinghy is only worth a few thousand dollars, yet the Bouhouche Gang were prepared to kill police officers. A short while later they ambush the police officers at the Diable Amoureux, using the same technique they planned to use in the dinghy robbery—all that for loot worth less than a dinghy. However, keep in mind that the Bouhouche Gang is not just stealing the dinghy or the tin cans to hide explosives; they are stealing what they need to get 30 million Francs or more in their extortion project (approximately US $845,000; that's US $2.2 million in 2018). They want to steal what they need so there is no evidence trail back to them from purchases. They know they had a close call with the purchases they made for the Goffinon bomb in 1981. They don't want the same problems with authorities again.

During the ambush that followed the Nivelles Colruyt attack, two friends of Bouhouche Gang were identified as the shooters. One of them was a Gendarme that a witness knew personally.

When they need to get rid of their broken down Saab Turbo in haste, they couldn't get rid of all the evidence. The Saab Turbo carried false plates with the same technical glitch used in the mold of the other Bouhouche Gang fake license plates. The license plates were also all aged artificially using the same process. Remember this is the only forensic evidence ever linked to a suspect of the Brabant Killings that has not been discredited to date.

BIRTH OF THE INSANE KILLERS

The Nivelles attack is the public birth of the Brabant Insane Killers. They become a huge media phenomenon. They are quite aware of this and will play along to serve their own purposes to terrorize the people of Belgium.

Before the Nivelles attack, their arms of choice are large caliber pistols and revolvers. They'll also use a .22 LR, likely fitted with a silencer for close quarter kills. However, because of their Nivelles attack, they'll forever come to be associated to pump-action. The press coverage took off, decrying these deranged criminals shooting on police with shotguns. Sales of pump-action shotguns shot up among the public. The Killers took note and deliberately used pump-action shotguns from then on to brand one of their attacks.

As for the black hats associated with the Killers, it comes from them forgetting a black hat in the Saab after the Nivelles attack. They rarely, if ever, used hats before that. The Brabant Killers are practical shooters and police officers, so they are quite conscious of the risk of weapons failing. That's why they bring so many to a simple robbery like Nivelles.

After being forced to abandon the Saab they illicitly commandeered to steal equipment, the Brabant Killers look for a new car to use while committing their crimes. They set their sights on a car in the parking lot of the Aux Trois Canards Restaurant in Ohain, striking in October 1983.

They probably wanted the Porsche as it was a dark-colored, fast, powerful car like the Saab, but they end up being stuck with a flashy red Golf—which is less than ideal. There's also no ballistic link between Aux Trois Canards and all their other attacks, which is a problem because if someone is arrested for the Brabant Killer crimes, there's still this separate investigation not focusing on the Borains that will stay open. They're in a bit of a bind, so to get out of it they need to link the red Golf—which they paint a less flashy black—to the other Brabant Killer attacks. They also use the opportunity to make it look as though they're not based in Ixelles in Southern Brussels to throw investigators off their tracks.

At this point, they know they've messed up big time. Both Nivelles and Ohain have been bungled. They're the talk of the country and they even have the government's attention. Police forces are looking at ways to adjust and the Gendarmerie is setting up a task force. It's time they get the Borains, their designated fall guys, arrested. They activate their Gendarmeries contacts, who go along deliberately or are manipulated without being quite aware what was happening. The Borains are arrested.

Because they absolutely did not want to link up to the Aux Trois Canards botched carjacking of November 1st to the other Insane Killers attacks, they brought different weapons. Unfortunately, this makes this one attack that can't be linked ballistically to all the others. It's just a question of time before authorities who suspect a link is possible between Ohain and the other attacks, realize there isn't one. This would establish a second set of perpetrators unrelated to the Borains.

Consequently, they need to find a way to link up the Ohain attack to all the other Brabant Killers attacks. They use the opportunity to make authorities think the Insane Killers are not centered in Southern Brussels. They drive the now black Golf all over a crescent, going from Namur to the lower Borinage to make sure the car is seen by as many people as possible. To ensure there's no confusion that this vehicle is linked to a Brabant Killer crime, the "I Love Australia" sticker that was on the Red Golf when they stole it from the Aux Trois Canards Restaurant is still prominently displayed on a window. They likely stick it on and off at the right opportunity. They then begin to prepare for an attack against the Beersel Delhaize supermarket.

All the attacks and the murders happened just south of Ixelles and every attack escape heads toward Ixelles, never toward the Borinage. The only exception is their attack in Maubeuge in France. The taxi driver was found in Mons, which is the capital of the Borinage. However, the murder itself happened not far from Ixelles and the vehicle was driven to Mons afterwards to benefit from contacts inside the Gendarmerie there.

BEERSEL DELHAIZE

The Beersel Delhaize supermarket attack is different from all their other supermarket armed robberies. The Delhaize Genval, the Delhaize Uccle and the Colruyt Hal attacks were committed with the intention of filling their coffers. The Beersel Delhaize attack is committed to fix a mistake. It's a false flag attack to link the Aux Trois Canards Restaurant attack in Ohain to all the other attacks committed by the Brabant Killers. The Delhaize Beersel is the first of the Brabant Killers contrived red herring attacks, followed by all of their Second Wave supermarket armed robberies.

To make very sure that the Beersel attack links up all the attacks together, they purposely make sure investigators find the bench from the repainted Black Golf that they left behind in the Beersel Delhaize parking lot.

They Beersel Delhaize attack will become the blueprint for the Second Wave attacks. Speed is not of the essence; the purpose is not to accomplish a typical stealth hold up with a stopwatch. The most important thing is for them to get in and get out safely while accomplishing their goal. They covered each other just as if they were executing a swat operation. One of the Brabant Killers had an extensive background in the Special Forces. Their cool calmness during this brutal attack is dumbfounding. This is likely exacerbated by the fact that at this time the Giant could not run as he had major problems with his leg, which meant the other two had to move at the same pace.

While tall guys had been noted in prior attacks, this is the first supermarket hold up attack since the Insane Killers became a media phenomenon. During the Beersel attack, as soon as they come in, the manager tries to intervene and he's shot down immediately. The customers are in shock. The presence of a very tall muscular man strikes the customers and they call him a Giant. After the media birth of the Insane Killers, this is the media birth of the Giant.

The Giant is a head taller than the other two Insane Killers, the Psycho and the Old Man. The other two are likely present in all the other attacks. However, there's anecdotal evidence that in a pair of earlier attacks the third wheel wasn't nearly as big as the Giant. He was slimmer and shorter. There's of course a big problem in having such an identifiable physical specimen in a group of perpetrators. The Insane Killers are aware that as well as his beneficial Special Forces skills and involvement in the extortion plot, the presence of the Giant helps to brand a crime as an attack by the Brabant Killers. As for the Old Man, he is likely about the same age as the Psycho. He just happens to be a master in the art of makeup and dressing up.

Until the Aux Trois Canards Restaurant attack of October 1983, the Killers would mask their faces with makeup, ski masks or anything else. They might have even used carnival masks once before. So when they wanted not to be identified as the Insane Killers, they wore carnival masks, pink kitchen gloves, bell-bottom pants and talked gibberish. Because they had messed up, they had to do the opposite to make sure the authorities didn't pursue other people instead of the Borains. So, during the Beersel Delhaize attack, they wore carnival masks. The Killers quickly became associated with wearing carnival masks in the media.

There's a huge manhunt after the Beersel Delhaize attack. Anyone driving a Volkswagen Golf in Belgium that looks a bit suspicious is stopped. This is when a dark Volkswagen Golf became associated with the Insane Killers. Like the Delhaize, it could have been any another car. They used several other cars, but there was never a public manhunt to look for those kinds of cars.

BOMBING CAMPAIGN

The Anderlues jewelry store attack is their first known attack where they get back on the program of stealing items after Nivelles. It's also the last attack associated to the Insane Killers during the First Wave. The Bouhouche Gang is trying to figure out how they'll place bombs in supermarkets that can be triggered later. Their bombs are to be ignited by two means: by timers or remote controls. The motive for the Anderlues jewelry attack is to steal the alarms they could use as timers for their explosives, but they messed up again.

They planned to shoplift the stuff and leave while the jeweler was three rooms away from the showroom. There was no need to ring the bell for the jeweler as the items weren't locked up. The Killers didn't know that the jeweler's wife was lying down, resting in the dark room on the other side of the door. When she started running, they didn't want a witness and employed their shoot-to-kill policy. Then they also had to kill the jeweler, who emerged from where he was working, armed with an Arminius handgun.

As mentioned earlier, the jeweler's expertise was clocks and timepieces—his store was called "Jewelry and clock maker" Szymuzik. Only a part of the store's stock and business was dealing in jewels, the other part was clocks, alarm clocks and timepieces. Among the items the Brabant Killers stole were plain alarm clocks, some with quartz batteries. The brands stolen included Lorus, Peter, Bayard and Europa. It's only after a detailed inventory review that investigators could determine that the Insane Killers actually stole anything at all because everything looked untouched. Their plan was just to go in, grab alarm clocks and leave.

The fact that in both Nivelles and Anderlues they left behind many more valuable items, the robbery motive makes no sense and should have brought up a bunch of red flags. Some saw it as a reaffirmation that they were dealing with very simple-minded criminals who had trouble differentiating the value of things. Others saw it as a sign that these were terrorist attacks as they were clearly fake robberies, but both motives are very forced and don't quite fit.

Add to the large tin buckets of cooking oil and alarm clocks several remote controls that were found after the Second Wave, and it's clear whoever the Brabant Killers are, they're engaging in some sort of bombing campaign. Looking around in late 1983 at who was using or preparing to use explosives for criminal purposes in Belgium, the choices are limited. There's the CCC, but not much else other than our prime suspects, the Bouhouche Gang members who are also preparing to blow up pressure cooker bombs in supermarkets. And which of the bombing suspects would have killed for tin buckets or timers? Certainly not the CCC… The Bouhouche Gang absolutely needed these items and had no choice but to steal to get them.

Unfortunately for the Borains, they fit the profiling of the investigators at the time as poor, illiterate, dumb drifters who would do anything to kill for a buck. In both Nivelles and Anderlues they just grabbed anything: Cooking oil, gold and diamonds. Same difference… But the Borains are in jail. How could they have done Anderlues robbery? Common wisdom held it must have been committed by other Borains who hadn't been arrested yet.

Whether deliberate or not, the Brabant Killers made their Anderlues mistake in the zone where they wanted to be seen. They travel the same large crescent going from Namur to Anderlues, far from Southern Brussels and closer to the Borinage. If someone died, it needed to be with weapons linked to the Insane Killers that would keep everything linked to the Borains. Despite the fact the key Borains were in jail, the Killers still do the Anderlues attack. They are very self-confident that this attack will also be linked to the Borains and that investigations will continue going the way they want.

The torching of the car in December 1983 brings the First Wave of the attacks to a close. Now two out of four phases of their extortion project are finished: The Funding Phase and the Equipment Phase, which matched the exact timeline of the First Wave of the Brabant Killers attacks. They now go to phase three, the Digging Phase. In early 1984, they rent the Buanderie building, which is close to the Brussels sewer system and start digging.

They disappear for one year and a half. While they dig, it's the pause in the crime spree of the Brabant Insane Killers. They continue digging until mid-1984, when Bouhouche's extortion plan is abandoned because it becomes unfeasible. They never get to the Extortion Phase, which is when they would threaten the directors of the supermarket chain, bomb or poison food in the supermarkets if they had to, and secure blackmail money. Once they stop digging, if they commit other crimes, they have no need to ensure they are attributed to the Insane Killers or link them forensically to keep the investigation focused on the Borains. For the couple of months that follow the end of digging, they mostly focus on arms schemes and fraudulently selling sensitive documents for politicians. While they're preparing their next big thing, they kill a money transporter leaving the Walibi amusement park in August 1985. They didn't put on their Insane Killers costumes or disguises. They commit this crime as common murderers.

CHAPTER 30

LOOKING FOR THE REAL KILLERS

AFTER THE EXTORTION PLAN BECOMES UNWORKABLE, THE GANG IS broke. They killed and injured countless people to prepare for an extortion project that failed. The other money-making crimes they toyed with, like selling information to politicians, have come to nothing as well. What do they have left? They have created the Insane Killers brand and they have brand recognition. Is there any way to make money off it?

Their big project is to now get the reward the supermarket association is offering for information that leads to the arrest of the Brabant Killers. They need to find another Gang like the Borains to take the fall. Or find the elusive "other Borains" who could have committed the last First Wave attack when the Borains were in jail. The Bouhouche Gang successfully directed the investigation to put the Borains in jail the first time, and they feel they can do it a second time. All they need is to find marks that match the descriptions. For example, they need to find a Giant.

They're helped by the fact the Borains investigation has not progressed since the discovery of the Ruger in Mons and the unending cycle of confessions and retractions during interrogations. Beyond a few First Wave attacks where they feel they can stitch something together based on the Ruger, they can't link them to many of the major First Wave attacks. The supermarket association has never withdrawn their offer for information that leads to the arrest of the Brabant Killers.

By January 1985, they've started building files of potential suspects. This time the Bouhouche Gang is building a case based on a political arc. Not only was 1984 the year of the Westland leader Paul Latinus was murdered, it's also the year when the Far-Left CCC started its bombing campaign.

They target at least three French citizens using a political angle. They have informants following their marks everywhere. One of their marks is Adriano Vittorio, the Borain nicknamed King Kong because of his girth. He's a French citizen. They promote that he's part of the SAC, a Right-Wing Gaullist-linked organization that had just been disbanded by the French government. It grew from a group of De Gaulle's political supporters and mutated into a mob-like criminal gang that committed murders.

The Bouhouche Gang members who were the Brabant Killers still had some evidence on hand from their First Wave. They were getting ready to frame Bouhouche and others for the Brabant Killings to pick up the ransom. So it's really the Brabant Killers looking for fake Brabant Killers.

THE RANSOM

By Mid-1985, the Gang members are busy planning their next criminal scheme and discussing all the money on the way.[346] The numbers the Bouhouche Gang members have in mind are making at least 10 million Francs (or 250,000 Euros) per participant.

There's obviously a huge discrepancy between the amount offered by the supermarket association, and the huge amounts being bandied about by the Bouhouche Gang. About three to four times as much... The actual reward from the supermarket association is only 10 million.

The Second Wave is all intended to get the supermarket associations to raise their ransom. Once it's high enough, which they evaluate to be around 30 million or more, they'll give their evidence that leads to the arrest of the Fake Brabant Killers and collect the reward. How can they increase the reward money? Commit more attacks! The Gang is quite aware that their last two supermarket attacks at the Halle Colruyt in March 1983 and the Delhaize Beersel in October 1983 resulted in the association of supermarkets raising the reward each time. Remember that this is a Gang that's very self-aware; they're known to discuss amongst themselves the public reactions to their hit.

The day after the attack of the Halle Colruyt in March 1983, the Colruyt stores promised a reward of 5 million Francs for anyone who gives information that leads to the arrest of the assailants. The Brabant Killers weren't even a concept yet and the Colruyt attack had not yet been linked to any other attacks. After the Beersel Delhaize attack in October 1983, the Colruyt and the Delhaize chains got together with the supermarket association called the "Directions des enterprises de supermarches et grands magasins de Belgique" and everyone affiliated put reward money in a common pot. Very quickly the reward money is doubled from 5 million to 10 million. The Association is now responsible for paying out the ransom. After this last attack, the media and the public have branded the perpetrators the Brabant Insane Killers. These attacks really damaged the grocery business, causing 40 percent fewer people to shop in supermarkets during the evenings in Belgium.

Now, the Brabant Killers discontinued their crime spree in 1983, and it is now 1985. What if the Brabant Killers show up again? Would the supermarket association feel obliged to increase the reward money even more? After the two previous attacks they did, so logic would dictate that they would do it again—especially if the Brabant Killer attacks are even more indiscriminate and more vicious. The more violent the attack, the more likely they feel the reward price will be increased.

Suiting Up

Wouldn't the supermarket association just keep their reward the same but change the terms? One example would be to pay out the reward for solving any string of murderous supermarket hold-ups committed. So the Bouhouche Gang would only get 10 million under that conjecture, even after having committed more attacks.

The solution is that it has to be immediately clear that the Brabant Killers are back in action, not some random murderous killer gang. The Bouhouche Gang members are very conscious that they've built the Brabant Killer brand with the media and the public. What easier way can they accomplish this goal than by suiting up as the Brabant Killers for a second go around?

They carefully accumulated a list of elements unquestionably linked to the Brabant Insane Killers. What easier plan could they unfold than to attack Delhaize with a dark Golf car and shot guns? They'll be there, all three wearing carnival masks. With the giant, no getaway car driver, a hostage and ripping out telephone wires. They'll rob the front cashes and the back-office vault. And of course, they'll need to bump up the level of ultra-violence to give the supermarket association no choice but to react.

Braine-l'Alleud and Overijse

To make it crystal clear they're back, they'll attack not only one, but two Delhaize supermarkets back to back—both in the Brabant, but one in French-speaking Wallonia and the other in Dutch-speaking Flanders. It'll rile up both communities…

By late summer of 1985, the supermarkets and the public were no longer on high alert for attacks. They were less fearful of the Brabant Killers and the vigilance and security measures were relaxed again. The public was comfortable, feeling that the Killers might be gone for good. However, a security guard who was on duty at the Overijse Delhaize supermarket before the attack said that the only law enforcement agent he ever saw on site before the attack was a friend of Bouhouche. At the time, this associate was supposed to be stationed in another area of the country.

They still have the Saab radio and pump-action shotguns in working condition left from their First Wave Brabant Killers attacks. They start lining up their ducks. Playing their contacts in the Gendarmerie, they get a police contact to write a report the week before the Braine and Overijse attacks that concerns the radio from the Saab. It's all a huge setup and the report includes the description of a transaction for the stolen radio. The seller is allegedly Adriano Vittorio, a Borain. The other two guys alleged to be present for the sale are an informant used in the past by the Bouhouche Gang who had been spying on Vittorio full time, and the informant's best friend. Shortly after Bouhouche is jailed, in the early summer of 1986, the informant was told to drop his spying on Vittorio. It doesn't fit in with the Gang's plan anymore.

The double Braine-Overijse attack is successfully executed. There is no doubt in the mind of witnesses and the media that this robbery is the work of the Brabant Insane Killers. They are back, but they've returned much more violent—killing kids, cashiers and customers. They had not resorted to this level of brutal violence during the First Wave. They attacked just before closing time, arriving in a stolen, dark Volkswagen Golf GTI. They are three and the Giant is there. There are the dark hats and the carnival masks. They emptied the front cashes and the back-office vault. The Killers reused the same pump-action shotguns as the First Wave and they indiscriminately grab hostages.

However, their renewed efforts to terrorize Belgium did not bring the desired effect for the Brabant Killers: The supermarket association did not raise the reward money. They did, however, motivate the rest of the country to take action. The public is in a state of panic and authorities establish extreme security measures, which makes it more complicated if they try to commit another attack.

Fortunately for the Bouhouche Gang, they have a contact in the new supermarket security cell. Consequently, they're able to access the security team's top-secret plans to monitor and protect the supermarkets . The Gang is able to obtain all the security and surveillance specific to the Delhaize stores.[347] They even learn where the snipers stand on the roof of the store. They knew the zones that were most highly guarded and where the security was less intense.

The Bouhouche Gangs now knows which supermarkets to attack,

when and how. All their preparations to secure the stores throughout the country are useless. It'll be the Aalst Delhaize in the heartland of Dutch-speaking Flanders. The new target for their most violent attack is just comfortably out of the highest protection zone of the supermarkets. A picture taken in 1985 before the Aalst Delhaize attack is later found in a Bouhouche acquaintance's home; he claims he took the picture when he was working for a client on some unrelated business. They scout the location carefully and one of the men is even confronted by a local, but he can't respond because he doesn't know Dutch. The Brabant Killers need to bump up the level of ultra-violence for the attack, so they shoot indiscriminately at employees and customers inside and outside the store. They also kill, kick and brutalize. They still won't discriminate between men, women, or children. In fact, they'll go much further and target kids specifically to up the horror factor and give the supermarkets association no choice but to react. On top of the bad press, they're losing lots of money.

Fifteen minutes before the Aalst attack, witnesses notice two men whispering in French and sipping drinks in the Christoffelken bar not far from the Delhaize. The two men are just staring at traffic as it passes by the window. Three witnesses identify one of the two men as a Bouhouche Gang member in a photo line-up.

Just as they did before the double Braine and Overijse attacks, the Insane Killers prepare carefully and double-check their marks. On November 7th, two days before the Aalst attack, they extract information about Brahim Larbi from the Gendarmerie computer terminal. This is an individual not linked to any of the cases the Gendarme is working on—and in fact lives in France, just on the other side of the Belgium border. He's a Frenchman just like Adriano Vittorio and he also happens to be a Giant. His nickname is Le Negro for his dark complexion.

The Brabant Killers study this man's circle of relations and his personal characteristics. It's no coincidence that the Giant in the Aalst attack is the only one without a mask. He even wears makeup to darken his face and witnesses report he was wearing an afro wig. When the Insane Killers first surprised nine-year-old David Van Den Steen and his family in the parking lot, the boy wondered why this guy was dressed up like Zwarte Piet. This Moorish character has an afro and accompanies Saint Nicholas during the local St-Maartens Feast, which happened to be the same day as the attack.

AALST ATTACK

Earlier that day various objects the Brabant Killers were trying to get rid of were found in a fire in the Houssière Forest. In addition to the remote controls they were using for their extortion project, there's a bill for the restaurant The Toucan in Nivelles. The Toucan just happens to be where the Bouhouche Gang members plan their actions. That's where they planned their extortion project they were forced to abandon. That's where they met to sell objects from the extortion project they were no longer using and had to get rid of. It's roughly at an equal distance from Brussels, the Borinage and the western part of the Brabant where three key Bouhouche Gang members live. It links up to the Bouhouche Gang and the Bouhouche Gang alone.

Also dumped in the same fire are remote controls, which include the brands such as Bang & Olufsen, Grundig, Philips, Korting and Panasonic they had collected to activate explosives. It's part of the now useless equipment stolen for the extortion project, they need to get rid of. They try to sell what they can. Otherwise, if the material is sensitive, they throw what sinks into the bottom of canals and burn what doesn't sink. They tried to sell off their explosives to the highest buyers, but they still had some left in 1987. Some were rotting. They also still had pickaxes, spades, rubber boots, dust masks, helmets, fire extinguishers and a life jacket.

Despite the ultra-violence of Aalst, the reward money is never raised. The Gang gives up, settling for the 10,000,000 Francs each out of the existing reward money.

In early 1986, Bouhouche tells the Gendarmes working on the Brabant Killing attacks: "Anyways, what you're looking for is the Walloon Brabant [Killings]? Don't bother, there won't be anything more."A This is Bouhouche's way of telling them I know who did it, and they'll be arrested soon. At the time of his arrest, Bouhouche considered himself as a detective, not an arms dealer. He was freelancing to find—really, frame plausible suspects—the Brabant Killers.

Unfortunately for Bouhouche, he'll be arrested in the Mendez murder case before the Bouhouche Gang can offer enough evidence to tie Vittorio and the other marks to the crimes. When Bouhouche is arrested, it throws all the Bouhouche Gang's plans up in the air. The key focus quickly moves to getting him out of jail instead of picking up the 10 million ransom. This is why the Brabant Insane Killers disappear and are never heard of ever again.

At some point in 1986, the Gang members dump weapons in the canal. They also make sure the information makes its way to the Delta investigation for the perceived benefit of having two separate investigations chasing two separate gangs for the same set of crimes. What investigators find in the canal is useless and doesn't help the investigation in any way. However, the small-caliber Kriko hunting rifle recovered from the canal is significant. Investigators always wondered why someone would force on a silencer on a hunting rifle. Well, it matches the description of the sniper rifle used by the Bouhouche Gang for their MDA assassination contract. The plan had been to assassinate the second in command of the Algerian regime, Sherriff Messaadia. They needed a hit man because Messaadia was coming to Paris. The European-based MDA wanted to assassinate him on the Champs-Élysées, outside the most prestigious nightclub in Paris, the Fouquet. They took the hit job for a price of 12 million Belgian Francs (or US $2 million).[348]

It was decided the hit man would kill Messaadia outside in front of the bar with a sniper rifle as he exited his car. The contract killer would use a small caliber rifle from a distance. The Gang affiliate involved explained that he was using a 22-caliber with a scope because it was very precise and he could have used it to assassinate the Algerian politician without anyone being able to establish a link between the assassination and the weapon, even if the weapon was ever recovered. The Brabant Killers were known to have a 22-caliber silencer they could use on the

Kriko. They could assassinate Messaadia up to a distance of more than two hundred meters, which would have kept the hit man safely away from Messaaddia's bodyguards. The Killers dumped it in the canal because the murder contract didn't end up going forward.

One of the Bouhouche Gang associates had once been a sniper in a special unit, where he had learned that using a special small caliber sniper rifle was optimal because .22 small caliber ammo could stop an attacker without being dangerous to bystanders, women and children. According to his thinking, it wasn't possible with a much more powerful ammo. If Messaadia survived, an associate of the contractor would probably throw a grenade inside the Fouquet. Coincidentally, a grenade is found in Ronquières. The Kriko and the grenade are also the only two weapons that otherwise can't be linked to Brabant Insane Killer attacks.

There would have been 3 men presenting themselves as Gendarmes that showed up to pick up a bag, right before the Ronquières discovery of November 1986. The men received a burlap bag from a diver and disappeared in a Beige Renault 4. We know one of the members of the Bouhouche Gang was driving a Beige Renault 4 during this time frame.

The small gains in the Second Wave are more linked to the ridiculous risks they took and the murder and carnage they wrought. This further reinforces that terrorism and robbery motives are inaccurate and illogical. The reason for this disparity in both waves is that the huge bulk of their money was coming from two different fraudulent schemes. Their take from the supermarket robberies was pocket change for them. In the First Wave, they were after the money they would extort from a supermarket chain, while in the Second Wave their goal was to secure the reward put up for their Brabant Killer avatar.

MAPS

Acknowledgments

First and foremost, I would like to thank my wife for her undying support throughout the entire process of writing this book. Without her encouragement, this book would have been impossible. I would also like to thank Isabelle for spending her holidays scouting crime scenes in Belgium with me. I wholeheartedly thank Martin, for slogging through the first manuscript of this book, and Leona, for her support and insightful suggestions. My deepest gratitude goes to Karen, for making this project what it is, and to Lili and Jennifer, for their assistance in finalizing this project. Additionally, I would like to thank Rashad and Caryn for all of their valuable input. Without all of you, this book would never have made it this far.

PHOTO CREDITS

ENDNOTES

Introduction

[1] Daniele Ganser, *Les Armées secretes de l'Otan* (Paris: Editions Demi-Lune, 2005).

[2] Robert C. Davis, Carl J. Jensen, Lane Burgette, and Kathryn Burnett, "Working Smarter on Cold Cases: Identifying Factors Associated with Successful Cold Case Investigators," Journal of Forensic Sciences 59, no. 2 (2014): 375-382. https://doi. org/10.1111/1556-4029.12384

[3] J.E. Douglas and C. Munn, "Violent Crime Scene Analysis: Modus Operandi, Signature, and Staging," FBI Law Enforcement Bulletin 61, no. 2 (1992): 1-10.

[4] Ibid.

Chapter 1: Shoplifting, Carjacking and Break-In
(March–May 1982)

[5] Belgian Federal Police,"Toonbankdiefstal in de wapenhandel Bayard", http://killersbrabant.be/facts/1982/bayard-nl.html

[6] Gilbert Dupont and Paul Ponsaers, *Les tueurs six années d'enquête,* 1988, 11-12.

[7] Ibid.

[8] Hilde Geens, Beetgenomen, Manteau, 2013, 19.

[9] "Warenhuis overvallen: 100.000 frank". *Het Nieuwsblad*, 8 May 1982 posted by Merovinger at https://www.bendevannijvel.com/forum/viewtopic.php?id=2135

[10] Belgian Federal Police, "Vol d'une Austin Allegro avec menaces par armes à feu", http://killersbrabant.be/facts/1982/austin-fr.html

[11] Geens, 20.

[12] Gilbert Dupond, "Il y a 35 ans commencaient les tueries du Brabant *DHnet. be.* http://www.dhnet.be/actu/faits/il-y-a-35-ans-commencaient-les-tueries-du-brabant-59135d5fcd70022542bf0c37

[13] Belgian Federal Police, "Vol qualifié d'une VW Santana au garage Brichau." http://killersbrabant.be/facts/1982/brichau-fr.html

[14] Gilbert Dupond, "Il y a 35 ans commencaient les tueries du Brabant *DHnet. be.* http://www.dhnet.be/actu/faits/il-y-a-35-ans-commencaient-les-tueries-du-brabant-59135d5fcd70022542bf0c37

[15] Belgium. Federal Parliament. House of Representatives, Enquête parlementaire sur la manière dont la lutte contre le banditisme et le terrorisme est organisée, 59/8 - 1988, 103.

Chapter 2: Grocery Store In Maubeuge (August 14, 1982)

[16] Belgian Federal Police, "Diefstal met braak in de kruidenierswinkel Piot gevolgd door een schietpartij met de Franse politie." http://killersbrabant.be/facts/1982/piot-nl.html

[17] Dupont and Ponsaers, 13.

[18] Anna Luyten, "Hoe het spoor van de Bende van Nijvel naar Lembeek en Maubeuge leidt", *Knack*, 16 May 2007. https://www.knack.be/nieuws/belgie/hoe-het-spoor-van-de-bende-van-nijvel-naar-lembeek-en-maubeuge-leidt/article-longread-916205.html

[19] Ibid.

[20] Ibid.

[21] Michel Leurquin and Patricia Finné, L'histoire vraie des tueurs fous du Brabant, la manufacture de livres, 2012. 18.

[22] Dupont and Ponsaers, 14.

[23] Ibid.

[24] Ibid. 14-15

[25] "Drame mystérieux à Soignies - Le père d'un garagiste blessé d'un coup de feu" *La Dernière Heure*, September 20, 1982" posted by Merovinger at https://www.bendevannijvel.com/forum/viewtopic.php?id=1558

Chapter 3: Wavre Gun Shop (September 30, 1982)

[26] Belgium. Federal Parliament. House of Representatives, Enquête parlementaire sur la dont la lutte contre le banditisme et le terrorisme est organisée, 59/8 - 1988, p. 97.

[27] Ibid, 98.

[28] *Les tueurs du Brabant Wallon,* RTBF, 1985. Television. Documentary.

[29] Ibid.

[30] Belgium. Federal Parliament. House of Representatives, 98.

[31] Ibid.

[32] Ibid., 99.

[33] Ibid.

[34] Ibid.

[35] Belgian Federal Police, "Fusillade à Wavre et à Hoeilaart." http://killersbrabant.be/facts/1982/wavre-hoeilaart-fr.html

[36] Belgium. Federal Parliament. House of Representatives, 100.

[37] Ibid.

[38] Ibid.

[39] Ibid.

[40] Ibid.

[41] Belgian Federal Police, "Fusillade à Wavre et à Hoeilaart."

[42] Geens, 22.

43 Ibid., 48-49.

44 Belgian Federal Police, "Vol à main armée de l'armurerie Dekaise." http://killers-brabant.be/facts/1982/dekaise-fr.html

45 Leurquin and Finné, 21.

46 Geens, 29-45.

47 Gilbert Dupont, "18km aux trousses des tueurs," DHNET.be, last modified September 28, 2007. http://www.dhnet.be/actu/faits/18-km-aux-trousses-des-tueurs-51b7be68e4b0de6db98b462e

48 Belgium. Federal Parliament. House of Representatives, Enquête parlementaire sur la manière dont la lutte contre le banditisme et le terrorisme est organisée, 59/8 - 1988, 103-104.

49 Geens, 49.

50 Guy Bouten, Tueries du Brabant: le Dossier, le Complot, les Noms (Brussels: Les éditions de l'arbre, 2009), 49.

51 Belgium. Federal Parliament. House of Representatives, dont la lutte contre le banditisme et le terrorisme est organisée, 59/8 - 1988, 104.

52 Ibid.

53 Geens, 24.

54 Belgium. Federal Parliament. House of Representatives, Enquête parlementaire sur la manière dont la lutte contre le banditisme et le terrorisme est organisée, 59/8 - 1988, 104.

55 Geens, 24.

56 Ibid.

Chapter 4: Het Kastel Inn Restaurant (December 23, 1982)

57 Haquin, René, "Le concierge de l'auberge du château de Beersel tué pour quelques bouteilles... " Le Soir. 26 December 1982.

58 Belgium. Federal Parliament. House of Representatives, Enquête parlementaire sur la manière dont la lutte contre le banditisme et le terrorisme est organisée, 59/8 - 1988, 111.

59 Ibid.

60 Ibid., 112.

61 "Gruwelijke afslachting in restaurant van domein van Beersel" [Horrific Slaughter in restaurant in Beersel property], Het Lasste Nieuws, December 27, 1982, posted on October 29, 2018 by Merovinger at https://www.bendevannijvel.com/forum/viewtopic.php?pid=51443#p51443.

62 Geens, 65.

63 Belgium. Federal Parliament. House of Representatives, Enquête parlementaire sur la manière dont la lutte contre le banditisme et le terrorisme est organisée, 59/8 - 1988, 111.

64 Geens, 66.

Chapter 5: Taxi Ride From Ixelles to Mons (January 9, 1983)

65   Belgian Federal Police, "Meurtre de Angelou Constantin." http://killersbrabant. be/facts/1983/angelou-fr.html

66   Belgium. Federal Parliament. House of Representatives, Enquête parlementaire sur la manière dont la lutte contre le banditisme et le terrorisme est organisée, 59/8 - 1988, 114.

67   Belgian Federal Police, "Meurtre de Angelou Constantin."

68   Belgium. Federal Parliament. House of Representatives, Enquête parlementaire sur la manière dont la lutte contre le banditisme et le terrorisme est organisée, 59/8 - 1988, 113.

69   Geens, 71.

70   Ibid., 70.

71   Belgium. Federal Parliament. House of Representatives, Enquête parlementaire sur la manière dont la lutte contre le banditisme et le terrorisme est organisée, 59/8 - 1988, 114.

72   Philippe Brewaeys and Jean-Frédéric Deliège, *De Bonvoisin et Cie*, 1992, 143.

73   Belgium. Federal Parliament. House of Representatives, Enquête parlementaire sur la manière dont la lutte contre le banditisme et le terrorisme est organisée, 59/8 - 1988, 115.

74   Ibid.

75   "Interview Pierre Dumont," *Humo,* accessed November 15, 2018, https://bendevannijvel.com/motief/afpersing/interview-pierre-dumont/

76   René De Witte and Dirk Selleslagh, "Delhaize niet zes, maar mogelijk zeven keer slachtoffer van Bende van Nijvel", *De tijd,* April 1, 1997.

77   Charge sheet. Borains. 51-52.

78   Ibid.

79   Gilbert Dupont, "Le témoin n'avait jamais été réinterrogé - Retrouvée par la DH, la veuve de Raymond Dewee a maintenant 90 ans." *La dernière Heure,* February 2, 2013.

80   One early Dutch expression to identify him was the Maniac.

Chapter 6: Delhaize Supermarket in Genval (February 11, 1983)

81   Charge sheet. Borains.

82   Belgian Federal Police, "Hold-up op de DELHAIZE te Genval." http://killersbrabant.be/facts/1983/ delhaize-genval-nl. html

83   Ibid.

84   Charge sheet, Borains.

85   Belgian Federal Police, "Hold-up op de DELHAIZE te Genval."

86   Charge sheet. Borains.

87 Ibid.

88 Ibid.

89 Belgium. Federal Parliament. House of Representatives, Enquête parlementaire sur la manière dont la lutte contre le banditisme et le terrorisme est organisée, 59/10 - 1988, 390.

90 Ibid., 429.

91 Belgian Federal Police, "Vol d'une VW Golf immatriculée DTX079 à Plancenoit." http://killersbrabant.be/facts/1983/plancenoit-fr.html

92 Charge sheet. Borains. 14.

93 Bouten, 76.

94 Belgian Federal Police, "Diefstal van een witte Audi 100 met nummerplaat DKC 329 in de garage VAG te Walerloo." http://killersbrabant.be/facts/1982/waterloo-nl.html

95 Ibid.

96 Gilbert Dupont, "Un fait élucidé sur le site officiel des tueries du Brabant," *DHNET.be*, last modified December 5, 2017, http://www.dhnet.be/actu/faits/un-fait-elucide-sur-le-site-officiel-des-tueries-du-brabant-5a25a71dcd70b488f-b052a83.

Chapter 7: Delhaize Supermarket in Uccle (February 25, 1983)

97 Belgian Federal Police, "Hold up au Delhaize d'Uccle." http://killersbrabant.be/facts/1983/delhaize-ukkel-fr.html

98 Ibid.

99 Charge sheet. Borains. p. 17.

100 Geens, 73-74.

101 Geens, 73.

102 Belgian Federal Police, "Diefstal van een witte Audi 100 met nummerplaat DKC 329 in de garage VAG te Walerloo."

Chapter 8: Colruyt Supermarket in Halle (March 3, 1983)

103a Guy Bouten, De Bende van Nijvel. Verrad, Manipulatie, Geheime Diensten (Leuven: Van Halewyck, 2015), 137.

103b Bouten, 77.

103c Roland Planchar « La profileuse contre les tueurs fou », Lalibre.be, 9 octobre 2007. https://www.lalibre.be/actu/belgique/la-profileuse-contre-les-tueurs-fous-51b895bae4b0de6db9b09db6

103 Belgian Federal Police, "Hold-up op de Colruyt te Halle." http://killersbrabant.be/facts/1983/colruyt-halle-nl.html

104 Charge sheet. Borains. 17.

105 Hugo Gijsels, *L'enquête, 20 années de déstabilisation en Belgique* (Brussels: La Longue Vue, 1989), 60.

[106] Bouten, 77-78.

[107] Jeroen Wils, *Bloed zonder tranen: het gangsterleven van Patrick Haemers* [Blood Without Tears: The Gangster Life of Patrick Haemers] (Antwerp: Manteau, 2008), 183.

[108] Denise Tyak, *Ma Vie avec Patrick Haemers*, 2012, Ebook. À la rue. 6.

[109] Tyak, Ibid., À la rue. 6.

[110] Ibid.

[111] Ibid.

[112] Ibid.

[113] Ibid.

[114] Jos Vander Velpen, Guère civil: de la gendarmerie à la police unique (Brussels, 1998), 71.

[115] Geens, 316.

[116] Ibid., 318.

[117] Ibid., 345.

[118a] Gijsels, 28.

[118] Ibid., 295.

[119] Belgium. Federal Parliament. House of Representatives, Enquête parlementaire sur la manière dont la lutte contre le banditisme et le terrorisme est organisée, 59/10 - 1988, p. 496.

[120a] "De moordaanslag: 26 Oktober 1981", www.bendevannijvel.com, https://bendevannijvel.com/daders/bouhouche-beijer/feiten/

[120] Ibid., 499.

[121] Ibid.

[122] Vander Velpen, 65.

[123] "Interview with Arsène Pint," accessed at November 15, 2018. https://bendevannijvel.com/onderzoek/belgische-rijkswacht/interviews-arsene-pint/

[124] Ibid.

[125] Vander Velpen, 67.

[125a] Jean-Paul Collette, « Affaire Swarts : de nouvelles questions dérangeantes à la Sabéna et à la Justice », 7 february 1984.

[126] Gilbert Dupont, "Un nouveau fait attribué aux tueurs du Brabant!" *La dernière Heure*, Septembre 28, 2015.

Chapter 9: Braine Car Dealership (June 8, 1983)

[127] Belgian Federal Police, "Vol d'une Saab 900 Turbo au garage Denuit à Braine-l'Alleud." http://killersbrabant.be/facts/1983/brainelalleud-fr.html

Chapter 10: Temse Fabric (September 10, 1983)

[128] Belgian Federal Police, "Diefstal gewapenderhand in de fabriek Wittock-Van Landeghem te Temse."
http://killersbrabant.be/facts/1983/temse-nl.html

[129] Dupont and Ponsaers, 38.

[130] Ibid., 37.

[131] Ibid.

Chapter 11: Colruyt Supermarket in Nivelles (September 17, 1983)

[132] Ibid., 41.

[133] Belgian Federal Police, "Vol à main armée au Colruyt de Nivelles."
http://killersbrabant.be/facts/1983/nivelles-fr.html

[134] Dupont and Ponsaers, 41.

[135] Ibid, 42.

[136] Ibid.

[137] Leurquin and Finné, 45.

[138] Belgian Federal Police, "Fusillade à Braine-l'Alleud au "Diable amoureux"."
http://killersbrabant.be/facts/1983/diable-fr.html

[139] Ibid.

[140] Dupont and Ponsaers, 44.

[141] Belgian Federal Police, "Fusillade à Braine-l'Alleud au "Diable amoureux"."

[142] Dupont and Ponsaers, 45.

[143] Geens, 78.

[144] Belgium. Federal Parliament. House of Representatives, Enquête parlementaire sur la manière dont la lutte contre le banditisme et le terrorisme est organisée, 59/10 - 1988, 402.

[145] Ibid., 59/9 - 1988, 86.

[146] Ibid.

[147] Ibid, 59/10 - 1988, 402.

[148] Details of the formation and accompanying graphic are found in Manual MCWP 3-11.3 of the U.S. Marine Corps 17 April 2000 called "Scouting and Patrolling."

[149] According to the Manual, "This formation subjects the enemy to both enfilading and interlocking fire. The "V" formation is best suited for fairly open terrain but can also be used in close terrain. When established in close terrain, the legs of the "V" close in as the lead element of the enemy force approaches the apex of the "V," and opens fire at a close range." Ibid.

[150] Bouten, 455.

Chapter 12: Aux Trois Canards Restaurant (October 2, 1983)

[151] Charlie Hedo, *Het Rattenkwartier : Een Blik in het Nest va de Bende van Nijvel*, 2015, Smashwords, ebook.

[152] Jean Mottard and René Haquin, Les *tueries du Brabant: enquête parlementaire sur la manière dont la lutte contre le banditisme et le terrorisme est organisée* (Brussels: Éditions Complexe, 1990), 116.

[153] Belgian Federal Police, "Moord op Jacques Van Camp en diefstal van Volkswagen Golf in het restaurant "het restaurant"." http://killersbrabant.be/facts/1983/canards-nl.html

[154] Leurquin and Finné, 68.

[155] Mottard and Haquin, 116.

[156] Dupont and Ponsaers, 51.

[157] Belgium. Federal Parliament. House of Representatives, Enquête parlementaire sur la manière dont la lutte contre le banditisme et le terrorisme est organisée, 59/9 - 1988, 356.

[158] Belgian Federal Police, "Moord op Jacques Van Camp en diefstal van Volkswagen Golf in het restaurant "het restaurant".

[159] Mottard and Haquin, 117.

[160] Belgian Federal Police, "Moord op Jacques Van Camp en diefstal van Volkswagen Golf in het restaurant "het restaurant".

[161] Ibid.

[162] Hilde Geens, "Interview with Catherine Van Camp," *Humo*, October 2004. www.bendevannijvel.com

[163] Ibid.

[164] Bouten, 60-61.

[165] Haquin, René, Des taupes dans l'extrême-droite, EPO, 1984, 216 pages.

Chapter 13: Delhaize Supermarket in Beersel (October 7, 1983)

[166] Dupont and Ponsaers, 54.

[167] Ibid., 56.

[168] Belgian Federal Police, "Hold up au Delhaize de Beersel." http://killersbrabant.be/facts/1983/delhaize-beersel-fr.html

[169] Dupont and Ponsaers, 56.

[170] Ibid, 54.

[171] Belgian Federal Police, "Hold up au Delhaize de Beersel."

[172a] "Les mystérieux tueurs fous", Temps présent, RTS, Directed by Paul Seban, 16 october 1986.

[172] Dupont and Ponsaers, 54-55.

[173] Ibid, 55.

[174] Belgian Federal Police, "Hold up au Delhaize de Beersel."

[175] Ibid.

[176] Dupont and Ponsaers, 55.

[177] Belgian Federal Police, "Hold up au Delhaize de Beersel."

[178] Ibid.

[179] Gijsels, Hugo, L'Enquête, 1989, 143.

[180] Gilbert Dupont, "L'inconnu des Trois canards - Tueurs du Brabant: un nouveau portrait-robot est dressé d'après le témoignage d'un carrossier" *La Dernière Heure*, 31 october 2002.

[181] Vander Velpen, 71.

[182] Statement of Pierre Beduwe, PV, Jumet, February 17, 1988.

[183] Statement of Mohamed Asmaoui, PV 21165, CBW, January 27, 1988.

[184] Statement of Daniel Choquet, PV 21244, Jumet, February 11, 1988.

[185] *Dossier Noir, Les Tueurs fous du Brabant*, directed by Daniel Remi and Jean-Michel Dehon, La Radio-télévision belge de la Fédération Wallonie-Bruxelles (RTBF), December 19, 2007.

[186] Bouten, 454.

[187] Les Tueurs fous du Brabant, *Dossier Noir*, RTBF, 19 December 2007.

[188] Vander Velpen, 70.

[189] Ibid., 74.

[190a] Ilegems, Sauviller and Willems, 14.

[190b] Ibid., 15

[190] Belgium. Federal Parliament. House of Representatives, Enquête parlementaire sur la manière dont la lutte contre le banditisme et le terrorisme est organisée, 59/9 - 1988, 87.

[191] Ibid., 59/9 - 1988, 86.

[192] Ibid., 59/10 - 1988, 389.

[193] Ibid.

[194a] Belgium. Federal Parliament. House of Representatives, Enquête parlementaire sur « les tueurs du Brabant », 573/8 - 95/96, 125.

[194] D. Ilegems, R. Sauviller and J.R Willems., *De Bendetapes*, 1990, 11.

[195] Ibid., 26.

[196] Vander Velpen, 75.

Chapter 14: Jewelry Store in Anderlues (December 1, 1983)

[197] Belgian Federal Police, "Vol à main armée et double meurtre dans une bijouterie à Anderlues." http://killersbrabant.be/facts/1983/anderlues-fr.html

[198] Leurquin and Finné, 80.

[199] Geens, 89.

[200] Ibid., 87.

[201] Belgium. Federal Parliament. House of Representatives, Enquête parlementaire sur « les tueurs du Brabant », 573/11 - 95/96, 72.

[202] Ibid.

[203] Belgium. Federal Parliament. House of Representatives, Enquête parlementaire sur la manière dont la lutte contre le banditisme et le terrorisme est organisée, 59/10 - 1988, 429.

[204] Gilbert Dupont, "Qui a voulu faire taire Pierre Romeyer," *La Dernière Heure*, July 18, 2016.

[205a] Bende van Nijvel website. Posted by site administrator Ben https://www.bendevannijvel.com/forum/viewtopic.php?id=1064

[205b] Ilegems, Sauviller and Willems, 35

[205] Geens, 59.

[206] Panorama La Radio-télévision belge de la Fédération Wallonie-Bruxelles (RTBF), 1995. *Panorama*, Television documentary, November 1995.

Chapter 15: Bouhouche Gang Extortion

[207] Geens, 349.

[208] Ibid.

[209] Bouten, 455.

[210] Geens, 350.

[211] Ibid.

[212] Guy Bouten, *De bende van Nijvel en de CIA* (Leuven: Van Halewyck, 2011), 259.

[213] Testimony of Christian Amory, PV 21184, January 30, 1988.

[214] Bouten, 455.

Chapter 16: The Death of Paul Latinus

[215] Belgium. Federal Parliament. House of Representatives, Enquête parlementaire sur la manière dont la lutte contre le banditisme et le terrorisme est organisée, 59/8 - 1988, 83.

[216] « Spéciale Tueries du Brabant » Devoirs d'Enquête, (RTBF), October 22, 2014. (video documentary)

[217] Haquin, 22.

[218] Tim Weiner, *Legacy of Ashes: The History of the CIA* (London: Penguin, 2011), 346-348.

[219] "Operation Gladio: The Foot Soldiers," *Timewatch*, directed by Allan Francovich, BBC, June 24, 1992.

Chapter 17: Difficulties for the Bouhouche Gang

[220] Geens, 351.

Chapter 18: Haemers and De Staerke's New Gangs

[221] Tyak, À la rue, 5.

[222] L'île Maurice, 7.

[223] Ibid

[224] "Enquête : Patick Haemers", *L'autre vérité*. Originally aired in 1989 https://www.youtube.com/watch?v=Zy8j9tWZsYE&t=3s. (video documentary)

[225] The De Staerke Gang actually have many more members but this is the core Gang that will go in the spree of hold ups in 1985.

[226a] Geens, 112.

[226] Lépold, Van Esbroek, *Lettre ouverte aux tueurs du Brabant Wallon*, 1998, 114.

[227] Van Esbroek, 67.

Chapter 19: Walibi Amusement Park

[228] Geens, Ibid., 95.

[229] Ibid.

[230] Ibid.

[231] Geens, 95.

[232] Belgium. Federal Parliament. House of Representatives, Enquête parlementaire sur « les tueurs du Brabant », 573/11 - 95/96, 59.

[233] Ibid., 16.

[234] Ibid., 573/10 – 95/96, 121.

[235] Renaat Landuyt and Jean-Jacques Viseur, *Enquête parlementaire sur les adaptations nécessaires en matière d'organisation et de fonctionnement de l'appareil policier et judiciaire, en fonction des difficultés surgies lors de l'enquête sur "les tueurs du Brabant,"* (Brussels: Federal Parliament House of Representatives, 1997), 60-61.

[236] Belgium. Federal Parliament. House of Representatives, Enquête parlementaire sur « les tueurs du Brabant », 573/10 - 95/96, 130.

[237] Ibid., 127.

Chapter 21: Delhaize Supermarkets in Braine & Overijse (September 27, 1985)

[238] Belgian Federal Police, "Hold up op de Delhaize te Eigenbrakel." http://killersbrabant.be/facts/1985/delhaize-brainelalleud-nl.html

[239] Dupont and Ponsaers, 69.

[240] Geens, 95.

[241] Ibid.

[242a] Les Tueurs fous du Brabant, Dossier Noir, RTBF, 19 December 2007.

[242] Dupont and Ponsaers, 69

[243a] "Reenactment of the Braine and Overijse attacks", France television, RTL-TVI, Directed by Patrick Volson, 2001.

[243] Ibid.

[244] Leurquin and Finné, 68.

[245] Dupont and Ponsaers., 69

[246] Ibid.

[247] Ibid., 70

[248] Leurquin and Finné, 69.

[249] Geens, 95.

[250] Belgian Federal Police, "Hold up op de Delhaize te Overijse." http://killersbrabant.be/facts/1985/delhaize-overijse-nl.html

[251] Ibid.

[252] Ibid.

[253] Geens, 96.

[254] Ibid.

[255] Ibid.

[256] Ibid.

[257] Belgium. Federal Parliament. House of Representatives, Enquête parlementaire sur la manière dont la lutte contre le banditisme et le terrorisme est organisée, 59/10 - 1988, 528.

[258] "Zoeken naar 'rode draad,'" Het Nieuwsblad, Oktober 14, 1983, posted at https://www.bendevannijvel.com/forum/search.php?search_id=1707453473&p=3.

[259] Geens, 95.

[260] Vander Velpen, 89.

[261] Ibid. 89.

[262] "Beveiliging supermarkten in het week-end," Panorama, VRT, November 21, 1985.

[263] Testimony of Christian Amory, PV 21184, January 30th, 1988.

[264] Van Esbroeck, 106.

[265] Belgium. Federal Parliament. House of Representatives, Enquête parlementaire sur la manière dont la lutte contre le banditisme et le terrorisme est organisée, 59/10 - 1988, 418.

[266] Raf Sauviller and Hilde Geens. "Interview with José Mendez", *Humo*, September 1997. www.bendevannijvel.com.

[267] Vander Velpen, 90.

Chapter 22: Delhaize Supermarket in Aalst (November 9, 1985)

[268] Belgian Federal Police, "Découverte d'un foyer d'incendie à Braine-Le-Comte." http://killersbrabant.be/facts/1985/braine-le-comte-fr.html

[269] Dupont and Ponsaers, 76.

[270] Geens, 105-106.

[270a] Dupont and Ponsaers, 76.

[271] Damseault, Ibid.

[272a] Van de Steen and Bulté, 17.

[272] "De Slachtpartij in Aalst" Panorama, special number, 1985, posted at https://www.bendevannijvel.com/forum/viewtopic.php?id=1031

[273] David Van de Steen and Annemie Bulté, *Ne tirez pas c'est mon papa! Un survivant des tueries du Brabant raconte* (Paris: Éditions Journdan, 2011), 16.

[274a] Geens, 101.

[274b] Ibid.

[274] Aalst beleefde zijn meest tragische nacht. De Voorpost 15-11-1985

[275] Leurquin and Finné, 81.

[276] Belgian Federal Police, "Hold up op de Delhaize te Aalst." http://killersbrabant.be/facts/1985/delhaize-aalst-nl.html

[277] Belgium. Federal Parliament. House of Representatives, Enquête parlementaire sur la manière dont la lutte contre le banditisme et le terrorisme est organisée, 59/9 - 1988, 35-36.

[278] Ibid., 36.

[279] "Interview with René De Witte", accessed at November 15, 2018. https://sites.google.com/site/tueriesdubrabant/interviewren%C3%A9dewitte

[280] Belgium. Federal Parliament. House of Representatives, Enquête parlementaire sur la manière dont la lutte contre le banditisme et le terrorisme est organisée, 59/9 - 1988, 36.

[281] Ibid., 112.

[282] Ibid., 59/10 - 1988, 420.

[283] Ibid., 419.

[284] "De Slachtpartij in Aalst" Panorama, special number, 1985, posted at https://www.bendevannijvel.com/forum/viewtopic.php?id=1031

[285] Ibid.

[286] Ibid.

[287] Geens, 99.

[288] Belgium. Federal Parliament. House of Representatives, Enquête parlementaire sur « les tueurs du Brabant », 573/15 - 95/96, p. 67.

[289] Bouten, 293-297.

[290] Ibid., 293.

[291] Geens, 107.

[292] Ibid.

[293] Police statement- PV 525

[294] Geens, 106.

[295] Dupont and Ponsaers, 77.

[296] Ibid.

[297] Belgium. Federal Parliament. House of Representatives, Enquête parlementaire sur la manière dont la lutte contre le banditisme et le terrorisme est organisée, 59/8 - 1988, 102.

[298] Ibid., 59/9 - 1988, 27.

[299] Belgium. Federal Parliament. House of Representatives, Enquête parlementaire sur « les tueurs du Brabant », 573/11 - 95/96, 121.

[300] Geens, 153

[301] Van Esbroeck, 104.

[302] Belgium. Federal Parliament. House of Representatives, Enquête parlementaire sur la manière dont la lutte contre le banditisme et le terrorisme est organisée, 59/10 - 1988, 419.

[303] Ibid, 59/9 - 1988, 27.

[304] Ilegems, Sauviller and Willems, 91.

[305] Ibid.

[306] PV 100198 Termonde Gendarmerie.

Chapter 23: Assassination of Juan Mendez

[307] Geens, 325.

[308] Raf Sauviller and Hilde Geens. "Interview with José Mendez", *Humo*, September 1997. www. bendevannijvel.com.

[309] Belgium. Federal Parliament. House of Representatives, Enquête parlementaire sur les adaptations nécessaires en matière d'organisation et de fonctionnement de l'appareil policier et judiciaire, en function des difficultés surgies lors de l'enquête sur « les tueurs du Brabant », 573/11 - 95/96, 276.

[310] Belgium. Federal Parliament. House of Representatives, Enquête parlementaire sur la manière dont la lutte contre le banditisme et le terrorisme est organisée, 59/10 - 1988, 478.

Chapter 24: Discovery in Ronquières (November 1986)

[311] "Het web rond de Bende van Nijvel," Panorama, originally aired on January 8, 1990, VRT NWS Channel https://www.youtube.com/watch?v=yJVUJOqp-GAE

[312] Van de Steen, David and Bulté, Annemie, *Ne tirez pas, c'est mon papa!*, 2011, 142.

[313] Belgium. Federal Parliament. House of Representatives, Enquête parlementaire sur la manière dont la lutte contre le banditisme et le terrorisme est organisée, 59/10 - 1988, 391.

[314] Geens, 385-386.

[315] *Dossier Noir, Les Tueurs fous du Brabant*, directed by Daniel Remi and Jean-Michel Dehon, RTBF, December 19, 2007.

[316] Geens, 314.

Chapter 25: Terrorism and Gladio

[317] Vander Velpen, 93.

[318] Van de Steen and Bulté, 233.

[319] Ibid, 234.

[320] Belgium. Federal Parliament. House of Representatives, Enquête parlementaire sur « les tueurs du Brabant », 573/9 – 95/96, 73.

[321] Christian Carpentier, Christian and Frédéric Moser, *La Sûreté de l'état*, 1993, 187-189.

Chapter 26: The Gendarmerie

[322] Vander Velpen, 93.

[323a] Geens, Hilde, Het Nieuwsblad, 11 oktober 1983.

[323b] Geens, 86.

[323] Gilbert Dupont, " Le soir de la tuerie d'Alost, qui était Gudule?" *Derniere heure*, 19 July 2016.

[324] Quoted by site manager Ben on www.bendevannijvel.com https://www.bendevannijvel.com/forum/viewtopic.php?id=29&p=2

[325] Vander Velpen, 94; also see: "Interview with Arsène Pint," www.bendevannijvel. com https://bendevannijvel.com/onderzoek/belgische-rijkswacht/interviews-arsene-pint/

[326a] "Interview with Arsène Pint", www.bendevannijvel.com, https://bendevannijvel.com/onderzoek/belgische-rijkswacht/interviews-arsene-pint/

[326b] Ibid., "Interview with Arsène Pint".

[326] see Daels, Kris, *Alpha 20 – Un agent secret belge raconte*, PIX, 2014, which describes life working as a Dyane operator.

[327] Plantinga, Adam, 400 things cops know, 2014, 24.

[328] Arnold Wielenga, "Contacten Politie met Bende van Nijvel", *Het Nieuwsblad van het Noorden*, 15 November 1985.

[329] Gilbert Dupont, « 18km aux trousses des tueurs » *DHNET.be*, 28 september 2007. http://www.dhnet.be/actu/faits/18-km-aux-trousses-des-tueurs-51b7be68e4b0d-e6db98b462e

[330] Belgium. Federal Parliament. House of Representatives, Enquête parlementaire sur la manière dont la lutte contre le banditisme et le terrorisme est organisée, 59/10- 1988, 375.

[331] Ibid.

[332] Ibid., 478.

[333] Ibid

Chapter 27: Putting a trial together

[335] Bill of indictment, Madani Bouhouche et al.

[336] Some debate that the Audi was not stolen by the Brabant Killers. The current investigative cell still consider that it was.

[337] René Haquin, «Tueries: un lien avec un hold-up à Wavre en 1985? Walibi: des similitudes troublantes... », *Le Soir*, April 14, 1998 posted on http://tueriesdubrabant.winnerbb.com/t309p50-walibi-le-15-08-1985 by site adminstrator Michel.

[338] The Bouhouche Gang was never charged with the Walibi murder. However, the circumstantial evidence in the case is overwhelming that they were involved.

Chapter 28: Evidence

[339] Ibid.

[340] Leurquin and Finné, 213.

[341] Questions Magnee, posted by Boomerang on www.bendevannijvel.com. https://www.bendevannijvel.com/forum/viewtopic.php?id=1083&p=4

[342] *Le Vif*, posted by www.bendevannijvel.com site manager Ben, https://www.bendevannijvel.com/forum/viewtopic.php?id=76

Chapter 29: With Arms, with hate, with violence

[343] Geens, 95.

[344] Ibid.

[345] Bouten, 455.

Chapter 30: Looking for the real killers

[346] Ibid

[347] Belgium. Federal Parliament. House of Representatives, Enquête parlementaire sur les adaptations nécessaires en matière d'organisation et de fonctionnement de l'appareil policier et judiciaire, en function des difficultés surgies lors de l'enquête sur « les tueurs du Brabant », 573/11 - 95/96, 276.

[347] Geens, 351-352.

Index

BIBLIOGRAPHY

Beijer, Robert. *Le dernier mensonge*. Brussels: Editions Luc Pire, 2010.

Bouten, Guy. *De Bende van Nijvel en de CIA*. Leuven: Van Halewyck, 2011.

————— *De Bende van Nijvel. Verraad, Manipulatie, Geheime Diensten*. Leuven: Van Halewyck, 2015.

————— *Tueries du Brabant: le dossier, le complot, les noms*. Translated and adapted by A. Jourdan and E. Timmermans. Brussels: Les éditions de l'arbre, 2009.

Brewaeys, Philippe and Jean-Frédéric Deliège. *De Bonvoisin et cie: de Liège à Bruxelles, les prédateurs et l'État*. Brussels: Éditions EPO, 1992.

Bultot, Jean. *Le livre que personne n'osa publier*. E-Book posted online May 7, 2008 at http://mozsnake.skyrock.com/1741484384-Le-livre-que-personne-n-a-ose-publier.html.

Candidus, P.S. *Les Tueurs du Brabant wallon*. Scaillet, 1988.

Carpentier, Christian and Frédéric Moser. *La Sûreté de l'État: Histoire d'une déstabilisation: le service secret belge dans tourmente*. Ottignies: Quorum, 1993.

Daels, Kris, *Alpha 20 – Un agent secret belge raconte*, PIX, 2014.

Damseaux, Gérald. *Les années noires vous intéressent?* Paris: Société des écrivains, 2015.

Davis, Robert C., Jensen, Carl J. Burgette, Lane, and Burnett, Kathryn, "Working Smarter on Cold Cases: Identifying Factors Associated with Successful Cold Case Investigators," *Journal of Forensic Sciences* 59, no. 2 (2014): 375-382. https://doi. org/10.1111/1556-4029.12384.

De Witte, René and Dirk Selleslagh. «Delhaize niet zes, maar mogelijk zeven keer slachtoffer van Bende van Nijvel", *De tijd*, April 1, 1997.

Douglas J.E. and Munn C., "Violent Crime Scene Analysis: Modus Operandi, Signature, and Staging," *FBI Law Enforcement Bulletin* 61, no. 2 (1992): 1-10

Dupont, Gilbert and Paul Ponsaers. *Les tueurs: six années d'enquête*. Anvers : Éditions EPO, 1988.

Dupont, Gilbert. "18km aux trousses des tueurs." *La Dernière Heure,* September 28, 2007. http://www.dhnet.be/actu/faits/18-km-aux-trousses-des-tueurs-51b7be68e4b0de6db98b462e

————— "Il y a 35 ans commençaient les tueries du Brabant." *La Dernière Heure*, May 10, 2017. http://www.dhnet.be/actu/faits/il-y-a-35-ans-commencaient-les-tueries-du-brabant-59135d5fcd70022542bf0c37.

————— "Un nouveau fait attribué aux tueurs du Brabant!" *La Dernière Heure*, Septembre 28, 2015.

————· "Un fait élucidé sur le site officiel des tueries du Brabant," DHNET.be, last modified December 5, 2017, http://www.dhnet.be/actu/faits/un-fait-elucide-sur-le-site-officiel-des-tueries-du-brabant-5a25a71dcd70b488fb052a83.

————· "Le soir de la tuerie d'Alost, qui était Gudule?" *La Dernière heure*, 19 July 2016.

————· "Qui a voulu faire taire Pierre Romeyer," *La Dernière Heure*, July 18, 2016.

————· "Le témoin n'avait jamais été réinterrogé - Retrouvée par la DH, la veuve de Raymond Dewee a maintenant 90 ans." *La dernière Heure*, February 2, 2013.

————."L'inconnu des Trois canards - Tueurs du Brabant: un nouveau portrait-robot est dressé d'après le témoignage d'un carrossier" *La Dernière Heure*, 31 october 2002.

Ganser, Daniele. *NATO's Secret Armies: Operation Gladio and Terrorism in Western Europe*, London: Frank Cass, 2005.

Geens, Hilde. *Beetgenomen: zestien manieren om de bende van Nijvel nooit te vinden*, Antwerp: Manteau, 2013.

————· "Catherine Van Camp Interview." *Humo*, October 2004. Posted on bendevannijvel.com

Gijsels, Hugo. L'enquête, *20 années de déstabilisation en Belgique*. Brussels: La Longue Vue, 1989.

Haquin, René and Stéphany, Pierre. *Les grands dossier criminels en Belgique*. Brussels: Racine, 2005.

Haquin, René. Des taupes dans l'extrême-droite. Brussels: Éditions EPO, 1983.

————· "Le concierge de l'auberge du château de Beersel tué pour quelques bouteilles… " Le Soir. 26 December 1982.

————· "Tueries: un lien avec un hold-up à Wavre en 1985? Walibi: des similitudes troublantes... ", Le Soir, April 14, 1998 posted on http://tueriesdubrabant.winnerbb.com/t309p50-walibi-le-15-08-1985 by site administrator Michel.

Havaux, Pierre and Pierre Marlet. *Sur la piste du crocodile: VdB de 1919 à nos jours*. Brussels: La Longue Vue, 1994.

Hedo, Charlie. *Het Rattenkwartier : Een Blik in het Nest va de Bende van Nijvel*, Smashwords, 2015.

Hermanus, Merry, *L'ami encombrant* (Liège : Liège Pire, 2013).

Ilegems, Danny, Sauviller, Raf and Willems., *Jan De Bende-tapes*. Leuven: Kritak, 1990.

Leurquin, Michel and Patricia Finné. *L'histoire vraie des tueurs fous du Brabant*. Paris: Manufacture de livres, 2012.

Luyten, Anna. "Hoe het spoor van de Bende van Nijvel naar Lembeek en Maubeuge leidt" Knack, May 16, 2007. https://www.knack.be/nieuws/belgie/hoe-het-spoor-van-de-bende-van-nijvel-naar-lembeek-en-maubeuge-leidt/article-longread-916205.html.

Massart, Victor. *Les dés étaient pipés: conspirations à la sûreté de l'état*. Ottignies: Quorum, 1997.

Masset, Adrien. *L'enquête criminelle sur les "tueurs du Brabant": enquête parlementaire sur les adaptations nécessaires en matière d'organisation et de fonctionnement de l'appareil policier et judiciaire, en fonction des difficultés surgies lors de l'enquête sur les "tueurs du Brabant."* Leuven: Presse Universitaire de Louvain, 1997.

Mottard, Jean and René Haquin. *Les tueries du Brabant: enquête parlementaire sur la manière dont la lutte contre le banditisme et le terrorisme est organisée.* Brussels: Éditions Complexe, 1990.

Offergeld, Jacques and Christian Souris. *Euroterrorisme, la Belgique étranglée.* Paris: Scaillet, 1985.

Plantinga, Adam. *400 Things Cops Know: Street-smart Lessons from a Veteran Patrolman.* Fresno, CA: Quill Driver Books, 2014.

Sauviller, Raf and Geens, Hilde. "Interview with José Mendez", Humo, September 1997. www. bendevannijvel.com.

Tyak, Denise. *Ma Vie avec Patrick Haemers.* Brussels: Racine, 2012. Ebook format.

U.S. Marine Corps. "Scouting and Patrolling." *U.S. Marine Corps Manual MCWP 3-11.3*, April 17, 2000.

Van de Steen, David and Annemie Bulté. *Ne tirez pas c'est mon papa! Un survivant des tueries du Brabant raconte.* Paris: Éditions Journdan, 2011.

Van Esbroeck, Leopold. *Lettre ouverte aux tueurs du Brabant wallon, Texte imprimé souvenirs d'un ex-gangster.* Brussels: La Longue Vue, 1998.

Vander Velpen, Jos. *Guère civil: de la gendarmerie à la police unique.* Brussels: EPO, 1990.

Weiner, Tim, *Legacy of Ashes: The History of the CIA* (London: Penguin, 2011).

Wezel, Guy. "Mons 8 April 1988." *De Morgen*, April 9, 1988.

Wielenga, Arnold. "Contacten Politie met Bende van Nijvel", Het Nieuwsblad van het Noorden, 15 November 1985.

Wils, Jeroen. *Bloed zonder tranen: het gangsterleven van Patrick Haemers* (Antwerp: Manteau, 2008), 183.

"Drame mystérieux à Soignies - Le père d'un garagiste blessé d'un coup de feu" *La Dernière Heure*, September 20, 1982" posted by Merovinger at https://www.bendevannijvel.com/forum/viewtopic.php?id=1558

"Interview with Pierre Dumont", *Humo*, accessed at November 15, 2018. https://bendevannijvel.com/motief/afpersing/interview-pierre-dumont/

"Interview with Arsène Pint," accessed at November 15, 2018. https://bendevannijvel.com/onderzoek/belgische-rijkswacht/interviews-arsene-pint/

"Interview with René De Witte", accessed at November 15, 2018. https://sites.google.com/site/tueriesdubrabant/interviewren%C3%A9dewitte

"Aalst beleefde zijn meest tragische nacht". *De Voorpost*, November 15, 1985. https://aalst.courant.nu/issue/DVP/1985-11-15/edition/0/page/2?query=

"Gruwelijke afslachting in restaurant van domein van Beersel", *Het Lasste Nieuws*, December 27, 1982, posted on October 29, 2018 by Merovinger at https://www.bendevannijvel.com/forum/viewtopic.php?pid=51443#p51443.

"Zoeken naar 'rode draad,'" *Het Nieuwsblad*, Oktober 14, 1983, posted at https://www.bendevannijvel.com/forum/search.php?search_id=1707453473&p=3.

"Warenhuis overvallen: 100.000 frank" *Het Niewsblad*, 8 May 1982 posted by Merovinger at https://www.bendevannijvel.com/forum/viewtopic.php?id=2135

Police Statements

Belgium. Federal Parliament. House of Representatives, Enquête parlementaire sur la manière dont la lutte contre le banditisme et le terrorisme est organisée, 1988.

Belgium. Federal Parliament. House of Representatives, Enquête parlementaire sur « les tueurs du Brabant », 1996.

"Les tueurs du Brabant." Site officiel de la police fédérale. Last accessed 15 December 2018. http://killersbrabant.be/index-fr.html

Police Statements (PVs) from Cellule Brabant Wallon, Termonde (Delta), Cellule Info and other law enforcement department in Belgium.

Charge sheets. Borains and Bouhouche Court Cases

Videos

"Les Tueurs fous du Brabant." Dossier Noir, RTBF, 19 December 2007..

« Spéciale Tueries du Brabant » Devoirs d'Enquête, (RTBF), October 22, 2014.

"Het onderzoek: De Bende van Nijvel," *Panorama*, originally aired in 1995, VRT NWS Channel. https://www.youtube.com/watch?v=9mhPAGwQr5Y

"Het web rond de Bende van Nijvel," *Panorama*, originally aired on January 8, 1990, VRT NWS Channel https://www.youtube.com/watch?v=yJVUJOqpGAE

"Les mystérieux tueurs fous", *Temps présent*, RTS, Directed by Paul Seban. 16 octobre 1986

"Operation Gladio: The Foot Soldiers," Timewatch, directed by Allan Francovich, BBC, June 24, 1992.

"Enquête : Patick Haemers", *L'autre vérité*. Originally aired in 1989 https://www.youtube.com/watch?v=Zy8j9tWZsYE&t=3

Lightning Source UK Ltd.
Milton Keynes UK
UKHW041845020720
365951UK00004B/117/J